# THE AFRO-CENTRIC SCHOOL

# Endorsements

Nah Dove's *The Afrocentric School – A Blueprint* is a masterpiece. More than a "blueprint," it is offers us educational guidance centered in African cultural values and beliefs that we need "to be human in this era." This vitally needed and incomparable volume is an absolutely essential resource for our re-Afrikanization. A philosophical and pedagogical *tour de force*, Dr. Dove brilliantly re-writes knowledge and curriculum across the disciplines to enable educators to conduct our children's "journey" toward self-knowledge and spiritual and educational awareness. I am deeply grateful for scholarship and love for our children, and I can't wait to engage my students with this wonderful, truly liberating work!

> Joyce E. King, PhD
> Benjamin E. Mays Endowed Chair for Urban Teaching, Learning & Leadership
> Georgia State University
> Past-President, The American Educational Research Association

"Drawing on a lifetime of unique personal experience and scholarly research, Dr Nah Dove has delivered a remarkable pedagogical blueprint that rightfully centers Africa and offers a timely, visionary and transformational approach to education."

> Margaret Busby
> Publisher, Writer, Broadcaster.
> Editor, *New Daughters of Africa: An International Anthology of Writing by Women of African Descent.* 2020 list of 100 Great Black Britons. Honorary title: Nana Akua Akon.

*The Afrocentric School – A Blueprint* skillfully guides the Afrocentric educator, providing a framework of over 5000 years and an understanding of how and why Eurocentrism has attempted to erode African knowledge and truth. I would highly recommend this text to those who wish to teach from an African centered perspective and equally for those responsible for educating children and young people of African ancestry and heritage.

> Dr Sally-Ann Ashton
> Dr of Egyptology and Dr of Psychology
> Professor at Edge Hill University, UK

Dr. Dove's *The Afrocentric School – A Blueprint* is a godsend and "dream come true" for PanAfricans! Finally, we have the seminal document of research-based curricula that will connect the global African family around the important issue of true education for all our children–a long-time goal of Afrocentric schools. *The Blueprint* will be welcomed in any education setting where the vision is to instruct young learners and by anyone who has the will to teach African children, parents included. Dr. Dove's goals are to train up scholars who will be spiritually balanced; who will know the majesty and brilliance of their African ancestors and the truth about their impact on the world; and who will seek cultural unity as a result of the awareness of their true his/herstory. Lessons are enhanced by pictures, diagrams, active websites and sample stories. *The Afrocentric School – A Blueprint* is truly a testimony to Sankofa!

Charlotte Forté-Parnell, Ed.D.<br>
Dean, Language Arts/Academic Development<br>
Retired

*The Afrocentric School – A Blueprint* is a major contribution towards transforming the education of the Black race. In the Afrocentric school Nah Dove has written a Blueprint for all that would like to improve the education of all children and in particular the education of the black child. The book offers all teachers, school administrators and curriculum officers, a practical, research-based model for excellence in pedagogy derived from the best of our African philosophies and traditions. The present-day achievements and challenges of the African people are based on centuries of Western acculturation, an oppressive and exploitative process wherever one group of people come under the economic, political, and social domination of another people. *The Afrocentric School – A Blueprint* constitutes one of the few promising practical approaches to educating the African in his/her own system. It also offers a rare combination of vision and pragmatism in line with the scholar-activism paradigm in Afro-centric education. It is a must read by teachers, school administrators, parents, teacher trainers and curriculum developers.

Dr. Augustine Obeleagu AGU<br>
International Consultant on Education and Social Policy<br>
(Former UNICEF Chief of Education and Social Policy Adviser)

Dr. Dove renders Afrika a distinguished service in meeting perhaps the most important challenge facing Afrikans at home and abroad: educating our generations. The solution is clear. The only appropriate education for Afrikan people is learning and teaching in our own tradition, with our own methods, from our own perspectives. This is Afrikan education for Afrikan people. Field based as well as thoroughly theoretical, this Afrocentric study is grounded in a commanding familiarity with the deepest tradition of Afrika and its contemporary manifestations on the continent and in its communities abroad. Carefully and knowingly graduated to meet the learning needs of different age groups in rural and urban communities, this text is inclusive, wholistic and Pan Afrikan. This is a foundational text of Afrikan education.

Dr Kimani Nehusi, International Scholar, Kemetologist,<br>
Department of Africology<br>
Temple University, Philadelphia.

# THE AFROCENTRIC SCHOOL

[ a blueprint ]

**NAH DOVE**

Universal Write Publications LLC

No part of this publication may be reproduced in whole or in part, or stored in a retrieval system, or transmitted in any form or by any means, electronic, mechanical, photocopying, recording or otherwise, without written permission from the publisher, except in the case of newspapers, magazines and websites using quotations embodied in critical essays and reviews.

**The Afrocentric School: A Blueprint**

Copyright 2021 @ Nah Dove

All rights reserved.

Nah Dove
'The right of Nah Dove to be identified as the author of this Work has been asserted by him/her in accordance with sections 77 and 78 of the Copyright, Designs and Patents Act 1988.'

Book Designer: AuthorSupport.com

For information:
Website at www.UniversalWrite.com and www.UWPBooks.com
Publisher: Universal Write Publications LLC

Mailing/Submissions
Universal Write Publications LLC
421 8th Avenue, Suite 86
New York, NY 10001-9998

ISBN: 978-1-942774-05-1

# TABLE OF CONTENTS

| | |
|---|---|
| Foreword | xi |
| Introduction | xiii |

## Part I: Overview

| | | |
|---|---|---|
| 1 | THE RACIALIZATION OF HUMANITY | 3 |
| 2 | RECLAIMING AFRICAN KNOWLEDGE | 9 |
| 3 | A CULTURE-BASED STUDY | 19 |
| | Essential factors | 21 |
| | Findings from the Study | 33 |
| 4 | AFROCENTRIC CURRICULUM AND ASSESSMENT | 53 |
| | Conceptual Framework Based on Age and Educational Attainment | 56 |
| 5 | LOCATIONS OF AFROCENTRIC SCHOOLS | 81 |
| | Model 1: The Community based Afrocentric School | 81 |
| | Model 2: Urban-based Afrocentric School as US Charter | 83 |
| | Model 3: The Independent Urban-based Afrocentric School | 84 |

## Part II: Lesson Plans

| | |
|---|---|
| LESSON PLANS FOR AGES 3-5 YEARS | 89 |
| Overview | 89 |
| Language Arts | 92 |
| Sociocultural Studies | 97 |

| | |
|---|---|
| Mathematics | 100 |
| Science | 109 |
| Music | 111 |

## LESSON PLANS FOR AGES 5-6 YEARS — 113

| | |
|---|---|
| Language Arts | 113 |
| Wisdom and Ethics | 116 |
| Mathematics | 119 |
| Geography | 121 |
| Science | 122 |
| The Arts | 126 |

## LESSON PLANS FOR AGES 6-7 YEARS — 129

| | |
|---|---|
| Geography and Sociocultural Studies | 130 |
| Mathematics | 140 |
| Science | 151 |

## LESSON PLANS FOR AGES 7-8 YEARS — 157

| | |
|---|---|
| Sociocultural Studies | 158 |
| Rhetoric and Writing | 160 |
| History | 163 |
| Mathematics | 168 |
| Science | 172 |
| Music | 175 |

## LESSON PLANS FOR AGES 8-9 YEARS — 177

| | |
|---|---|
| Language Arts and Sociocultural Studies | 177 |
| Logic | 182 |

| | |
|---|---|
| Science | 185 |
| Music and Dance | 192 |

## LESSON PLANS FOR AGES 9-10 YEARS — 195

| | |
|---|---|
| Language Arts and Sociocultural Studies | 195 |
| History | 198 |
| Mathematics | 205 |
| Science | 211 |
| The Arts | 215 |

## LESSON PLANS FOR AGES 10-11 YEARS — 217

| | |
|---|---|
| Language Arts and Sociocultural Studies | 218 |
| Science | 228 |
| Mathematics | 234 |
| Music | 239 |
| Kemetic Yoga | 239 |

## LESSON PLANS FOR AGES 11-12 YEARS — 241

| | |
|---|---|
| Language Arts and Sociocultural Studies | 241 |
| Science | 248 |
| Mathematics | 256 |
| The Arts | 260 |

## LESSON PLANS FOR AGES 12–13 YEARS — 265

| | |
|---|---|
| Language Arts and Sociocultural Studies | 266 |
| Logic and History | 275 |
| Mathematics | 284 |
| The Arts | 290 |

| | |
|---|---|
| LESSON PLANS FOR AGES 13-14 YEARS | 295 |
| LESSON PLAN FOR AGES 14-15 YEARS | 323 |
| Conclusion | 329 |
| Bibliography | 333 |

# FOREWORD

During the past fifty years, there has been a global rush to create schools centered on the cultural narratives emanating from the people who were marginalized in the colonial and imperial quest to dominate the world. Africa and its diaspora were severely impacted by the work of those who sought to turn African children into black and brown copies of Europeans. This was a crime against humanity perpetrated by powers that had little interest in the maturation of African and African descendant children. Lacking cultural rudders, African children and adults were tossed by the Western or Arabic educational systems into stormy seas or desert sands with little guidance, grounding, and direction. Whatever they brought to the table was thrown out, and they were made to eat what was pushed before them, even if the meal was something that would damage their self-concepts and historical legacies. Nothing could be more crippling than an educational system that took children away from their parents, their cultures, and their societies, so that they could no longer remember the names of their generations or the traditions that made them great farmers, explorers, doctors, or students of astronomy.

When I opened the pages of Nah Dove's manuscript to read what she had written about African education, I immediately felt that I had finally seen an important work about education that all teachers should have in their classrooms and home offices. It was a book that grew out of the combination of her intelligence, will, and determination to correct what had been written or told about Africa. In writing this book based on her on ground research, Dove, with her doctorate in hand from the State University of New York at Buffalo and confidence through her association with UNICEF, was able to provide the reader with a concrete example of the Afrocentric model of education.

There is nothing more important for children than the application of knowledge for the interpretation of their own histories, experiences, and possibilities. But, as Dove knows, in Africa and outside of Africa, black and brown children are frequently alienated from their own roots and made to believe that they have no culture, no science, no mathematics, no poetry, and no responses to nature. Education is derived from the deepest well of a people's thinking about relationships. How we relate to the universe, to nature, to animals, to plants, and to each other. Our educational compass, like our moral compass, is rooted in the very way we approach reality, and that is a gift to us from the ancestors who laid the first sense of value in our midst so that we could show justice, balance, truth, harmony, and order. Nah Dove with this breathtaking book that is sure to be a classic much like Amos Wilson's Blueprint for Black Power has taken the philosophical leadership in the Afrocentric education field. What I most appreciate is the ability to see the connection between the African concepts and the realities of actually educating children. Nah Dove has finally produced the book, The Afrocentric School: A Blueprint, for which an entire cadre of teachers has been looking forward to reading.

Molefi Kete Asante

# INTRODUCTION

I have written *The Blueprint for Afrocentric Schools* for the African diaspora, teachers, and students wherever they exist in the world. Teachers have often asked me for information about Afrocentric information, and I have been eager to give them the benefit of my training, experiences, and research in a format that will make sense. It is the aim of this book to offer the teacher, school administrator, and curriculum officer, a practical, research-based model for excellence in pedagogy derived from the best of our African philosophies and traditions.

This critical and necessary Blueprint for an Afrocentric school offers a foundational curriculum geared to educate girls and boys globally. The blueprint is grounded in a belief in the potential and ability of children to reveal their special genius when they are taught from an Afrocentric perspective. Created from over three decades of research in education and the development of Afrocentric Schools in both the U.K. and U.S., along with the findings of a baseline study carried out on the African continent, the curriculum offers possible models and a guide to appropriate curriculum for all children aged between 2-15 years. It is the intention of this blueprint to enable children to understand more clearly, not only the nature of anti-African cultural constraints that are cruelly imposed upon them, but also how cultural knowledge counteracts its effects.

Schools are "educational" institutions, culturally shaped and defined to be used to provide information deemed necessary by the authority of the rulers of nation states. These authorities plan and oversee what citizens learn and what is regarded as relevant to the continuation of their culture and society. If the citizens of that society suffer inequalities, it is an unjust society. If the culture of that society despises your humanity, it is not your culture. In this case, an "education" that supports that society's inequalities and injustices is corrupt. In fact, it cannot be called an education, rather as Mwalimu Shujaa says in his work *Too Much Schooling, Too Little Education* (1994), it is merely schooling. In this light, what may be regarded as "relevant" may oppose the personal and social development of people, whether privileged or underprivileged, depending on the cultural aims and inequities that are being upheld in that society.

From his work *Revolutionary Pedagogy* (2017), Molefi Kete Asante says,

> I cannot accept the educational status quo in either the elementary or secondary schools in America, I can neither accept nor appreciate the structure and scope of the curriculum in most universities. Consequently, I am forced by circumstances to be against the status quo, to seek its overthrow, to obliterate its racist ethic, and to demand a new vision of education for all children.

Following this line of reasoning and logic and in opposition to maintaining inequalities and injustices, the Afrocentric School, must be regulated by people who wish to teach children literacy, numeracy, science, and philosophy through knowledge of their cultural history and herstory so that they will know who they are, their potential, and what they might become. In this way, cultural identity takes on a major role in the educational development of children.

These schools vary depending on where they are located in the world. Location, whether urban or rural will dictate the resources available to support this kind of education. Becoming literate is a fundamental requirement for Afrocentric Schools. Depending on circumstances, not all educators involved in these schools may be highly literate but their knowledge will be used and translated for children gaining literacy. What is of greatest importance is, as follows:

- The *knowledge* of the teachers, children, and their local communities
- The teachers' love for the children
- The teachers' vision of a better world

The Afrocentric School places Africa, the birthplace of humanity and civilization, at the center of knowledge development. This concept is itself radical, as it defies the logic of today's thinking and schooling about Africa and her people and Diaspora. Yet, it is a cultural historical journey that must be taken in order to understand the story of humanity and why we are in this place at this time in the world.

The Afrocentric School aims to:

- Help children to become literate in Reading, Writing, History, Geography, Science, Philosophy, Music, and Mathematics, so that they can compete in the greater society and participate in making decisions about their futures. In this way, they can help to change the inequalities and injustices in their societies.
- Help children and their families learn the Truth of history and herstory. For this Blueprint, herstory is deemed as critically as important as history. For African descended women, men and children, herstory is viewed as marginalized in the reconstruction of cultural knowledge. This will become clear in the following work as African cultural values and beliefs become more specific. In this way they will have the ability to see outside the imposition of a false cultural identity based upon the fabrication of history.
- Help the children to build a foundation for learning skills, including Agriculture, that can help their communities.
- Encourage the Artistic and Musical features of their lives.

It is believed that the Afrocentric School will help to develop the mind, skills, and potentiality of children and therefore the communities in which they are located.

After over 40 years as an educator Molefi Kete Asante says,

"I have never found a student that I could not reach using pedagogy based in Afrocentric theory" (2017, p.x).

Much of what has been written about Africa has supported the idea that the "wholesale exploitation" of Africa, her people and recognized Diaspora, has been justified. In order for this to have taken place, a culturally developed lie was malevolently devised to restructure the epistemology of the world's people – that we humans are divided into races and that our value can be identified and determined by the color of our skin. The ramifications of this cultural belief include untold genocide and both psychologically and spiritually damaging repercussions on the lives of the people of the world, in particular those with the darkest skins, wherever they live and whatever cultures they espouse.

For over two thousand years there has been a concerted effort, by differing cultural groups of people, to debase and demonize the continent of Africa and her people. Eurocentrism is a conceptual framework, used in the majority of the world, which places Europe at the center of human civilization and world history, beginning with Greece. This framework, which is the predominant worldview in which history is taught, encompasses the misconception that the epistemology or knowledge defined within this framework, is true. Those outside of this framework are viewed through a Eurocentric lens, deeming them objects or others in the Eurocentric retelling of history. Africa is the mother of humanity and where we find the earliest and most foundational civilizations of the world. Why should we not respect our place of origin and where we come from? Why would history begin from outside of the birthplace of humanity? These are questions that a number of people have been asking for some time; some still living in Africa and members of the Diaspora who inhabit the rest of the world, who see beyond the falsehood, and recognize with pride, their African Ancestors and origins.

Africa has been a major source of wealth for the "development" of the countries that have oppressed her for centuries, and indeed the world. They have collectively exploited Africa through the use and misuse of women, men and children's energies, lands, food, agriculture, medicine, science, spirituality, mathematics, astronomy, astrology, architecture, and historical, philosophical, ecological knowledge as well as her mineral wealth in precious metals and jewels.

For this Blueprint, it is understood that Africa is inarguably the place of origin of the human race. Today everybody's mitochondrial DNA can be traced back to an African mother who lived between 100-200 thousand years ago. Homo sapiens sapiens, the humans who inhabit the earth today have resided in Africa for at least 250 thousand years. Some remained in Africa and others left Africa and populated the world between 80-50,000 years ago. Our human phenotypes changed in differing climates over time; thus, all people at one time were African, highly pigmented (melanated) and what we consider today Black. White skinned people whose heartlands are in the colder Northern cradle or the Western world are descendants of Black African people as are the yellow, red, and brown people who inhabit different parts of the world. The color of skin is based on its melanin content. The whiter or lighter the skin color, the less melanin it contains.

# PART I

# Overview

CHAPTER 1

# The Racialization of Humanity

The theory of race is a cultural construction created by patriarchal societies in their justification for the conquest of Africa. This will be explained using Cheikh Anta Diop's cradle theory which is recognized as fundamental to Afrocentric theory. Those most involved in the enslavement and colonization of Africa, using the race paradigm, are the people from Euro-Arab patriarchal cultures. They have used "race" as a detrimental way of determining levels of human status and the value of human life. Race has influenced not only our thinking but also the ability of people to survive. By the end of the 18th century and continuing throughout the 19th century, the pseudoscientific concept of race and the belief in white superiority were developed systematically by European academics including explorers, biologists, anthropologists, linguists, historians, physicians, and others.

Simply put, European academicians, researchers and writers constructed a cultural belief largely based on skin color which placed humanity in a color-coded hierarchy denoting superiority and inferiority. European women and men were placed at the top of the hierarchy as white people, the most superior, with the Blackest woman and man (African) considered the most inferior at the base. In between are the yellow, red and brown types. Within this patriarchal perspective, women are considered inferior to men, although based on skin color the white woman is viewed as superior to all other men and women except for the white man. This cultural belief became a comprehensive doctrine that was/is used to justify white global and local control and their appropriation of non-white peoples, their energies, lands, knowledge, wealth, minerals and other resources.

Within this Eurocentric cultural conceptualization there was the belief and fear that these so-called races could not and should not mix. If they did mix, then the children would inherit the devised inferiority of the Black parent which would contaminate the purity of the white or that the Black child would be brought to a new level of advancement by the forged purity of the white parent. Nowhere is this Manichaean concept more apparent than in Brahmanism, the Indo Aryan construction of Hinduism. Importantly, these ideas and behaviors are not recent. They can be identified over two thousand years ago during so-called Semitic and European conquests across Africa beginning with Kemet (Ancient Egypt), in religious texts and societal formations.

Within the Hebraic-Talmudic-Christian religion the bible supplies the notion of the races of humanity in Genesis 9:23, in the story of the sons of Noah; Ham, Japheth, and Shem who were responsible for peopling the world after the great flood. Essentially, Ham would father the Black people, Hamites; Shem, the mixed-race Semite; and Japheth the white Aryan. It is said that Ham saw his father Noah's nakedness and drunkenness but did not cover him. Then, Noah cursed Ham by condemning Ham's fourth son Canaan and his children to a life of servitude (enslavement) to his uncles, Shem and Japheth. It is important to reiterate here that humans originated in Africa, and were highly melanated/Black prior to travelling outside of Africa and populating the globe so these stories do not align with the true human story in which all people were originally highly melanated/Black and remained so for 200,000 plus years.

The earlier version in the 6$^{th}$ century CE Babylonian Talmud, which evolved from 100 BCE was part of the Tanakh and prior to the coming of Muhammed and Islam, supplies a reason for the "curse." Noah's son Ham supposedly saw his father sleeping naked in the night and castrated him for no apparent or stated reason. When Noah awoke he cursed his son Ham telling him that as a result of not being able to have a fourth son, Ham's fourth son Canaan would have children who were ugly because of the crime, black because of the night time when it occurred, with twisted hair for turning to see his nakedness, with red eyes and swollen lips because he made fun of his father, naked because Noah was naked, and with long penises. These offspring would be called Negroes (Poe, 1997, p.370). They would more likely have been called "abd" a derogatory Arabic word to define a Black person or an enslaved person who was Black that could be used interchangeably to describe an obscene person lacking morals, a filthy person or a person practicing a non-Muslim religion; like the Nuba of South Sudan who are historically enslaved to the Islamic Arabs (Jok, 2001, pp.8-9).

Influenced by the Hebraic tradition, the Arab-Muslim-Shem version is that Black people are cursed to be slaves and menials, Arabs are blessed to be prophets and nobles, while Turks and Slavs are destined to be kings and tyrants (Lewis, 1990, p.45). These ideas are reinforced by the blasphemous descriptions of African people throughout the literature.

These thoughts are mirrored in India in Brahmanism, the Hindu religion based upon ideas of reincarnation, composed by the conquering Indo Europeans (Aryans) around 1000 BCE. The Indo Aryans arrived in the Indus Valley around 1500 BCE, contemporaneous with when the Hyksos were conquering Kemet. The Black indigenous people, Kushites, who were builders of the Indus Valley complex, the Harappan civilization, were both literate and matriarchal people 1,000 years before the Indo Aryan conquest of this region. They brought with them their spiritual knowledge from Africa. Reinterpreted in the "holy" scripture, the Rig Veda professed that there are essentially four castes (colors) but five statuses. White was associated with the Brahmins who were the teachers and priests, red with the Kshatriyas, the warrior caste, yellow the Vaishyas, the merchant caste, and Black the Sudras, the subservient caste; finally, the Black Dalits born of forbidden liaisons within the castes are kept outside the four races. Born as sinners, the Dalits live a debased life as "untouchables," their lives must be lived in servility (enslavement), humiliation and degradation, spurned and abused by the others in the belief that their very shadows pollute the earth (Ben Levi, 1986; Chandler 1988; Fairservis Jnr 1988; Rajshekar 1987; Rashidi & Van Sertima, 1988). The Sudras and Dalits are the Black descendants of the builders of the Harappan civilization.

Evidence shows that Africa was conquered primarily for her incredible wealth of knowledge, including the spiritual, medicinal, astronomical, astrological, mathematical, scientific, musical, literary, artistic endeavor, urbanization and nation state development etc. Those who have conquered, imperialized, plundered, looted, stolen, murdered, enslaved and maligned African integrity have sought to create a false epistemology and reconstruct a history within which they are saints, heroes and heroines. Thus, much of the academic teaching, writing, research, thinking, philosophy, theology, artistry, music, agriculture etc., is problematized by the egregious lack of truth. These beliefs justified both the ancient and ongoing usurping of lands and wealth, the demonization of Africa and her people, and the heinous and brutal enslavement of African women, men and children by the Arab–Semitic or Middle Eastern populations and Europeans.

It is well documented through writings by Greek scholars that the ancient Egyptian Kemites were their teachers; many of them were educated there and developed their philosophical thoughts through these teachings. The fall of Kemet (Ancient Egypt) augured a time described by Chancellor Williams as the *Destruction of Black Civilization* (1987). It may also be viewed as the destruction of Maat – Truth, female-male reciprocity, balance, justice and harmony and righteous universal order.

As Cheikh Anta Diop, the African multi-genius told us, "The history of Africa will remain suspended in air and cannot be written correctly until African historians connect it with the history of Egypt" (Diop, 1991, p.xvi).

This necessary cultural link has been a challenge to those academics and educators in particular, grounded in Aryan-Euro-white culture as well as those grounded in Arab-Middle-Eastern-Semitic culture and the racist epistemology that their forefathers have created and which they have relied upon to develop their theories and paradigms.

As Diop's meticulous research revealed, the cultural beliefs and practices found in Kemet, which was by all accounts a highly evolved civilization, can be found across Africa. In fierce corroboration with maintaining the race paradigm, there continues to be a concerted effort by European so-called Egyptologists, historians, anthropologists, archaeologists, and other "pseudo-experts" on Kemet (Ancient Egypt) and Africa, to challenge and destroy the credibility of scholars of any discipline, female or male of any color, who claim that African women and men on the continent of Africa who resided in and ruled Kemet for thousands of years were indeed African.

The paradigm of Afrocentricity, as developed by Molefi Kete Asante, embraces the works of all those throughout time who have contributed to understanding the significance of Africa to humanity. Afrocentricity, through logic, challenges Eurocentric epistemology and information that places Europe as the wellspring of human knowledge. Instead, Afrocentricity places Africa at the center of the story of humanity, thus providing the theoretical and conceptual framework, the basis of an epistemology within which the truth of the totality of the human experience has the potential to come to light. It enables people to locate themselves in the his/herstory of the cultural journey from Africa until now.

In the words of Molefi Kete Asante, Afrocentricity is a process in education that seeks to locate or relocate African people and phenomena within the context of African historical and cultural agency.

CHAPTER 2

# Reclaiming African Knowledge

The Euro-Arabic schooling of people has been critical to maintaining power over the spiritual, psychological, political, social, and economic development of Africa and her Diaspora across the world. The institution of "Education" has been absolutely vital to providing misinformation to enable people to know their "roles" in societies.

Carter G. Woodson brought to mind in *The Mis-Education of the Negro* (1933) that the school cannot provide a real "education." Woodson believed that being taught European-white (Eurocentric) economics, history, philosophy, religion and literature could only train the mind of the African-Black person to know her/his restricted place in society. In this way s/he will continue to support the power of the oppressor. It was clear that Woodson saw cultural distinctions between the experiences of European and African people and the negative impact of Eurocentric ideas on the African psyche. Woodson's idea was that to have "real" knowledge (Truth) would enable the liberation of the African mind and the destruction of false information.

This is why understanding and respecting the cultural link to Africa, challenges perpetual falsehood. It can open up a way of thinking about the self and the world, that promotes the re-awakening of ancient memory. In this way cultural identity can be formed that is true to the heart and soul of the African child as s/he is formulating her/his understanding of reality.

All cultural groups invest in the development of their people so that members may survive and flourish individually and collectively. Within this cultural matrix, the love of one's humanity is a vital component of culture. *If the culture despises your humanity, it is not your culture.* Vital to the shaping of a society is the molding of the mind and the intellect; how these evolve is crucial to the development of cultural identity, and thus knowledge of self and society. For those whose ancestors were conquered, enslaved, and colonized, the development of African cultural identity has been compromised and altered, through the systematic efforts that have endured for centuries, to debase and demonize Africa and her people.

The conquest of Africa required the disruption, degradation, demonization and devaluation of its cultural history as a method of political, religious and economic control. The imposition of various forms of foreign cultural domination, have been fundamental to this enterprise. The conquering men and women have effectively trained, through the use of violence and later rewards, African women and men to become emissaries of their cultural beliefs in order to work on their behalf in the effort to maintain control over resources. Unfortunately, the culturally antithetical differences in major conquering thoughts have not always been viewed as critical to the divisions among African people, by African people. Thus, liberation theories of African unity like Pan Africanism often fail to recognize the significance of what Afrocentric theory understands; the potential for African unity is based on African cultural unity. Diop warned us that unless we link ancient African cultural history to today, we shall never know our true his/herstory.

According to Diop (1991) a major factor in cultural identity development, the basis for the development of cultural unity, is the history of a people; this is the cultural "glue" that unifies a community with a sense of belonging in that its collective experiences over time are part of a historical continuity. It provides a consciousness that enables people to identify themselves as part of a population connected in ways that define their traditional similarities and distinctions from other cultural groups. People want to understand, appreciate, and live their historical legacy and transmit their cultural memory or heritage to their descendants.

The psyche underpins the development of identity, personality, and consciousness. Humans need to feel safe, loved, appreciated and respected as they grow to understand the collective ideals of culture from pre-birth to adulthood within their societies. In this way, they can locate themselves, fulfill their potential, and contribute to the future of both self and society. Identification of this cultural characteristic has been indispensable to understanding the psychosocial cultural realities of living in an essentially Europeanized (Aryanized) and Arabized (Semitic) cultural environment.

An important prerequisite for developing cultural identity, requires a clear sense of one's spiritual connection to the universe. The knowledge of self is the foundation of True knowledge. Imposed religions based on corrupted interpretations of Ancient African knowledge, have undermined the development of cultural identity. As Wade Nobles poignantly teaches in *Seeking the Sakhu* (2006), the Greek word *psyche*, itself rooted in the Kemetic word *sakhu*, means the "soul of being." Human mind and human behavior cannot be separated from the spirit as they shape concepts of humanity and understandings of "self." Thus, the cognitive recognition of and the spiritual connection to the ancestors and their historical and cultural significance, can support the development of cultural identity for people of African descent.

The earliest educational institutions that we are aware of, arose in Africa. As Asa Hilliard (1984) and George James (1954) informed us, long before recorded invasions, the ancient records show that the African system of classical education that developed in Kemet was the model upon which later systems in Europe evolved, through the Greeks and Romans.

In Kemet, rose the focus on Grammar, Rhetoric and Logic as moral disciplines centered in Truth. Mathematics, Geometry, and Astronomy dealt with the knowledge of the destiny of humanity in individuals, societies, and nations. Music was viewed as the living practice of philosophy, the route to harmony with the Divinity–the unseen, the unknowable, the mother and father. Music was used in the cure of disease. These seven disciplines were the basis of the Seven Liberal Arts; the foundation of western higher education.

These disciplines, although separated as a method of learning and developing, are all part of the same whole; developed within a cosmological reality and belief that everything in life and nature that exists, ever was, and ever shall be, is connected. This learning method is a way to begin to understand the enormity of what that means. Essentially, in its truest form, education is the process of becoming enlightened by gaining intelligence as the basis for inner vision.

**Language arts** In this educational setting, speech itself was sacred as was the expression of it in writing; the Mdw Ntr (Kemetic text) literally means Divine word. The Ancients knew that the symbol and sound of the word or speech emit vibrations as part of the vibrational environment that life exists in.

As Wayne Chandler (1999) explains, in the Principle of Vibration everything is moving, nothing is still, whether we are aware of it or not. Scientific instruments are able to detect vibrations in their slightest motions. They vary in speed, and the rate and frequencies determine the form they take. It is considered the substance of universal matter moving towards positive or negative. Moving towards the positive pole is moving towards self-awareness and realization. In this way, the Mdw Ntr as both speech and symbol is part of the higher vibration and learning.

**Rhetoric** is oratory and considered to be the study of the technique of using speech. In KMT it was an Art to use the voice, its vibrational sound, to heal. The concept of "good speech" and righteous speech is linked to the vibrational sound.

**Philosophy and Logic** is the study of the interpretations of theory, subject, and matter. The mind–thought, can investigate and determine the truth or falsehood of the theory.

**Mathematics** is the study of numbers, configurations, quantity, shape, space and the metaphysics of being.

**Geometry** is the branch of mathematics concerned with the properties, relationships, and measurement of points, lines, curves and surfaces.

**Astronomy** is the scientific study of celestial bodies and the universe as a whole. It branches into Astrometry, Astrodynamics, Cosmology and Astrophysics. The study looks at the measurements of the positions of bodies in space as well as seeking to find their properties and origins.

**The arts**, particularly music, were perceived to be the living practice of philosophy; the route to harmony with nature, the celestial bodies, Divinities, and used in the cure of disease.

From George James' *Stolen Legacy* (1989, p.27), we learn that in

KMT students undergoing training to become Priestesses and Priests, competent in their fields of study, comprised 3 grades.

1. **The Mortals**, probationary students who were being instructed, but who had not yet reached "Inner Vision."
2. **The Intelligences**, those who had attained the "Inner Vision."
3. **The Creators**, those who had become united with "True Spiritual Consciousness."

The individual was expected to cultivate the Arts and Sciences along with Virtue, and through this understanding seek to become divine while on earth. These seven disciplines remain in Traditional systems across Africa.

Much of the responsibility of learning, teaching and educating was held by the priests and priestesses all over Africa. No distinction was made between spirituality and education. In fact, spiritual and educational knowledge could not be separated. As Hilliard (1984) noted, the Temple complex of Ipet-Isut, meaning the holiest or select of places, was standing prior to the existence of Greece and was renamed Luxor and Karnak by the Arabs, who arrived a thousand years after the Greek invasion. These Temples housed libraries and professors, with more than 80,000 students attending. Even the "secret" or mystery systems (traditions of knowledge practiced in Kemet) were reflected in the teachings throughout Africa.

During the period of Kemet, there were specific times of indigenous African rule, as non-indigenous patriarchal rulers such as the Hyksos, Persians, Assyrians, Greeks, Romans and Arabs took over and tried to imitate what already existed. It was during indigenous African rule in pre and early Kemetic dynasties that most of the pyramids were built until the 12th century. During the 18th dynasty the building of magnificent temples and tombs took place and the 25th dynasty of Kushite Kings who brought back the Queens and high priestesses, placing them, once more in major roles of leadership. Ancient indigenous ways of male-female reciprocity returned to Maatic rule – order, an African renaissance.

Notably, sophisticated and complex systems of education flourished across Africa in rural as well as urban societies and communities. It was these spiritual based institutions that were targeted by the conquerors to undermine the strength of the people, so that their source of thousands of years of knowledge, cultural history and identity, spirituality, and skills development, could be appropriated, corrupted and destroyed. In this light, the forced imposition of foreign religions was viewed as an important tactic in controlling the passing on of culture and therefore knowledge.

The Arabs Islamized Ancient Egypt after its Christianization by the Romans; seizing the wealth of indigenous education for their own sociocultural development both in Egypt and where they had come from. In the same way as Europeans, the Arabs denied the African authenticity of their stolen knowledge. Similarly, Islamized Africans translated the knowledge of places like the University of Sankore in Ancient Ghana into Arabic. Ancient Ghana, contemporaneous with Kemet in its early development, akin to Kemet, focused on the promotion of higher education.

From current evidence it is clear that Africa promoted higher education and through its spiritual systems it has been a cultural and historical mainstay for the survival of her people. At the same time, it has been exploited to "educate" and "develop" western and Arab civilizations. Importantly, during European and Arab conquests, imperialism, colonization and enslavement of African people, many of these practices were transferred to the places that African people migrated or were forcibly taken to. Not to be taken lightly, the development of bone tools can be traced to African people who lived 90,000 years ago in the Congo region, previously Zaire. This discovery by Alison S Brooks and David M Helgren et al. in 1995 points to modern human inventions created by African ancestors. Findings such as this defy the inculcation that human advancements in civilization and inventions began in Europe.

Wherever African people travelled or were forcibly taken, the need for and belief in education as cultural knowledge was encouraged. There is evidence of education as higher knowledge all over the Americas, North, South, and Central through the First Nations people whose origins are African. David Imhotep's (2012) research into First Nations people uses genetic evidence to show that the *First Americans were Africans,* grounded in the logic of Africa as the birthplace of humanity and phenotypes changed. It may be said that alongside the arrival of later enslaved African women, men and children, that over the centuries, the descendants of Africa who recognize and respect their Ancestors and their Africa-ness, have tried to seek, understand, uplift and uphold the Ancient cultural values and beliefs. We are the descendants.

**Know Thyself**

S/he who knows not that s/he knows not, is a fool – shun him
S/he who knows not and knows that s/he
   knows not, is simple – teach him
S/he who knows and knows not that s/
   he knows, is asleep – wake him
S/he who knows and knows that s/he knows, is wise – follow him
All of these reside in you so to thine own self, be true

This ancient African wisdom is found written on the Ancient Egyptian Temple walls. This teaching applies to all of us.

The Educators in the ancient times across Africa were Priestesses and Priests who included their spiritual awareness in the way that they approached and taught the knowledge handed to them. They were the wise women and men that served as examples to the people of how they should live.

Afrocentric Educators are those who are educated in understanding the ancient African principles that guide our behavior and the way that we seek knowledge. They are seekers of Truth who recognize in humility that they must continually learn and grow. We are Students as well as Teachers; we are the Leaders as well as the Followers.

Afrocentric Educators are those who understand or are in the process of trying to understand the current conditions that have beset African women, men and children on a global scale. The history and herstory of Africa from an Afrocentric perspective is about placing Africa at the center of the story of humanity. This is critical to the educators' knowledge base. In this way, wherever the educator travels, s/he is able to use the Afrocentric paradigm to bring clarity to the assessment of the situation of women, men and children located in any place in the world.

S/he must understand the construction of race as a Eurocentric/Aryan and Arabic cultural creation. That the Blackest skinned person is the most maligned and mistreated. S/he must know that this cultural belief has been imposed upon the cultures of all people globally, epistemologically, religiously, psychologically, physically, socially and in any aspect of human endeavor and reality. S/he must know that skin color has not only determined the treatment and life experience of women, men and children, but impacts on her/his existence too, whether s/he has been privileged or not. Thus, s/he must be able to locate her own place in the construction of race so that s/he may understand the nature of discrimination and her responsibility to bring about enlightenment on the subject through teaching.

The Afrocentric Teacher must be educationally grounded in knowledge of the ancient African matriarchy which is based on female and male reciprocity–Maat. In this way, s/he will be able to make sense of the historical and cultural changes that have occurred globally through patriarchal domination, conquest, imperialism, colonization, enslavement and impoverishment, whether through Arabizing or Europeanizing models.

The Afrocentric Educator must be able to assess the current conditions of the women, men, girls and boys whom s/he will teach. Race and gender abuse appear in differing forms according to the cultural methods of domination. For example, whilst the continual police killings and containment of people of African descent in the US is rife, and re-enslavement is going on in the prison industrial complex as amplified by Ava Duvernay (2016) in the film *13th*; in Brazil 40 men are killed per day by the police and in Islamic Africa and the Middle-East, enslavement persists and African men continue to be castrated, while African women are concubines to the Arab/Semitic rulers.

A prerequisite is that the Afrocentric Teacher must love the children. As spiritual beings, the children will know if you love them or not. It is that spiritual connection that will enhance the education process. Too many of our children are taught by people who view them through the Aryan-Eurocentric-Arab-centric lens that debases the potential of the Black child. These people may be Black, white, red, yellow or brown. The child will react in different ways to this disrespect. A crafty, deceitful way of curtailing the development of the child in school is to emphasize behavior so that whilst the children are reacting to her/his unspoken but known psychological, spiritual, and social debasement, their actions are recorded as part of their profile as they are led on the path to their eventual "place" in society.

The Afrocentric Educator must understand her/his cultural identity. In this light, the Educator's work is to primarily develop the cultural identity of children by helping them to know who they truly are so that they are not bound by an imposed cultural belief in their inferiority accompanied by a false his/herstory of humanity. In this way, the children or even adults will be able to see outside the falsification of their societal conditioning and understand and realize their true potential.

Importantly, the Afrocentric Educator/Teacher is a role model and example to the students, their carers, and the community and society within which they live. One cannot have expectations of the students' behaviors and beliefs that one does not continually strive to practice.

The Afrocentric Educator must be aware of her/his ancestral relationship to those who have gone before. S/he must pay respect and recognition to the ancestors; setting an example for the students to honor those who came before us and without whom we would not exist.

It is known that we are living in times when Truth is depicted as a lie and lies are held up as Truth. To be human in this era is to be confused, and yet we must continuously learn, grow and develop. We are not perfect. We recognize ourselves as working towards our own betterment as we work towards the betterment of the world. In other words, we are all works in process and progress.

Thus, although the Afrocentric Educator must be an example, s/he must also recognize her/his own frailties and thus be understanding of the process that we are all undergoing, including and especially her students. Thus, s/he must be humble and at the same time confident that s/he can carry out the Afrocentric mission. The mission as it is understood at this moment in time is to globalize the Afrocentric School model so that we are continuously educating ourselves, researching and discovering, and disseminating True knowledge across the world in order to improve the life chances of our people and subsequently humanity as a whole.

The potential Afrocentric Educator must be trained in Afrocentric theory and understand both her/his Purpose and the immense responsibility with which the role of teacher in this form of education entails. This should ideally include a process of teacher training in order to qualify for this critically important role.

# CHAPTER 3

# A Culture-Based Study

## A Basis for setting Educational standards for Children of African Descent

In developing the Afrocentric School, it will be important to develop curricula and lesson plans that speak to the needs of the children, underpinned by expectations of their development at particular ages.

In light of this, the results of a baseline study carried out in Ghana are used to look at Indigenous Traditional Education Structures in mainly rural areas where the majority of children do not attend schools. This research applied Afronographic methodology to study the child upbringing practices among mostly culturally Traditional rural people. This methodology refers to the method of recording and writing the African experience from an Afrocentric perspective. The consultant coordinators and interviewers underwent an intensive Afrocentric orientation prior to the study. These findings are used to understand the children's developmental process from pre-birth to 9 years old. Whilst the majority of children were not literate, they were still undergoing an Educational process in learning the skills necessary in their communities.

A key recommendation from this study was to develop a plan for Community-based Learning Systems (CBLS), that would include the introduction of Literacy. It was clear to me through my research at the time that culturally affirming community-based learning systems would need to be a self-sustaining developmental project. The CBLS would call for recognition and need to apply Sankofa (the concept of reclaiming our past to understand the present and move forward) principles to connect the development of African children to Africa's own developmental and cultural standards. Thereby conserving African cultural specifications which would comprise the fulfillment of basic imperative needs such as clean water, food, electricity, roads and transportation. The respondents were willing and inspired to carry out the work of reconstruction to sustain the communities. Most importantly, the CBLS requires the knowledge and expertise of indigenous women, men and children, combined with Afrocentric knowledge on the true his and her story of African people and our achievements from ancient times to the present day.

The findings of this research provide the basis of the development of Afrocentric education which is viewed as the path to personal and social development, cultural identity and the route to intelligence and higher learning.

Education is looked at as a process of growth and development in learning about self and the world, how one should behave to honor the self and family, and what one can do to contribute to the society one lives in. For this research, literacy is not deemed as a panacea of intelligence if what one is learning in the process of becoming literate, is of no use to enhance life and is based on falsehood.

It seemed culturally relevant to primarily use the Mothers, the major transmitters of knowledge, for the study. They have the most direct and intimate knowledge of childrearing practices from the womb until 9 years of age. Both the Mothers and Fathers in the study came from rural communities and were principally farmers and petty traders. They lived mainly in compounds and small village communities in secluded areas. Although the Mothers were the main knowledge bearers for the Data, it was found that men played a critical role. The men were found to be amenable to the whole idea as Priests, husbands and fathers, trusting that the information would be used for good purposes.

The Fathers were interviewed about how supportive they would be to their girls and boys learning literacy. The Akan believe O̱bea ye̱ turom mu nhwiren; ne kunu nso ye̱ ne ho ban: A woman is a flower in the garden; and her husband the fence around it. This illustrates the strong held belief that the man in this capacity is the protector of the woman. Many nations whether patrilineal or matrilineal believe that Traditionally, the Father plays an important role in spiritual guidance and protection to the children also. Originally, 1,248 Questionnaire interviews of 835 Mothers and 413 Fathers took place. It was decided that 256 Mothers' Questionnaires would be randomly selected to remove the bias of the sameness in answers from the communities. Thus, 256 Mothers' interviews were used for this study.

## Essential factors

The Mothers practiced three main religions, Traditional African Spirituality, Islam, and Christianity. Most Mothers practiced Traditional beliefs even if they practiced another religion. The median age of the Mothers was 36 years, the median age for bearing her first child was 20 years and the median number of children was 3. The majority of the Mothers spoke 3 languages. They represented the Nations of Builsa, Dagomba, Konkomba, Bassare, Ewe, Krobo, Guan, Mamprusi, Kusasi, Busanga, Moshie, Bissa, Bimoba, Garuma and Akan – which although used as a classification is in fact a confederacy of Nations. Six of the seven districts where the Mothers lived were in the North and Upper East regions. They are the poorest regions and becoming increasingly poorer. The 7th district, the Eastern Region, although more fertile, is still impoverished. For these women, men and children, poverty or wealth rests with the sustainability of their lands and its ability to produce a good yield that can:

- Sustain the lives of the family
- Help others
- Be sold or exchanged for extra necessities

Importantly, the majority of the people in the Baseline Study did not have the following basic needs met:

- Clean water
- Water located close to the communities
- Sufficient amounts of food
- Electricity

- Roads
- Access to western health services

From a Eurocentric perspective, evidenced in countless studies, deprived social and environmental conditions appear to be culturally natural to Tradition based societies. For instance, women, girls and boys carrying water on their heads for miles is viewed as Traditional when in fact history shows that, prior to conquest, urban and rural development in Africa was built around the proximity of water and centralized water systems existed prior to ancient Ghana.

The communities that took part in the study believed there was a need for social change and that they would eventually be able to have basic needs met and become self-sufficient like their ancestors. They believed that their children would be a part of that movement.

## Indigenous Knowledge

The Foundation of Family and Community Cultural Values.

## Spirituality

In terms of the Traditional cultural spiritual beliefs of the Mothers and their families, the majority of Mothers have ancestral and family god/ess representations in their homes, compounds and communities. It may be surmised that some Mothers, owing to their religious affiliations with Islam and Christianity, do not use or did not admit to using the Shrines in their communities. However, it is safe to assume and moreover know that they are familiar with indigenous beliefs and practices around them. Since indigenous cultural values concerning Traditional practices are an integral part of the historical, deep and ancient social structure, it is logical that there exists a cultural unity of which Cheikh Anta Diop theorized, that underpins the more modern religious cultural impositions even after centuries of persecution. In this light it may be said that these rural communities practiced a more undiluted African culture than would likely be found in more urban areas. It is for this reason that the findings can help to link this knowledge to both the Ancient and modern Traditional African culture which can inform those of us who have become more westernized but seek knowledge of African cultural connections.

## Traditional Medical Practitioners

The earliest written records to date of Indigenous African medical treatments are documented on ancient papyri found in KMT. These records include methods of examination, diagnosis, and prognosis, in addition to surgical procedures and treatments.

Written records comprise 10 major medical papyri:

1. Kahun Papyri
2. Ramesseum Papyri
3. Edwin Smith Papyrus
4. Ebers Papyrus
5. Hearst Papyrus
6. London Papyrus
7. Berlin Papyrus
8. Carlsberg Papyri
9. Chester Beatty Papyri
10. Brooklyn Papyrus

The Edwin Smith Papyrus may go back as far as 10,000 years, according to Charles Finch (1990), Kemetologist (Afrocentric Egyptologist) and Medical Doctor. This Papyrus existed thousands of years before Hippocrates, the Greek father of Western medicine (5th Century BCE). According to these papyri the indigenous medical practitioners were able to perform highly sensitive operations. The Traditional medical practitioners of KMT were Priestesses and Priests and a critical part of treatments included a spiritual component.

Like the Ancients, today's Traditional Medical Practitioners (TMP) are Priestesses and Priests. As a result of the resourcefulness of indigenous people, they have maintained their Traditional Healthcare Structures over centuries of ongoing wars (whether foreign or national), conquests, and attempts to destroy their indigenous institutions–their power bases. It is known that 2/3 of the world's population rely entirely on TMP to stay alive. As Priestesses and Priests, the TMPs bring harmony back into communities as part of their work. Much of their training is done in secret, similar to the mystery systems practiced in KMT and all over Africa. The relationship between the Shrine and the TMP is based on a pact made by healer and the relevant Divinity. Protection for the healer is based on ethical conduct. It is believed that breaking these rules can end in illness or death.

A child may qualify to become a healer or TMP when and if:

- S/he shows a predilection for an interest in herbs.
- Is chosen by the Shrine e.g., the parents may be informed through the Shrine before her/his birth, of her/his past knowledge and s/he will be observed.
- S/he inherits the knowledge of healing from the family. Girls usually inherit from the Mothers and/or grand-Mothers and boys from Fathers and/or grand-Fathers.

The process of qualifying can be found in communities in the US displaying the same African cultural traditions as professor and author Stephanie Y Mitchem (2007) experienced growing up with healing knowledge all around her.

The girl or boy may be as young as 4 years; must have the required attributes like humility, compassion, thoughtfulness and obedience. S/he must have respect and be respected as well as be able to listen and concentrate carefully, follow instructions strictly, and have a tendency for introversion. In all, the child must possess evolved characteristics.

In the Asante tradition, accordingly both women and men are accepted for training. They must not break the vow of celibacy (if so, then they must make a sacrifice to the Shrine and then begin training again). They must not drink alcohol or quarrel. They must salute their elders by bending the right knee and touching the ground with the right hand. They must not command their god or goddess to harm or kill anyone. They must not visit the Chief's or High Priest/ess' court without permission and not go out at night with other young men and women. Apprentices will live in the grounds of the community Shrine and learn ritual under the tutelage of the TMP. The first year of training is a period of orientation during which the trainee is told very little. If s/he is not suitable, the family is informed and the training ceases.

It is clear that with the advent of some clinics and the availability of western medicines in the markets that their introduction has been made use of. Sixty four percent of the Mothers used both Traditional and western medicines, particularly with regard to their children. Some of the Mothers spoke of times when without Traditional Medicines they or members of their families would have died.

## Traditional Spiritual Protection

Within the Traditional Medical Structures, appeals to the Ancestors and Divinities are made, asking for the safety and protection of the children. Talismans, waist beads and wristbands are used to guard the children against negative forces. It was found that amongst the Muslim and Christian Mothers that many also practiced Traditional Spiritual protection for their girls and boys. Another aspect of Traditional child protection happens soon after the birth of the child, who is introduced to water. It is considered to be a welcome, and a libation is performed to thank the Creator for the safe arrival of the child. This ancient African ritual is not unlike the anointing of the Christian child with holy water.

## Funerary Practices

For African Traditional women, men and children, the funeral ritual is highly important because it takes place at the time that the soul, if the person is worthy, will enter the Ancestral realm. The sentiments of the family and community are critical in the transition of the soul to the spiritual realm. Becoming an Ancestor is highly desirable as it is a testimony to the life lived. Ideally, one wishes to have a life to be remembered as one who strived to live righteously and uplift others, and to become a role model for those remaining.

In this case, the desire and the attempt to live a righteous life and to be responsible to one's self, family, community and humanity is a reflection of the Ancient desire to do the same. Images and written information from KMT show the weighing of the Heart against Maat's feather of Truth as the test of the measure of one's moral obligation in the physical to live in Truth. This stage is the beginning of the transitional journey to the spiritual life and trials along the way to reach Ancestor-hood.

For the families, the idea comprises that at the end of physical life the children will remember you well and make sure that the funeral will enable you to enter the Ancestral realm. It is evident that the spiritual world is very real and in effect the physical is considered the manifestation of the spiritual. Death is the transition of the spirit from the material to the spiritual realm just as birth is the transition from the spiritual to the material realm.

For these people death and birth, as they are understood in the European and Arab world, does not occur. Ancestral spirits, particularly family Ancestors, still have an active involvement in the everyday lives of those who remain in the physical world. They are there to provide guidance, support, and direction to knowledge for those left in the material life. Some of the Ancestors will return to continue the cycle of life. Thus, the desire of members of the families to have good funerals is so that they may impact upon the life that they left and return as future babies with a benevolent purpose. In this way, incoming infants are often viewed as returning family members.

## The Significance of Song

Music and Song to Traditional Africa may be viewed as the spiritual-based cultural expression of the lived experience in every sphere of life, from the ritual to the socio-political. Music including Song cannot be separated from Philosophical beliefs, Rhetoric, Wisdom, Knowledge, the Arts, Mathematics, Logic, Morality, and the Sciences, Cosmology and Astronomy.

Linguistically, this expression is highly valued and must be used carefully to be significant to Traditional life. The corrupt use of sound and language can release negative forces. Song is used for example for amusement, rituals, and heroic accomplishments. Song is also used as an educational medium for teaching children about their culture, its history, values, beliefs, traditions, spirituality, and necessary behaviors. Songs convey deep meanings and involve parental participation as well as communal participation in the creation and understanding of it.

Findings from the study showed that songs sung during a child's infancy from pre-birth to birth are used to explain, for example, a difficult situation to alleviate the concern, worry or fear that the infant may be experiencing. Through song, the infant learns culturally relevant psychosocial skills regarding truth, patience, trust, security, tranquility and a sense of self. This type of song is the equivalent of the lullaby in the west. The infant understands the abstract nature of the messages and over time grows to understand the literal meanings. For instance, in the case where the infant's mother has passed, possibly during childbirth, which is common among these communities, owing to the lack of all kinds of social needs; the song is used to explain to the infant the unfortunate condition and is emotionally enabling.

There are songs of praise and sympathy for the mother as well as the father. Songs vary and are complex and may be used to learn responsibility, kindness, compassion and the values of womanhood and manhood. There is also the aspect of play and dance which is important for the all-round cultural development of children who often live in difficult, intensive laboring circumstances where the basic needs of their people are not met expediently or sufficiently.

Another important aspect of Song that emerged from the data showed that the need to stand up for one's self or one's community is sometimes critical. There are Songs referencing relationships between mother and daughter, father and son, and parents and children, and specifically women's issues and men's issues as well as deep friendships that can develop among people. In fact, Song is reflected in life and life is reflected in Song. Childhood development and adult development is contingent upon Music and Song. These developments are critical to the process of becoming a person. The unborn infants listen to the Music, and in this way are affected by and participants in the experience, even before their entry into the world.

## Parental Hope

Overall, the hopes of the parents for their girls and boys were simply that they should grow well, prosper and continue the practices that they were taught. The parents believe that their children are a blessing. Reasons for why they chose and wished for a particular number of children were based on the potential of the family in terms of:

- Extending the family
- Developing rural activities like farming, Weaving, hunting, trading, manufacturing etc.
- Becoming prosperous
- Having a good reputation
- Having a good funeral

Having many children provides a family with status. A Mother and Father who have many children are highly regarded in the community. The Data showed that careful consideration goes into deciding how many children Mothers and Fathers plan for. Economic and health deterrents are serious considerations. Polygynous families' decisions about how many children Mothers and Fathers have differ greatly. A man in whatever type of marriage or non-marriage may have a hundred children while a Woman must think of her physical and psychological potential limitations.

## *Mothers*

Their hopes for their children were the same regardless of nation, district and religion. Generally, the importance of girls becoming good Mothers and housewives and finding good husbands was mirrored in the desire for the boys to be good Fathers and good husbands who would find a good wife. Expectations for girls and boys to gain good positions in political life came from some Mothers, and some wanted their children to become learned in education. Schools that have risen in areas in the north have influenced many parents to feel positive about literacy. Traditional Mothers were concerned that their girls and boys retain and maintain their cultural values and beliefs. Some wanted their children to become Traditional Medical Practitioners (TMPs). They hoped that their daughters would produce grandchildren for them. All the Mothers were concerned that their girls and boys would eventually help them in their old age and provide them with a good funeral.

The Mothers all wanted their children to be respected and be respectful. They hoped that the children would be obedient to their parents, the Elders and community, and in turn be acceptable so that they fitted into the community. They wanted their children to work hard as farmers, or traders, parents, builders and whatever they needed to do to help develop family and community. Mothers prayed to the Ancestors for their children's well-being. Having a good name was very important.

## *Fathers*

The Fathers in the study were not married to any of the Mothers in the study. It was felt that their answers might have been compromised had they been married to each other. The Fathers wanted to offer help for their children's education and literacy. Their answers were separated into 5 categories. They were prepared to offer:

- Provision in moral teaching
- Care for their children's needs to attend school (food, drink, supplies if possible)
- Financial help if they could
- Help in the development of specialized skills
- Encouragement in the community to provide space or buildings for a school

These categories were prioritized differently in each district. All of the Fathers wanted their children to remain in the areas and utilize their cultural beliefs and practices.

## Traditional Educational Structures

The most well-known and influential theory of cognitive development is that of Swiss–French psychologist Jean Piaget on the intellectual and logical abilities of children. His theory describes the mind as proceeding through a series of "fixed" stages (stage theory) of cognitive (becoming aware) development, each being a precondition for the next, relating to the development of Intelligence. Since Piaget did not take spirituality into account, he did not acknowledge the reality that cognition is not limited to "fixed stages". In Europe, the idea of Intelligence has been grounded in the belief that it can be quantified in levels or stages as a psychological entity determined by genetic and/or cultural constructs. And that it can substantiate, through culturally biased testing, the inferiority or superiority of a person, cultural group or "race". Piaget has perhaps had the most impact on the development of current educational school structures, curriculum and pedagogy; essentially the method, practice and theory of teaching. Most western and westernizing teachers and scholars have been influenced by Piaget's work.

The idea of Intelligence in ancient Africa differs from European and Arabic thought as it is not limited by the construction of "race" as a cultural belief system. Within the "race" paradigm and the subsequent racialization of the notion of intelligence, levels of Intelligence are qualified, quantified, or measured by using Eurocentric class and culture biased tests. These tests may have little bearing on the knowledge base, literacy, educational attainment, experience and understanding, of children, particularly those of African descent.

The idea of Intelligence will be understood in relation to the cultural knowledge of African indigenous children, developing within Traditional Education Structures. This can help to bring a deeper awareness of African people more connected to their spirituality and retaining some ancient values, beliefs, practices and behaviors. In this way, we may gain some knowledge of how near or far that we have moved from them; as part of the continuing investigative quest to learn and develop, in whatever locations that we live and work. In this light, the ancient African model of education will be used as a guide to understand the growth of a child in relation to the specificity of the skills and disciplines being finely tuned toward higher learning.

The notion of Intelligence in the university-temple setting in KMT was based on the spiritual attainment of inner vision. It was the second of the three levels of students' educational attainment.

1. The Mortals, probationary students who were being instructed, but who had not yet reached "Inner Vision."
2. The Intelligences, those who had attained the "Inner Vision."
3. The Creators, those who had become united with "True Spiritual Consciousness."

The ability to reach these levels of spiritual and educational awareness cannot be separated from following the cultural moral path necessary to attain it, preferably from childhood.

The educational path includes the learning, understanding and application of the 7 disciplines needed to achieve human Intelligence/Inner Vision. Our existence is formed in a cosmic sea of Intelligence within which we, as humans, are seeking knowledge of self. The disciplines of Grammar, Rhetoric, Logic, Mathematics, Geometry, Astronomy and Music contextualized by Spirituality and Truth are the keys to knowledge and the unlocking of human Intelligence.

A perfect example of the meaning of Intelligence today from children is more fully understood through the work of Robert Serpell, who sought to find its meaning in a more Traditional environment. In Zambia among the children of the Chi-Chewa nation living in a cluster of villages, the majority of whom had never attended school; the meaning of Intelligence was highly complex. Social and moral responsibility is an important aspect of Intelligence so that, for example; a person who acts in a manner that is unconscionable (unprincipled, unscrupulous) cannot be Intelligent. In this case, it is the behavior and thinking that denotes Intelligence and it cannot be considered developed in this person.

Intelligence for the Afrocentric School is viewed as spiritually based and culturally oriented within a moral order (Maat). History and herstory show that African culture is the original culture of humanity. The spiritual feature of culture underpins Traditional life. To become a good person requires the necessary belief in the Logic of practicing values fundamental to the attainment of correct or appropriate behaviors from the personal to the cosmological.

It may be said that Intelligence is Spiritual and manifests in matter. It is associated with the "primeval waters of the nun" from which existence and humanity were born; to become conscious of physicality and its purpose in creating an environment that respects forms of life, of which we are a part and to which we are attached. The 7 disciplines are the laws of realizing our own human intelligence. In growing aware of them we become more able to define, maintain and retain the Maatic order.

The Afrocentric School will identify the ways that these skills develop, in order to introduce literacy that can enhance an identity of self in the history of humanity. The attainment of the disciplines as these rural Tradition based children mature, is used as an educational model that provides a set of standards from 0-9 years, that can be extended and applied to the educational expectations and accomplishments of children attending an Afrocentric School.

<u>Language arts</u> are recognized as inclusive of speech, which was sacred, and the symbolism called writing that is an expression of it. In KMT the Mdw Ntr was the first writing that we know of and it means Divine word. Its instructional and educational teachings in the Temples and Tombs exemplify its spiritual importance.

<u>Rhetoric</u> is oratory and considered to be the study of the technique of using speech. All over Africa the use of speech was/is held in high esteem and considered an Art. It is with this skill that great orators like the story tellers and historians have kept the people informed. In the

Asante nation the Akyeame is the Linguist who is a Priest/ess. With the position comes great responsibility as the word must be True or it brings harm. The child is learning the significance of speech from this vantage.

Philosophy and Logic is the study of the interpretations of theory subject and matter. The mind–thought, can investigate and determine the truth or falsehood of the theory. As the child is being taught about the values and beliefs, the child naturally uses her/his Logic to discern Truth in order to be balanced and learn of self in relation to everything.

Mathematics is the study of numbers, configurations, quantity, shape, space and the metaphysics of being. The child must have a mathematical awareness to try to understand her/his physicality and spirituality, in order to learn how to walk, understand ecosystems, grow plants successfully and relate to nature and others.

Geometry is the branch of mathematics concerned with the properties, relationships, and measurement of points, lines, curves and surfaces. Pyramids are evidence of the knowledge of properties, locations and relationships with the universe. Their designers exemplify the use of the highest level of this knowledge. Child's play with learning about the shapes and possibilities of objects from nature is a feature of attaining this knowledge.

Astronomy is the scientific study of celestial bodies and the universe as a whole. It branches into Astrometry, Astrodynamics, Cosmology and Astrophysics. The study looks at the measurements of the positions of bodies in space as well as seeking to find their properties and origins. For children this is the spatial reality that they must understand mentally and spiritually in order to make decisions about what they can achieve physically along with how and when.

Music is perceived as the living practice of philosophy, the route to harmony with nature, the celestial bodies, and the Ancestors. It creates cultural unity based on its harmonious link with the spirit and the universe. Its expression in dance and song create the physical and spiritual link to nature and the Divinities. Music is the message. Unborn infants respond to the sounds and meanings.

These disciplines are idealized and simplified in their definitions. It can be seen that none can exist without the other. They represent the order of the environment within which all humans are born. As we grow, we learn how to use them to survive as physical beings. Their realization and attainment serve as a set of standards that can be applied to the educational growth of the child. This differs from the narrow Eurocentric idea of Intelligence which has no spiritual, moral or cultural attributes in its definition. There is the recognition through the sacred writing, that human beings are part of a cosmic order of Intelligence and it is this mystery that we are trying to understand using every human faculty known and unknown.

## Findings from the Study

### *Skills Development*

The findings showed that the children are precocious by mainstream western standards in terms of the development of their skills and familial and social responsibilities, particularly by the time that they are 9 years old. Their potential may be recognized as universal.

Over 50 years prior to this study, carried out in 2001, Psychomotor Development tests (the relationship between the cognitive and physical) using western instruments of deduction, were carried out in Africa beginning with Mary Ainsworth's work (1977). Her research was followed by a plethora of studies that challenged the belief in the inferiority of African children. Amos Wilson provided a list of the comparative results from the Psychomotor Development findings.

1. Nine (9) hours old, being drawn up in a sitting position, able to prevent her/his head from falling backwards. It takes a European child six (6) weeks.
2. Two (2) days old, with head held firmly, looking into the face of the examiner. It takes the European child eight (8) weeks.
3. Seven (7) weeks old, supporting herself in a sitting position and watching her reflection in the mirror. It takes the European child twenty (20) weeks.
4. Five (5) months old holding herself upright. The European child takes nine (9) months.
5. Five (5) months old, taking the round block out of its hole in the form board. The European child takes eleven (11) months. Five (5) months old, standing against the mirror. It takes the European child nine (9) months.

6. Seven (7) months old, walking to the Gesell Box to look inside. It takes the European child fifteen (15) months.
7. Eleven (11) months old, climbing the steps alone. The European child takes fifteen (15) months.

The question of whether these research findings can be attributed to culture and the child-raising practices, breastfeeding, genetic makeup (melanin for example), or an amalgamation of these and other factors is ongoing, or in the main, not discussed.

# Tradition-based Rural Skills Development

|  | Girl | Boy |
|---|---|---|
| **Unborn child** | Physical aspects<br>Unborn child communicates satisfaction or dissatisfaction:<br>• Foods-sickness/nausea caused if diet not correct. Turns when hungry<br>• Mother will crave and eat what the baby wants<br>• Child may continue with same food preferences after birth<br>• Positioning-Mother/baby comply to ease condition<br>• If Mother over-exerts child will display movement until mother ceases<br>Sex of baby may be indicated by:<br>• Weight<br>• Feelings<br>• Position of child<br>Responses<br>• Reacts to pain<br>• Reacts to music<br>• Reacts to sound<br>Spiritual aspects<br>Some Mothers and Fathers are aware of the child's sex and nature before birth through spiritual consultation. Mothers may dream or "know" | Same |
| **0-3 months** | Observes; Smiles: Laughs: Sits in lap: Plays: Likes Mother's singing: Responds to name: Alerts Mother of hunger: Communication (through the winds, spirits and Gods) | Same |

|  | Girl | Boy |
|---|---|---|
| **3-6 months** | Listens: Sits independently: Crawls: Plays: Takes the breast independently: Takes weight on legs/stands: Discriminates against strangers: Understands instruction: Can look up and see an airplane | Same |
| **6-9 months** | Follows instruction: Obeys commands: Tries to speak single words: Crawls: Walks: Tries to walk: Plays with toys (objects): Laughs: Signals (shakes head etc.): Sings and dances: Carries small items: Misses Mother: Imitates others: Shows preference for something appealing | Same |
| **9-12 months** | Perfecting the above skills: Imitates chores (unskilled – destructive): Can articulate pain; not eating/uneasiness: Requests bath, plays with water: Independently plays, Takes food/breast: Requests play with others: Plays with objects of interest: Refuses to stop playing and to eat certain foods: Speaks sensibly (articulately) names and objects: Asks questions: Reports problems: Fetches calabash/ water / items: Helps with chickens: Tries to help Mother. | Same |

|  | Girl | Boy |
|---|---|---|
| **1-2 years** | Speaks well: Eats independently: Knows verbalizes illness: Mood changes: Tries to bath, not well: Toilet trained: Points out injuries, sores etc.: May asks questions on sexuality: Sings and dances: Plays independently and tries to be creative e.g. building with stones, broken calabashes, empty containers, leaves, sticks etc. Can play Ampe (Afram Plains) Can wash toys: Plays with others; Follows older children: Fetches stool for someone/visitor: Carries out simple errands in house: Purchase simple things (e.g., sugar, salt, toffee): Watches and plays with younger babies: Feeds fowl: Drives goats away: Washes with Mothers: Plans own entertainment: Can understand spiritual protection e.g. the role of amulet/bracelet/waste-band etc. | Same |

|  | Girl | Boy |
| --- | --- | --- |
| **2-3 years** | Visits other houses to play with friends: Can explain condition of health/sickness: Sings and dances (perfectly); Requests Mother to sing: Drives/feeds fowl: Washes bowls: May ask questions or be told of sexuality: Knows the names of animals: Tries to help in kitchen (pounds soup ingredients): Drinks/Eats independently: Sings: Follows siblings and Mother for water: Runs simple errands to neighbors: Sweeps: Throws away rubbish: Cares for babies (notifies Mother of problems): Can learn of specific herbs especially<br>• Through Spiritual choice. If shows extraordinary interest. Inherits from the family. | Helps Father with goats: Serves at the Father's table: Eats with Father: Receives Blacksmith training (observes/sits with Father, Uncles, senior brothers (Chiok Wiaga/Builsa): Visits other houses to play with friends: Can explain the condition of health/sickness: Sings and dances (perfectly): Drives fowl: Does Housework: Helps with sheep: Cares for babies (notifies Mother of problems): Can learn about herbs: Can be selected to learn of herbs<br>• Through Spiritual choice. If shows extraordinary interest. If inherits from the family. |
| **3-4 years** | Follows Mother to farm: Explains and knows illness: Sweeps yard and garden: Washes bowl after meals: Goes for water from the bore hole (carries small container): Cares for babies: Can tell stories: Alerts Mother of babies' needs: Carries out simple service for other adults e.g. watches and protects grains drying: Buys simple things: Can understand Spiritual protection. | Sets table for Father: Fetches water for the Father (greeting): Can enter Father's room: Clears table after meals: Washes bowls: Fetches fire wood: Drives fowl: Sweeps coop: Weeds compound: Collects cow dung: Carries out simple service for other adults e.g. watch protect grains drying: Buys simple things like bread: Cares for babies: Can understand Spiritual protection: Learns specific healing herbs. |

|  | Girl | Boy |
|---|---|---|
| **4-5 years** | Asks for medicine: Provides details of illness: Bathes well: Goes to collect water at bore hole/river: Washes cooking utensils: Washes her clothes: Helps in kitchen (cooks TZ): Sets the fire: Harvests groundnuts: Harvests/Trades Shea nuts: Mills flour: Pounds soup ingredients: Purchases goods: Carries messages: Weaving skills (baskets): Can draw. | Sweeps Father's room: Washes Father's bicycle: Follows Elders to care for cattle (to graze): Spreads Father's mat: Follows Father/Mother/brothers to farm. Asks for specific medicine: Provides details of illness: Bathes well: Cares for babies: Feeds fowl (finds white ants): Puts chickens in coops: Fetches water: Fetches water from the boat (Afram Plains): Harvest groundnuts: Carries messages: Sweeps compound: Can pray by himself: Learns fishing from the boat: Mends fishing nets: Plays football/oware: Draws. |
| **5-6 years** | Cares for babies/carries: Cooks simple foods for younger children (e.g. boils yam): Collects firewood/makes fire for cooking: Tries to protect privacy (personal) Bathes alone: Carries water from bore hole: Watches cattle: Assists in brewing: Dresses like Mother (woman); Harvests Okro/pepper (Mother's farm). | Farms with Father: Can farm without supervision: Farms with others (communal labor): Cares for goats and fowl: Can rear fowl: Fishes: Watches cattle: Sweeps compound: Hunts birds with catapult: Makes small farm. |
| **6-7 years** | Washes/Cooks/Feeds/for babies<br>Goes to farm<br>Collects food from farm<br>Understands Spiritual protection<br>Washes cooking pots<br>Fetches water<br>Learns Pito brewing<br>Focuses on personal hygiene<br>Fetches firewood for cooking<br>Cooks rice and stew | Spreads the Father's mat<br>Cares for the younger siblings<br>Helps feed the younger ones<br>Weeds<br>Makes his own farm (grows his own garden)<br>Looks after cattle<br>Search for sheep<br>Learns weaving<br>Understands Spiritual protection<br>Learns carpentry<br>Finds termites for chickens/fish |

|  | Girl | Boy |
|---|---|---|
| **7-8 years** | Cares for young ones (can bathe them)<br>Grazes cattle<br>Goes to market petty trading<br>Plants crops<br>Does threshing/winnowing<br>Learns about plant properties and healing<br>Helps to care for the house for Mother<br>Spinning skills<br>Washes clothes (personal)<br>Brews Pito | Assists Father with festivals and funerals<br>Weeds like adult<br>Fishes<br>Searches for feed for fowl/animals<br>Learns plant properties and healing<br>Dyes materials (smocks)<br>Cares for animals<br>Tries to make toys/musical instruments like flute, konde<br>Learns carving<br>Learns Blacksmithing<br>Learns to build ridges (possibly yam mounds)<br>Harvests crops<br>Rears goats/sheep/fowl<br>Rears fowl for sale |
| **8-9 years** | Cooks TZ<br>Pounds fufu<br>Grinds millet<br>Collects firewood<br>Can brew Pito & sell independently<br>Extract Shea Butter<br>Washes light clothes<br>Sells and buys (petty trading)<br>Carries out domestic work like Mother<br>Is responsible e.g. cares for the house in the absence of the Mother<br>Sells Cola nuts (for Shrine)<br>Helps the Elderly<br>Perfecting her womanhood<br><br>NB<br>Eating independently refers to the child's skill in eating at the same plate as the family | Assists Father during sacrifice<br>Is responsible e.g. acts as landlord in absence of Father<br>Understands men's activities<br>Protects house when Father away<br>Fetches water<br>Sets traps<br>Makes bow and arrows<br>Fishes and mends nets (Afram plains)<br>Learns Trade<br>Accomplishes most farm activities (foundation for farming as career)<br>Roasts yam for others<br>Washes clothes (personal)<br>Problem solves for younger ones<br>Cooks when Mother absent |

## The Unborn Child

The unborn child may be considered a returning ancestor and thus known to have abilities before birth. The child is already connected to the cultural ethos before birth through her/his awareness of the sounds of human, animal, nature, environment and music etc. S/he signals, influencing the Mother's choice of foods and movements and as well as warning sensations, like "turning", indicating discontent, if for instance, the Mother works too hard. Through modern scientific investigation it is known that the unborn child is also affected by light and sucks her/his thumb; both heat and cold have an effect too.

Because of the Mother's awareness of the child before birth, the effort is made to keep the child in an environment that is safe, both physically and spiritually. Pregnant Mothers cannot go to places where negative events might occur or have taken place, because of the spiritual vulnerability of the unborn. Places like markets have too much noise; funerals involve powerful spiritual activities as do Shrines. Forests, bush and rivers may also put the baby in a vulnerable position as particular places where ancestral wars have taken place.

The child and Mother are connected spiritually in what might be termed a symbiotic relationship where the unborn child is protected by, and helps guide, the Mother. In this way, s/he is a participant in her/his own life chances.

## Birth–3 months

The Mother, family and community play a critical role in the child's development. In compound or village life, the Mother is the primary carer but the infant has access to many caretakers, from siblings, to other wives (if a polygynous family) grandmothers, sisters, aunties, fathers, grandfathers, uncles and brothers. The psychosocial, spiritual and physical development is contextualized by the welcome expectations of all. They have a responsibility to educate the child to understand the nature of the environment and how to live in it.

The child observes, smiles (from birth), laughs and responds to hearing her/his name, which is given in a special naming ceremony, that takes place usually around the seventh day. The child may be named in relation to the timing of the birthing event, the expectations of the child, or a name associated with an Ancestor or Divinity. Naming is linked to Grammar and Rhetoric and its utterance must be grounded in the Truth of its meaning.

Breastfeeding is considered a valuable component involved in the loving and tender relationship between Mother and child as well as stimulating the child's awareness of self and others. This forms a basis of knowing love. The infant will communicate the need to be fed which her/his Mother is most times aware of, as often the milk begins to leak precisely at the moment that the infant needs/wants to be fed. Breastfeeding will continue for most of these Mothers until the ages of 2-3 years. Picking up the babies, holding and loving them, provide a way of preparing a child for independence. If the Mother is unable to breastfeed through illness or passing on, another relative will breast-feed the child.

Smiles and laughter are continuously encouraged by all, showing love and approval. S/he can sit and stand strongly in the Mother's lap because s/he wishes to. Here s/he is testing her/his Logic as well as Spatially the ability to balance and make choices to do so. The Mother understands the infant's desire to sit and stand, and carefully guides, supports and encourages. Linguistic and Musical connections to the spirit carry messages of all kinds from the personal to the collective. Babies are guided to understand them through the inclusion and responses of their family and community.

## 3-6 months

The infant is consistently honing her/his physical, psychological skills and acumen and building on them. Now, s/he can sit independently and take the breast when s/he wishes to and stands well balanced and is also trying to crawl. S/he is learning mathematically how to understand the physicality of her movements and Spatially the reality of how near or far her Mother might be as well as the separation of leaving and returning using these skills. At the same time s/he uses these skills to push away the stranger whom she can now discriminate against.

The child will be carried on the back or side of her/his Mother in an advantageous position to see what is going on, where the Mother is going, what she does and how people react to both she and the infant. Listening to Rhetoric as instruction is becoming more important as s/

he is learning how to follow instruction. The infant is constantly monitored and not left to her/his own devices. In this way, personal development is guided by family values. The infant is able to make a distinction between the engine noise of the airplane in the sky, its movement and distance away, as opposed to the distance and sounds of the birds in the sky. The birds will be a constant part of everyday life and the airplane is distinctly different. Mathematical/Spatial and Geometry skills will enable her/him, much in the same way as moving from or to the Mother, to work out how near or far flying entities may be.

## 6-9 Months

Rhetoric is now prominent for the child to follow instruction and to communicate. S/he becomes increasingly articulate, signals and gestures become clearer, and dexterity more specialized. The desire to achieve skills is more pronounced as s/he strives to achieve what the older children and adults can do. Fetching small items in obedience is a testimony to her/his observation and understanding of the needs of the culture. Crawling, trying to walk and walking as well as carrying small items calls for dexterity and balancing skills. At this point, Logical, Grammatical, Rhetorical, Mathematical and Musical disciplines overlap in the attainment of these skills.

What makes the infant laugh is couched in values. Laughing is encouraged. During religious events the infant is now taking part in the spiritual and moral values surrounding singing and dancing because of the community involvement. Her/his protective items are appreciated and understood so that she keeps them on her. Among Tradition based people, it is believed that the child is as close to the spirit world as the Elders.

The close attachment to the Mother leads her/him to miss her when she is away even though other Mothers assist in her absence. Separation is an aspect of becoming independent and yet still connected.

## 9-12 Months

By this age the child can indicate illness and articulate the location of the pain. Rhetoric and Mathematical disciplines create ways of understanding how sickness is curable. The art of speaking in order to make requests and ask questions is a powerful point in a child's life. Greater articulation in Linguistic and Musical speech, along with greater dexterity, presents the child with new possibilities of communicating and learning.

The love of bathing and water along with the idea of personal hygiene are learned from older siblings. In this communal setting, the older children are always guiding and teaching the younger children as they themselves are being taught and guided.

Independent play is a time of appreciating and accomplishing something alone and personal decisions are coming into effect. Wanting to continue to play when it is time to stop enables the child to understand the Logic of cultural rules defining her power. The discipline of Astronomy helps the child to understand her own physicality and its connection to understanding self in relation to the Mother, family, community and all that exists and therefore what is possible in this configuration.

Fetching items, imitating chores, helping with the fowl is indicative of following instruction by using play as fun, to become a viable member of a family and collective.

## 1-2 years

The family is the microcosm of the community and the child's engagement with those outside the compound or home. Family affirms the emotional and social skills around behavior, instruction, and obedience in the home. The growing Astronomical knowledge of self and the Logic of understanding the reality of community life, become more prominent, especially in shaping her/his responsibility.

Purchasing simple things requires Logic and Mathematics for calculating the worth of items, money and exchange. Until now, these disciplines have been used to make sense of cultural products. The early introduction of purchasing takes this education into another realm which is further developed by the older children's reasoning.

The majority of children are able to take solid food independently with their own bowls. They will not sit at the same plate as older siblings until they are around 2-3 years old.

Play has become more creative. The child begins to fashion objects like broken calabashes, stones, sticks, leaves, empty containers and so on; into constructions. At this point, Logic, Mathematics, Astronomy and Geometry intertwine to advance the creative skills that the child is physically able to undertake. Older siblings set the standards of expectations of what the younger siblings accomplish. Fetching the stool for a visitor as social play is the accomplishment of a social grace. To carry out this act without instruction is evidence of the personal recognition of the stool's cultural significance; framed by when, where, how and why?

Both girls and boys are learning of the relationship between humans, nature, and the animals that they care for. They feed the fowl and drive away the goats, learning of the boundaries that goats have. At the same time, they are able to distinguish the personalities of each of the fowl and goats. Understanding nature, its nurturing and its boundaries, movements and behaviors, are inclusive of calculating configurations, quantity, shape, physicality, spirituality and the metaphysics of being.

Children are being taught the protective role of amulets, bracelets and waist-beads which are blessed and used against negative forces. The children develop a holistic scientific understanding of the spiritual and material world.

The cleaning and relieving of self in the right location are highly valued social skills that the children can feel a measure of pride in accomplishing. Questions on sexual distinctions are answered simply and are underpinned by the female/male orientations.

## 2-3 years

Up until now there has been little difference between the girls and boys in expectations of learning, education and achievement. At this point, there are differing expectations about the children's cultural and social roles. The boy serves his Father's table and can eat and work with him. Girls follow their Mothers and assist in her work. Age differentiation is critical for maintaining Tradition based social order. The younger is a virtual life apprentice of the older and this relationship requires respect for the older who has responsibility for educating the younger.

In Chiok Wiaga (Bulsa), the son begins his apprenticeship for Blacksmith training. He will follow his father, Uncles, and senior brothers to sit with them and observe this ancient work. Like Blacksmithing, cooking is an important ancient science that requires the use of Mathematic and Logic as well as Astronomical knowledge. Girls begin to learn the art of cooking from 2-3 years old. Pounding soup is one of the many skills the girls will study during their apprenticeship. Boys will also be expected to have a good understanding of preparing food.

Caring for the babies helps both girls and boys to develop Mothering skills in order to become good parents, as well as community and nation members. They are able to identify with the needs of the babies because they are so emotionally close to them. They have the intensity, compassion and sensitivity to understand them. The child is highly developed in terms of forming symbiotic and empathetic relationships in order to know the temperaments and intentions of the babies in their charge. The children love to care for the babies. It is an honor to have this responsibility. These competencies require a holistic, spiritual and emotional awareness of infant needs so that the mathematical understanding of the metaphysics of being, along with Astronomical and Cosmic consciousness are critical.

The use of Logic is important in becoming a responsible person; for instance, when delivering a message, the child can see the relevance of the task personally and in the greater picture of human connectedness. The children are now skilled dancers. From the womb until now their relationship to Music and song continues to connect them to their culture, family, community, nation, humanity and the Creator.

The children follow their mother and older siblings to fetch water and they learn how to carry the bowl on the head. They use little bowls and learn how to develop the strength, balance and dexterity necessary for the work. Carrying the water helps the child learn of the spatial and physical reality, the social necessity for water to survive and the great/life and death responsibility it holds for the carriers to bring it home to the families. Whilst this domain is essentially for the girls, if there are no girls in the family, the boys necessarily do what girls will do and vice versa in all skills development.

Learning about the medicinal properties of herbs requires the overlapping of the disciplines of **Grammar** through instruction, **Rhetoric** through explanation, **Mathematics** through study, **Astronomy** through cosmological awareness, and **Logic** to understand how. This training begins at the ages of 2-3, developing through the following years. Most children will gain some knowledge of herbs and some children will become apprentices of herbalists and gain a deeper awareness in order to become Traditional Medical Practitioners.

## 3-4 years

The majority of the children are no longer breastfeeding and there is a looser physical attachment to the Mother. The children are more grounded in community expectations and the foresight and self-assurance to realize them. Girls and boys use Rhetoric (good speech) and Music to sing to babies to reassure them and help them sleep. Memories coupled with a profound understanding of songs help children retell them to babies in their own words.

A deeper knowledge of science-based Logic is critical for the child learning of spiritual protection. The child is preparing to heal and use Shrine ritual in this undertaking.

The girls and boys are developing more complex relationships to their Mothers and Fathers respectively. The girl follows the Mother to the farm who is introduced to farming (subsistence), to learn how to sustain family. She will learn agricultural processes from planting, growing, harvesting to the final product. In this way, she will learn of ecosystems and nature and prayer in this regard. Both girls and boys are introduced more fully to the social order and their expected roles and duties to maintain the stability of the family and community.

Throughout their childhood the children meet to play and take time to communicate with each other outside the earshot of their parents and other adults. They discuss privately both in the home and the community. Mostly, they congregate under a shady tree. During these times they pass information and share ideas. Younger siblings and friends listen and learn from each other. Communication among children provides the greatest form of educational transmission.

## 4-5 years

Children of these ages are quite accomplished with regard to personal hygiene, the articulation of their health standards, and their ability to undertake and complete tasks more competently.

The girl is working closely with her Mother, learning cooking from preparing fresh ingredients that have been grown or traded, to cleaning up afterwards. She is purchasing goods in preparation for trading. Mathematical Logic must be at a substantial level because her family depends on these skills. Her introduction to weaving baskets is both artistic and useful. Basketry weaving is an ancient skill, the product of which is considered a form of symbolic expression like Literacy. In fact, the Kemetic symbol for the K is a basket. The girl employs her Mathematical, Geometric and Grammatical knowledge for this work.

The boy goes with his elders to graze the cattle. He can find food for the chickens, feed them and put them in the coops. Elsewhere, he is fishing and mending nets requiring his artistry and patience.

Girls and boys are introduced to the rigors of harvesting groundnuts and shea nuts, which is meticulous work demanding great concentrative skill and patience. The ability to be patient has been nurtured in children since birth. Concentration, patience and observation are fundamental to learning how to accomplish and complete tasks from fetching water, caring for children, caring for animals, hunting, fishing, milling flour, pounding soup ingredients, to weaving and harvesting etc.

## 5-6 years

The children are competent to work on their parents' farms. The boy can farm independently, that is, without supervision. The girl needs privacy in her personal care and desires to imitate and dress like her Mother. This situation signals a stage of maturity in her thoughts about her identity as a woman. The recognition of her feminine identity is shaped by the family and community. These desires are linked to the physiological changes that girls are undergoing. These changes are catered to in some societies through rites of passage.

Observation, obedience, and the desire to succeed, are the attributes necessary for any scientific undertaking. The attainment of these skills can produce a cultural product, like Pito brewing, a responsibility of women, that will be consumed in the communities and used to bring money into the family. Pito is made from millet and includes several stages of fermentation; it is not purely an alcoholic drink. In the first stage the millet is boiled and can be used as an herbal remedy; it is rich in iron. It goes through stages of maturation and the alcohol strength differs at every stage until it is fully matured. It is used as a social drink and as a Shrine offering.

Girls and boys are dexterous and boys can hunt wild birds with a catapult. The boy is able to make deductions about the nature of the bird and its habits based on his Cosmological, Mathematical, Geometric knowledge of nature, of which he is a part. The development of his practical and symbiotic relationship with nature has been ongoing since the age of 9-12 months when he fed the fowl.

In terms of Rhetoric, the children are learning with care, when and where it is appropriate to speak. They are also learning how and what to speak when there are adults around; as they are aware of sound and words and their spiritual impact in their lives and the lives of others.

## 6-7 years

The boy is learning of the complexity of the men's role in his family home and community. A symbol of his respect for his father is laying out his father's mat. It takes place at the time that he is learning how to weave mats. The overlapping of skills like Grammar in the creative art of weaving, Rhetoric for the instruction of learning, Logic to understand its value in the community, Mathematics in its configuration, Geometry in its spatial reality, Astronomy in its measurement, while Music is the mainstay of cultural/spiritual communication throughout the community experience.

Both girls and boys focus on personal hygiene that shall never end. At this age the girl and boy have their own garden in which to cultivate foods and healing herbs. They are very aware of their responsibilities regarding caring for younger siblings, respecting older siblings, looking after the animals that they are in charge of, as well as growing food and preparing it and learning of the connection between illness, healing and the spirit.

## 7-8 years

The girl is able to go to market and trade items that have been created and exchanged as well as foods grown. She is spinning, threshing/winnowing and caring for the young. The boys are using their artistic skills under the tutelage of an adult or elder like Blacksmithing, weaving, carving, caring for younger siblings, making musical instruments and dyeing materials.

Everything that is produced has an aesthetic quality that must fit into the requirements dictated by the spiritual world. The boys are involved in the spiritual arena, learning ritual. They imitate and accompany their fathers to festivals and funerals. Both girls and boys are more fundamentally aware about the properties of herbs and usage.

## 8-9 years

Skills development and achievement intensify by the time the child reaches this age category. Great expectations are held for the child's entry into adulthood. The child is able to run a home in the absence of either the Father or Mother. The girls can farm, trade, manufacture, and care for others; carrying out all the responsibilities of Mother. The boys can look after the land and younger siblings, hunt, care for the animals from feeding to guarding them, and protect the home like the Father. What the children are able to achieve by this age is as a result of what they have been learning in every age group.

As earlier noted, the gendered roles, chores or tasks will change according to the number of boys and girls in the family. Girls will do what might be regarded as boys' work and boys will carry out what might be regarded as girl's work. For instance, girls will graze the cattle and boys will collect the water.

## The process of Educational Development

An age appropriate comprehensive Education system is applied to the educational development of the children based on ancient African principles. Whilst the 7 disciplines are the basis of the 7 Liberal Arts, they also offer an explanation of the mystery of the cosmos into which we are born. Our ancient African teachers gave us a key to unlock the process of how to understand the complexity of the unknown that comprises aspects of life and existence and therefore what and who we are, within it.

The children are taught through a comprehensive system of Education. Children's achievable expectations are held within each age category. As each child transitions through the ages becoming more physically adept at carrying out tasks, s/he learns the fundamentals of the spiritual world applied to the physicality and materiality of life. Parents, older siblings, adults and elders are the teachers and the evaluators of the standards of the skills expected.

Through this model and process the children learned:

- To care for and raise their younger siblings as well as look after the Elderly (exhibit Mothering skills like compassion, love, care, empathy and responsibility).
- To farm; employing the skills of plant nurturing and ecosystem knowledge.
- They are gifted in creative works like singing, dancing and producing forms of artistry like making and mending fishing nets, basket and mat weaving (there are other things like wind protectors and boundaries that they weave too), carving, iron shaping etc.
- How to apply their spiritual knowledge to healing and ritual.
- How to use the sciences for small scale manufacturing like brewing *pito* and extracting oil from peanuts and shea butter.
- How to nurture, raise and care for animals.
- How to hunt and fish.
- How to take care of their personal hygiene.
- To carry out domestic duties in cooking, cleaning and washing clothes.
- Trade.
- To make important decisions and carry out adult roles and responsibilities by the time they are 8-9.
- To be spiritually and socially aware as well as good people.

These accomplishments reveal the precocity of children whose lives are endangered. They do not have their basic needs met; they are the survivors of centuries of persecution and continue to be marginalized. Their cultural values and beliefs are considered archaic and of no value or use to modern society. The ability to spread and develop their knowledge and create, is limited by their lack of freedom from Westernizing/Arabizing State political power, ideology, imperialism and impoverishment. In reality, indigenous, Traditional African women, men and children are of infinitesimal value to the survival of the country and the world.

**CHAPTER 4**

# Afrocentric Curriculum and Assessment

Curriculum is based on a Latin word that means "a race" (as in running) or "the course of a race". More appropriately it should mean a planned journey to self-knowledge.

The Ancient African system of Teaching requires a holistic approach to education so that each subject is viewed in relation to the others in the way that the 7 disciplines overlap. This is how the curriculum will be taught. Underlying the teaching process is the knowledge that the African Education system was run by Priestesses and Priests and is actually, in the ancient way, teaching the children how to become enlightened. Most of us will be neither Priestesses nor Priests but this is a standard by which to understand the original role and objective.

As Afrocentric Educators, by being the best that we can be, we are training the children to be the best that they can be in their own development. There is evidence to show that the children in some rural areas who practice their parents' Traditional Spiritual Systems, and work to support their parents and family survival, far from being passive as Eurocentric research claims, are learning how to become spiritually aware persons–the best that they can be, respecting their Elders, teaching their younger siblings and others, obeying their parents and thereby learning cultural and social responsibilities.

Curriculum refers to the assignments and projects given to students;

the books, materials, videos, presentations, and readings used in a course, along with the type of assessment used to evaluate student learning. These materials will be tempered by the resources available in the communities in which the schools will be developed and also by the resources made available by charities, donors or area investments etc. In areas where no electricity is provided, simple solar systems should be built to generate electricity for light and appliances like computers, laptops, tablets, mobile phones and recording equipment etc., useful to the schools.

The Afrocentric School will aim to create an environment that will encourage the highest performance among its students. The Educators will have high expectations of their students, as they do for themselves and will work toward the delivery of excellent academic content knowledge, including the Arts.

The expectations of children's learning are based on the model provided, that is grounded in the findings of research carried out to learn child-raising practices among Tradition based people in Ghana. The idea is that all children are capable of developing the 7 disciplines. The works of African Psychologists like Amos Wilson, Asa Hilliard, and others who specialize in understanding the effects of racist cultural domination and oppression in the early development of children of African descent, particularly in urban areas; will be invaluable.

Books, videos and teaching materials will be provided by Publishing companies with a focus on Afrocentric education. The Molefi Kete Asante Institute (MKA Institute) is a great source to find materials that will be appropriate for the ages of the children being taught.

Afrocentric Materials in the US surpass much of the materials on offer to children elsewhere in the world. There has been much effort to challenge the purposeful invisibility of Black people in the US and the world. The use of Black owned Publishers, Bookshops, and African centered schools, who have developed their own curriculum specific to the needs of African children in particular, but all children generally, should be approached to potentially donate or help to supply these schools. These Black/African institutions can be asked to assist in creating Curriculum and Pedagogy for the children wherever they reside. This is part of building and utilizing the community around the Afrocentric School in order to find strength and support in people who would want to see this type of school succeed. The translation of

Curriculum materials into the appropriate languages will be important and will rely on the resources available in the US, the Caribbean, South America, Africa, Europe and whichever countries in which the schools will be embedded.

The nature of the curriculum can be adjusted to suit the immediate conditions of the environment. A goal is to nurture each student's ability to create innovative and scientific solutions to complex problems in their communities so that they may bring higher levels of economic attainment and socially progressive change. This will eventually erase the need to rely on "outside" help. In another study, *Listening to the Children* (Dove, 2003), in some African rural communities, the children aged from 4-9 were asked what they would hope to achieve through their literacy attainment. They all chose careers/skills relating to the inadequacies of their communities so that they could transform the social conditions of impoverishment that their communities suffered.

Reading, Writing, Speaking, and Listening skills in the teaching of Afrocentric History, Science, Mathematics, the Arts (including Music) and Language will be promoted.

Truth is the basis of critical thinking which is crucial to the attainment of Literacy. Students need to be able to understand how to distinguish false information from valid information, racist information from non-racist information, colonized information from decolonized information and so on. This knowledge will provide the basis for writing Truth. The Educator will have done her/his research to understand the historical and herstorical cultural background of the locality in which s/he will teach, so that students will be taught over time the background to their own cultural legacy, local, global, and ancient. Thus, reasons for current social situations and the need to install Africa into academic disciplines like History, Language, Mathematics, Literature, the Sciences, Theology, Philosophy, Architecture, Ecosystems, and expressions of Dance, Music and the Arts; like Painting, Carving, Weaving, and Sculpturing and so on, will be explained. At the same time there is the expectation that problems within communities can be resolved, and plans on how to accomplish this will materialize during the Education of the girls and boys.

At the end of each year as each child reaches a particular standard in literacy shaped by her/his understanding of, and educational

Achievement in, each of the disciplines, a special certificate will be awarded to record the accomplishment. The family and carers will be invited to celebrate the child's success.

Wherever it is that we are creating the school we shall take note and do our best to be inclusive of children who may be extremely poor and/or not easily mobile.

## Conceptual Framework Based on Age and Educational Attainment

In a classroom setting which may be in many different forms, from a room in a home to a place under a tree, the images that should be impressed on children should exist long before the children can understand them. For instance, a Shrine, where the children and Educators can remember the ancestors, whether it is placed in a corner of the educational setting or beside a tree outside. Also, positive images of African ancestors both ancient and modern, cultural symbols like the Ankh and the Sankofa bird, carvings, masks, a map of Africa, a map of the world, a map of the locality, a map of planets and the globe etc. should be on display. The students will become familiar with them and then over time, the images and symbols can be explained, at first simply and then more deeply and profoundly in line with the children's curiosity and lessons.

### 1-2 years

*Language arts*

The introduction of letters as symbols will be interesting for the children. Memorizing them adds to the capacity to deeply understand what is necessary to their community. The repetition of sounds that each letter makes along with its relationship to the alphabet can produce a lovely sound.

*Rhetoric and Sociocultural Studies*

Stories through the use of song, have been told to these children from their birth. This should continue throughout each age. Aesop's fables will be enjoyed throughout each year group. The moral meaning becomes clearer as the child gets older. These morals fit entirely into the social fabric of being African. Images of the animals in the stories will be very important as many of the children will not have seen these creatures before, so they should be realistic representations of the authentic animal rather than cartoon like characters.

## *Logic*

The reasons why the children are becoming literate will be explained as they have fun with being in a different space with other children whom they might not know. All that they learn will be based in Logic, reasoning and understanding. Asking questions will be welcomed so that the children are developing an understanding of Logic through Truth based teaching. Learning to respect and be with each other will be monitored so that the children feel safe and supported. Most gatherings and welcoming of the children will take place in circle groups to help this process.

## *Mathematics*

The introduction of mathematics will link the way that children learn how to use the concept of purchasing, exchanging and producing; for example, food grown, manufactured or bought and crafted objects or objects no longer needed. It will help the children know how, why and what their families purchase. The study will take into account social needs and introduce the children to the reality that social needs can be different between communities. Some people may have clean drinking water, others may live near mountains or rivers or even deserts.

## *Geometry*

Building with bricks, sticks and other objects will continue to encourage the idea of construction and architecture that the children have already been developing, added to by noticing the local architecture. Images locally and from around the world will show the variety of design and technology that goes into building and construction.

## *Astronomy*

A globe in the classroom and maps on the walls can be referred to as places in the world on the planet Earth. The miniaturization of the Earth will not really be understood but it is about developing a conceptual framework and familiarity with shapes like the globe and countries, continents, and seas for future reference regarding world history and location. Africa will take precedence as a shape that the children will become familiar with over time and its view from the moon will be interesting at a later date.

*Music*

The formalization of local songs and dances specifically for children to dance and sing together and their meaning would involve local musicians. The songs and dances can be filmed and recorded with permission to be used in other Afrocentric schools around the world. This would help in the identification of cultural similitude among children of African descent wherever they are located.

## 2-3 years

*Language arts*

Learning letters and words with cards or laminated paper can be used in memory games and to aid in the writing and drawing of them. The symbols for the child's name can be memorized and recognized along with the letters sounded out. We are learning these letters and sounds so that we can read signs and books and write our own books and stories when we are older.

*Rhetoric and Sociocultural Studies*

The children are articulating very well and can congregate with carers or older or younger siblings and explain what they know about animals and healing plants around them. A camera can be used to record these events as both a learning and teaching tool. Children love to see the images and sounds of themselves, friends, other children and family. Those children who do not know of animals and plants and their uses can learn from those who do and class journeys to see them should be planned.

*Logic*

Explaining to the children about the nature of rubbish/garbage/waste is both scientific and logical. They will learn how rubbish is created and how it is or should be discarded in a way to keep the environment safe. What happens to rubbish in the world and why and whether we should care? We can explain the concept of recycling which will be different wherever the children are; possibly linked to political, social and environmental factors outside the control of the children and their communities. This idea can be built upon as the children get older.

## *Mathematics*

Counting using fingers and toes and the numbers of people in the knowledge arena, whether it is in a closed space or outside. Introduce the symbols that represent the numbers so that counting and symbols interact.

## *Geometry*

Natural objects, where they come from, and what they do. An example might be a stone which the children can find and feel. They can examine the hardness, look at the color which can be defined, and explain simply their properties and use for building materials, ornaments and healing. Their use will be based on the ideas of the ancients. This will become more complex as the children get older. Photographs or books on stones can be used to show the enormous variety and introduce the places that they come from on the globe or the map. Today, we find that Africa has every semi-precious or precious stone as defined by the ancients and the west.

## *Astronomy*

Children can be taken on a journey by foot or in a vehicle to visit special sites and scenic places recommended by the parents and Elders. A simple example of this could be walking to the water (pond, lake, stream, canal, sea etc.) which may be some distance. The journey could be about observation and reflection on what we see that is both natural and manmade. Such an event can open the children and parents' minds to extraordinary views, horizons, sky and the concept of travel for understanding distance, time, learning and study.

## *Music*

The children are already able to sing and dance at home. They can teach each other songs and or dances and explain what they mean in the educational setting. In this way, they are teaching and learning from each other. Drumming has always been important for the message, movement and vibration. Skilled drummers can come to teach the children how to drum and its importance for specific reasons.

## 3-4 years

### *Language arts*

Dexterity in writing is enhanced by the use of wrists and hands in sweeping and weeding for example. The children will practice circular motions in artwork with finger paints and colors highlighting the relationship between these shapes to nature, trees and plants. Rock painting is one of the oldest records of events and the lives of African people, illustrated on rock surfaces. It is likely that these ancient images become the early symbols of writing. Images of these beautiful paintings (such as the paintings in the Ennedi Mountains in Chad) will fuel a desire to continue the legacy so often undermined in the school setting. Laminated writing symbols on the walls are useful in the teaching of drawing them, as their images are memorized by the children. Drawing/writing letters is a work of art. The children should be taught how to write each letter on the board, slowly and clearly to show them how to do it and allow them to see its artistic nature and the importance of the letter to sound and communication.

### *Rhetoric and Sociocultural Studies*

Remembering how his/her name looks and sounding out the letters of the alphabet as well as trying to write the symbols is fun. Repeating names in order to show their link to the letters and the writing of them will help the children make sense of the relationship. Having a world map on the wall will help familiarize the children with the "world" and is useful to talk about people of the world with images either moving or still. What is the same and what is different in the places, how do the women and men dress and look and what types of food do they eat? Aesop's fables will be a mainstay for good speech along with other African stories. African stories predominantly have a moral thread running through to guide them and affirm, as well as confirm to the children about what is good and what is not. Simple examples from everyday life are helpful. These teachings provide a basis for Logic.

## Philosophy and Logic

Learning history is a way of understanding and developing the concept that events that happened a few moments ago are historical and have an impact on what we choose to do. An example can be enacted in comedic fashion, for example if a person isn't looking where s/he is going (looking at a mobile phone or event happening) and bumps into a wall, that person can learn that s/he needs to learn from the present, which in moments, becomes the past, to be aware in order to be safe and put more focus into where s/he is heading from that moment on. The introduction of the history of the children's people, wherever they live can be introduced simply from the example of the teacher's history, where s/he came from and why s/he is teaching in this school.

## Mathematics

The development of the idea of trading, purchasing, producing and manufacturing will help the child understand how and why this takes place. From the growing and making of the product to the selling or exchanging of the product, introduces the child to the idea of the holistic nature of what is happening. In this way, the counting of objects and their worth, which is valued against the worth of other objects in terms of where it was made, how long it took to make, and what it is made of, helps to introduce money as a different object.

## Geometry

Distance and time can be more clearly understood and employed to show that measurement is important to architecture, and use as an example the homes that the children live in. The children can be shown a demonstration of how to, and then be helped to build a simple construction with cardboard and glue or clay.

## Astronomy

The globe should always be around to refer to and explain the planet Earth, where we are located on it, and the shapes of the countries and continents, particularly Africa. The children will have fun identifying Africa.

For learning the concept of time and its African origin, the children can look outside and learn about the Sun and its significance to Earth, nature, the universe, and humanity. This awareness can be followed by the explanation of how the Moon shines and lights the Earth. By using the globe, one will explain the position of it in relation to the Sun and Moon (bring in other balls reflecting their size) and discuss how we come to understand the days, weeks, months, years, hours and minutes.

*Music*

This is a perfect age for drumming, dance and song. Explanation of its historical significance and meaning will enhance the children's existing feeling that they receive from playing, dancing, and listening to the drum as it touches the heart and spirit evident in their movement. Drumming should be a welcoming expression of unity at the beginning of the day when the children are meeting together before the lessons begin.

## 4-5 years

*Language arts*

The instruction of writing and reading the meaning of words, should relate to the experiences of the children in learning their responsibilities and knowledge that they have acquired. At this age, they are able to understand the plants for healing (diagnose) and to ask for medicine. For children who have no knowledge of healing, books should be created to approach the subject as a norm. Watching the growth of plants and recording/writing about the changes, is in sync with the development of the child. The reading books which will be available in the environment, should relate to their lives. Certainly, some children's books in Ghana for example, are far more sensitive to realistic accomplishments and adventures of African children. The children can copy a sentence that the teacher has written slowly and carefully, to help them understand what to say and how to write it.

*Rhetoric and Philosophy*

High expectations of the children's ability to speak well and in Truth is emphasized throughout the educational process, but particularly at this age. For children who may not be able to speak Truth through their training and survival process, the meaning of its importance can be taught using the idea of the need for it in speech (based on ancient African beliefs) and the repercussions of not speaking it. Aesop can be useful, e.g. *The Boy Who Cried Wolf.* The children can be involved in acting the parts and speaking the parts.

## Logic and Sociocultural Studies

Caring for the younger siblings, washing her/his items and utensils, helping with the cooking, fetching water, feeding and caring for animals and plants are responsibilities that help children understand their significance. They can see how much better able they are to accomplish tasks as they get older. This gives them a feeling of pride. The children by this time are able to see a product from beginning to end and understand its value. The child may make a basket from the local plants, prepare them, dry them, weave them and use them and possibly even sell them. Children who do not see the value of an item or object such as a chair or a necklace (anything), can be taught the history of how items and objects are made from the origin until the final product. This teaching can become more complex as the child gets older.

## Mathematics

The children may be using mathematics to measure and shape weaving materials and to mend the fishing nets or clothing. In the education facility, they should practice measurement using the heights of the children, teacher, and classroom objects. These measurements can be translated into numbers and written down. The history of measuring can be explained to the children as an African invention which can be related to the pyramids, how they looked, and their function. The shape will bring into account the significance of the triangle which will be linked to Geometry.

## Geometry

The teaching of shapes, like the pentagon, cone, triangle, pyramid, square and cylinder; along with trying to copy them and coloring them, will help with writing skills. These skills will overlap, as drawing and writing symbols is an artistic endeavor. At the same time, it is

Mathematical and Geometrical. This work will nurture the imagination regarding depth, symmetry, height and distance, along with learning about the pyramid and its significance to ancient African people. Exhibiting the products of art for others to see as well as communicating these images online and speaking with other children will provide value to their work and the potential of its use. The work of older children should be displayed to inspire younger ones.

*Astronomy*

As the children become more adept, they are attaching a historical understanding to their physical accomplishments. The girls and boys compare what they could do, to what they are currently accomplishing and hoping to accomplish. They can look to the examples of their older siblings, parents and other adults. Their spatial reality is being assessed all the time. Teaching about the spatial reality of what we understand about the Sun and Moon, the planet Earth, and the origins of time, will be making more sense with the use of the globe and other round objects representing the Sun and Moon and their relationship to each other. Images and photographs will help to define this cosmic design. Drawing them and coloring them will bring the children into the scientific realm of imagination. This work will nurture the imagination.

The children are aware of their spiritual engagement and need no religious undertones. They know how to give thanks, meditate or pray, and connect with greater positive energy. For students less knowledgeable, being taught that spirituality is a medium in which we physically exist will make sense. Also, the teachers' spiritual link with the scholars will be helpful in developing the concept of our energies and connectedness with all that is, was, and shall be. The concept of putting out positive energy that can surround you, bless others, and return to you should be practiced and discussed. If we go around putting out negative energy, how will this affect those around us, and how will it affect us?

*Music*

It is through the Music that the children most sense their spiritual connection to others and the universe. Music will never lose its importance to the children, so being very selective at this age is important as they are influenced by everything. Learning how to play drums and dance to them is directional and responsible as well as helping to exercise the body. Listening to world Music is valuable in linking the similitude across the African world. Learning about the role of music and the work of musicians, why they are musicians and so on will be linked to the instruments that musicians play. Ideally, musical instruments should be available to the children like thumb pianos (mbira) drums and flutes. Some could be made in card or wood or drawn and colored simply.

## 5-6 years

### Language arts

At this age, a child can grow her/his own foods. There is a high level of awareness of the mystery of nature; to plant, nurture, grow and harvest. The child sees the growth of the plant like the growth of self and the growth of animals. This is a good time to bring the concept of growth as an aspect of life, into the educational setting and as a subject to inquire and write about. The explanation of the impact of the Sun on the food, water, nature etc. is appropriate, and writing and explaining this opens the mind to further investigation. Asking questions regarding the children's own experiences is helpful for knowing what the children already understand, and how to use this to approach the lesson; in order to teach them what they need to know. The children must continually be shown how you want their writing to look as well as giving praise for their attempts. The children should be reminded that writing is an art and is therefore specific. Handwriting is disappearing as the computer takes over, so its importance must be impressed on the children.

### Rhetoric and Sociocultural Studies

Learning to speak well is indicated by the children's ability to diagnose verbally to parents and older siblings. The children are able to wash, feed, collect firewood, make a fire and cook simple food for the younger siblings. At the same time, the girls and boys are becoming more private about personal care as the girls learn to do what their Mothers do and the boys learn to do what their Fathers do.

Discussing the nature of responsibilities and what roles and chores the girls and boys carry out in the home will be very interesting. Each location will have differing social and political structures that impact on what can be or is done. Using the data from the study can teach the children what other children of their ages are learning regarding their skills and family responsibility.

Preparing the children to speak and recording their voices can be used to show them how important speech is and can allow them to create messages to other children from Afrocentric schools to listen to. Communication with other children through video calls can also be undertaken to show how they are all learning and make real the distances.

*Logic*

What is happening in the locality or across the world is of interest to children at this age. Children are involved in the effects of global political decisions although often not accounted for. They witness all kinds of events and happenings, and rarely is their awareness or the impact on their lives mentioned. Social changes that will enhance their circumstances will always be of interest to them. The need for clean or close water, the availability of different types of food, nature, the environment and its impact on life are important discussions. For instance, the value of trees, their sacred role in human survival, the killing of or sacrifice of trees to make space to do something that might be useful or harmful. These will be interesting discussions. Facts and figures about just how many trees are being lost in areas across the world and the reliance we have on them. Videos and books will help as examples in any discussion.

*Mathematics*

The girls and boys can go to market and exchange a product or money for an item or product. Examples of how this trading takes place from the production, perhaps growing the yam on the farm, to exchanging it for something which will be useful, can involve the children in the practicality of what that entails and even how the price for the item is decided. Some places have a particular price that cannot be changed whereas in some places, a discussion takes place whereby the seller and buyer come to an agreement (negotiation). In some places no agreement can be made and both parties are without an exchange. Mathematics should be understood as a holistic enterprise that is impacted by cultural values and beliefs. This understanding sets the stage for more discussion in the future concerning value in different beliefs. This will include the ancient African concept of Justice and Truth and the power it wields. At the same time, adding, subtracting, multiplication and division are fitting into the framework for making sense of the use for math in everyday life.

Mathematics is already a part of the discipline used in developing skills relating to the distance of the planets. The telling of time will be linked to the ancient Africans and the movements of the Earth, Sun, and Moon, along with the seasons resulting from their movements. Its introduction through literacy and symbol should relate to life

*Geometry*

The girls and boys are now able to weave mats and wind shields competently. They are able to understand Geometrically, how the pressure of each leaf against another and the weaving of the leaves, are a design specific to the use of the finished article. The article will either protect areas (possibly where plants are growing) from the wind or to carry objects (possibly to market). Weaving must be done well to perform well. At this age the children are efficient. Throughout the child's development of skills, the child is able to make mistakes in order to get better; it can be viewed as fun. Learning is not a stressful situation and whenever a child or an adult begins to learn a skill, there is a process of Learning. Boys and girls can be introduced to weaving to create something specific that is Art and design but forms a function and has depth, width and height. The item must have strength against the wind and be able to carry a circumscribed weight. There may be local people who make artifacts and can be invited into the school to give lessons. Photographs, pictures, or local objects and items, can be exhibited to show differences in height, depth, length, mass and so on. Objects from various locations in the world can be used to show differences. Questions on these areas will reveal how much the children understand. They will teach each other as they investigate.

The role of Mathematics and Geometry can be explained in technological development such as the fabrication of sun-dried earth bricks used to build homes and other constructions that remain cool in the sun. The antiquity of the quarrying and cutting of stones will be taught along with their use in building the pyramids, their purpose, and their relation to the Sun and other stars. The calendar, the Sun and the stars, can be explained more deeply to show the conceptual broadness of the way that Mathematics, Geometry, and Astronomy overlap.

*Astronomy*

The children are able to farm without supervision and thus know the correct time of planting for different vegetables. For this they understand the seasons and the appropriate times of planting and harvesting. Gaining the knowledge of the movements of the sun and moon and seasons is fundamental to being able to farm and care for the animals who will produce young and whose diets may change according to the season. The impact of these environmental and cosmological determinants on our lives are better understood by those closer to nature. Prayer is an important part of planting and harvesting. There is the hope for a good harvest and celebration of music and dance when it is good.

Planting a garden and growing food to show the children how the seeds grow into something amazing. If it is possible, there should be a garden for the 1-2 or 2-3 year-olds. By the time that the children are 5-6 years old they should be aware of their relationship with the plants and be able to speak, write about and illustrate plant life. Observation, care and watering etc. should be shown as a serious discipline in that growing food is a matter of life and death for all of us.

The introduction of how the ancient Africans knew how to balance their needs with what was available and how to produce and store food to care for societies, compared to how little respect there is for the environment today. Learning about the social relationships among nations that enabled the sharing of food during lean times for some, will help to increase the awareness of human relationships.

The children should be made aware of the danger to the world using GM foods made for profit not life. The globe, the planets and the map of the locality and the world will all be helpful in explaining where this GM food is grown and for whom it is marketed. In this way children can begin to understand cash cropping and the sacredness of seeds.

## Music

The computer opens up a world of communication; sanctioned in all the disciplines. Afrocentric schools will exploit this form of communication to meet each other. The children may speak, sing, dance, perform and play instruments or speak on their latest projects and achievements, and in this way inspire each other. Exchanges of ideas can take place as children discuss their locations, environments, and lifestyles. Their introduction to each other will be monitored to influence appropriate speech and content.

# 6-7 years

## Language arts

By this age the children are reading and writing well. The focus on teaching writing will still be necessary as it is an art form. If children are only just beginning to attend school at this age, writing and reading will require the same process as if the children started earlier. Their ability to write will be enhanced by their age as they will have learned wrist and hand movements necessary for writing. Reading instruction would be carried out the same way as the process for the younger children.

At this age boys and girls can be asked to take part in a project, like producing a school-paper with information about their personal interests, chores, tasks and outings. This information will become part of a historical documentation of the school to be shown to the parents, new children who shall attend, as well as children at other Afrocentric schools online. Drawings and photographs of their interests will be a part of the paper and presentation that they will speak on.

They are preparing for conferences that the Afrocentric schools will hold yearly. Important topics will be discussed by the children to help find solutions to difficult situations that affect them, wherever they live. Video calls and connecting through the computer can put the children in visual and audio contact. Even if the languages are different, their works will show the similarity of their ideas from which they can learn. Translators may be necessary in some instances.

Now that the children are caring for their personal hygiene it would be appropriate to introduce the model of a human body. There can be an explanation on what the model body is made of and why it is useful.

Identifying the body parts, what they do and how they work together will show them how to understand the miracle of the body. Over time the children will become familiar with the model and human physicality. Writing simple sentences about the parts as they learn about them will overlap with Grammar, Astronomy, Logic and Rhetoric.

*Rhetoric and Sociocultural Studies*

Learning how to give presentations to other Afrocentric schools will be developed in the educational setting where children are encouraged to speak of important issues.

At this age the children who set the educational standards for the schools are able to be responsible to their parents and the community. They care for their animals, feed them and keep them safe. Discussion on the animals that the children's families may keep and their role in the family will be a way of broaching the subject of animal care.

Going to visit places that animals live; farms, zoos, woods, forests and clearings can be arranged to familiarize the children with their spiritual and physical presence. Many urban children do not get the chance to see animals other than the dogs, cats, and domesticated pets that people may own in the neighborhood. At the same time, if the students are meat eaters, they do not necessarily equate what they are eating with the living animal or the process which it goes through to arrive on the plate. In the rural setting where the study took place, if the children eat meat, the animal that they will eat is considered to have an important spiritual value as wealth. The spirit of the animal or fowl when sacrificed carries the message given to the Creator. In this way, the animal or fowl are seen to have a sacred role in the lives of the people and are therefore not maltreated, the way that they might be in settings where animals are slaughtered on a large scale and for profit. Discourse on this social and spiritual factor will provide a good avenue of debate on various concepts such as ethics.

*Logic*

The Logic of the child has been used continuously to understand why things are carried out and to link that with outcomes. In the rural Traditional setting, Logic is unencumbered with lies and thus can work correctly. This should be the nature of setting in the educational space.

Some children may attend who have problems with Logic as a result of the confusion perpetrated about whom people of African descent are. The emphasis on the history of humanity with reference to the Ancestors and their role in our lives will help to heal the child. Stories of great cities and the accomplishments of great African women and men with pictures and videos will help to illustrate the opposite of what they may believe, and challenge the cultural and societal lies perpetrated both implicitly and explicitly, that undermine Logic.

*Mathematics*

The children in the study are able to go to the farm and market and have an overview of the worth of an object or item based on who they are selling to. The practicality of life and its relationship to mathematics is important. The child has been learning the value of growing, producing, creating an object and exchanging and selling it in the market and within the community. In this way the role of exchange and the value of money are understood.

By now, in the educational setting the child can count into the hundreds and understand addition and subtraction. The child will be learning multiplication, division and fractions like quarters and halves. They can work together in repeating numerical sequences such as the times table. These mathematical skills, techniques and strategies will be memorized so that they can translate from mind to literacy.

Counting has become even more important to the life of the child because we can now link the number system to reality. For example; how many people live in a particular community? How many of these people are women? How many are men? How many are children? How many of these children are girls and boys? How many of these children are under the age of 3 etc.? What does the community produce? What are the ways in which people earn a living? How do they survive and what do they need in order to survive better? Is money the answer to the people's needs? These types of questions prepare the child for research that is important to recognizing and changing the conditions that many people live in. Examples of lifestyles and social conditions and data linked to gross domestic product (GDP) which is the market value of all final goods and services from a nation in a given year, can be used to illustrate differences in different parts of the world. This is a way to introduce the concept of economies and economics.

The application of mathematics to life will proceed as children become more aware and can identify their personal relationship to numbers and its social use.

*Geometry*

The practical application of geometry to life is important so that the children can see its value. Any building is based on geometry. Photographs and footage of constructions locally and anywhere in the world can bring to mind for the child its importance. The history of Geometry as a Mathematical and Astronomical Science will begin with KMT, where incredible buildings were erected for specific reasons that the world copied and built upon using a different cultural logic. There are many examples of how others have copied the amazing historical constructions across Africa throughout time; such as the Temples of Greece and Rome.

*Astronomy*

Learning the communities' style of theatre and teaching, for example, the South African cultural style of drama is critical to encourage expression based on pan African fables and social issues. Video tapes of other children acting can become learning instruments for other Afrocentric schools wherever they are located.

Science is appropriate for this age as children are sophisticated in their understanding of the sciences through manufacturing and food processing, from planting, harvesting, hunting, to selling. This educational attainment indicates the level of understanding possible among the Afrocentric students. It will be useful for explaining and thinking about the relevance of manufacturing homemade products. In light of this awareness, the significance of ecology and the land will make sense; as will the effects of the Sun and Moon on the growth of plants and movements of the oceans and the oceanic animal life etc. Teaching about toxic waste and its impact on all life on Earth brings into account the responsibility of humanity and cultural differences and beliefs in reference to these issues.

## Music

Important events need Music to impose upon the mind, body and spirit, their significance. Children will be more skilled in the playing of their instruments and dance for performance in these events. The application of the children's love of music and performance on special days, chosen in relation to the movement of the stars, Sun and Moon, as well as awards and presentations, will be carried out with great accomplishment and pride. The children will continue to have lessons from local teachers until they leave school. In this way, the older children will be learning and teaching the younger ones. Videoing the music and dance will be a record of improvement that new children can emulate and that the children will be able to look back on historically at their process. As a result of the yearly Afrocentric Conference, held in a new location each year (where some schools will be able to travel to), those unable to travel will be linked online via live camera, and the children will see and converse with each other and be inspired to share their joy together.

## 7-8 years

### Language arts

Africology as a discipline will be an important part of the curriculum taught. Africology takes into account the teaching of Logic, Grammar and Rhetoric to the students. It will teach the children to understand the history of culture, society and social conditions, beginning with Africa, the birthplace of humanity and civilization. In this way the children will be able to locate themselves in human history.

The children can write to each other at Afrocentric Schools and speak of the personal and local social issues that their people live in. They will also identify long term strategies that they would want to implement to improve any negative social conditions. Life in South African Townships, for instance, and the history of how Townships were created and what life is like for the women, men and children, can be a topic of discussion. In this way, the children will gain an important overview of the reality of life for many people.

The symbol of the Sankofa bird is relevant to this discourse. Sankofa is not only a symbol and divinity of understanding true history, but it demands that one must look at the past and take from it the best of the achievements on which to build a future. The children may discuss their findings, hopes and possible strategies at the annual Afrocentric conference.

*Rhetoric*

The focus on speech will continue and the idea of the sacred nature of its use as sound can be taught. The correct use of Rhetoric will also be viewed as a method of healing; broadened by its value in Poetry, Song and Music. Rhetoric's link to writing brings in the concept of how sound is changed into symbol and how the sacred symbol was in ancient times a method to create an image. The image through its vibrational force could represent sound that could be understood in its silence through the brain and the spirit. At this age the history and study of Rhetoric can be introduced as a standard for one to achieve over life. This teaching will continue throughout the years and the results can be evaluated.

*Philosophy and Logic*

When Truth underpins the information that is given to the girls and boys; it is easy for them to follow the theoretical path, that for instance, if you do something well (in goodness) then you and others will benefit. The girls and boys in the study are able to see that when they care for their younger siblings, the seeds that they have sown, their animals, their personal items and so on, that things go well. Simply, they would understand that if care was not taken, then there would be negative outcomes such as the younger siblings would be unhappy, the seeds would not flourish, the animals would be in danger and personal items will be unkempt and so on. In this way, they make sense of what they are doing and why, because their educators have been thorough in showing them the results of their life's experiences in the communities. Logic in educating from an Afrocentric perspective runs through all the lessons, and the Logic of the children is guided by the spirit and thus will judge it.

The children should be able to ask about things that do not make sense and they can be guided by the educator to bring sense and reasoning to the discussion. Such discussions help the students to have clarity with what they know and begin to understand the significance of, and preparation for, research and study.

## *Mathematics*

Seshat, the ancient African Goddess of Mathematics, Knowledge, Writing, Architecture and more, can be introduced as a critical Divinity of time, measurement, and building in KMT, to show the great value placed on the understanding of these concepts. The role of Seshat can be linked to Geometry and Astronomy to show the overlapping of these studies that are often viewed as separate. In this light, the pantheon of Divinities can be approached that will include Sankofa discussed in Grammar. The IXL learning which is online can be a useful guide to mathematical expectations for the different ages.

## *Geometry*

The question of how the pyramids were built and measured is relevant because at this age the girls and boys should be able to measure circles, triangles, and angles, as well as draw 2-D and construct 3-D shapes. They should also now be able to identify parallel, vertical, horizontal and perpendicular lines. The work of Imhotep (a multi-genius Priest; Traditional Medical Practitioner; first Master Builder and first known pyramid designer) and Seshat, the Goddess of measurement, will provide a suitable context for understanding the relationship between the ancient focus on the Spiritual and the current focus on the material. Comparisons can be made. The images of Imhotep and Seshat will be helpful to this learning.

## *Astronomy*

The teachers can investigate the herbal remedies used in the locality of the Afrocentric School. In some cases, there is evidence that African people brought plants with them to places that they were taken or migrated to and continued their ancient spiritual Traditions of healing. The children can learn about the significance of healing and its relationship to modern medicine based on the properties of plants. At the same time, they can provide examples of ancient or modern medicine. Students can speak of and begin to document the names of herbs and their properties that they know of, especially in their communities.

This will formalize their knowledge and help in developing the idea of the relevance of literacy and record keeping. The significance of formalizing this knowledge is based on the idea of eventually building a pharmacopeia. This information can be added to by other Afrocentric school children and teachers. Herbal uses in medicine both nationally and internationally can be taught.

*Music*

Each child can begin to compose a musical piece with the instrument that s/he is learning and add other instruments to the composition. S/he will provide a name to the piece and discuss what s/he feels that s/he is saying through the music. Her/his work will be contextualized by a history of dance and Music that shows how it has been interpreted in different societies across the African diaspora still maintaining the power of communication and message.

## 8-9 years

*Language arts*

The student will be finding and naming the Divinities in the African world and their distinct roles in the lives of women, men, girls and boys. S/he will seek similarities in the roles of Goddesses and Gods across the African world. The context of their similarities will relate to the global movement of African people which can be traced on the maps and globe and in books. Later the student can find out about the Goddesses and Gods in other parts of the world, especially among indigenous people in particular lands including but not limited to Australia and the Americas. This will be particularly relevant not only in understanding history but also the cultural similitude for instance among the First Nation people who populate North, South and Central America. It is in this light that female and male reciprocity will be linked to their spiritual representation of the Goddesses and Gods and the idea of God as Divinity; Mother and Father; the Unknowable; the Mystery; existing in all that is, was and ever shall be.

The maps and globe will be useful to show the locations and movement of humanity from Africa and the location of the peoples of the Northern and Southern cradles of civilization including the zone of confluence where these different cultural groups overlapped over time. This conceptual framework provides the context within which to define culture.

*Rhetoric and Philosophy*

The discipline of Rhetoric is very much a part of the children's lives in the study. At this age they are familiar with the Shrine and ritual and the use of speech in this context. The children in the Study are also familiar with their responsibility and relationship to their family and community.

In light of this, students in the educational setting will be continuously reminded of the role of good speech in setting up a positive spiritual environment. Discussing the findings with the students will provide a context for discussing what they are doing in their families regarding younger siblings and family chores. In some cases, the students will be carrying out similar responsibilities and roles in their own lives. In this case, discussion on lifestyles and existence should be approached from a sociological and historical perspective to understand the differences, if there are any, between the lives of the students in the educational setting and those in the Study. The social conditions can be discussed in terms of the hopes and aspirations of the girls and boys.

*Logic and Sociocultural Studies*

The discipline of Logic is a good place to elucidate on what culture is and how different people have created different cultures; although the first human culture was defined in Africa. The values and beliefs that shape the mind and behaviors can be distinguished between Southern cradle and Northern cradle people. Female and Male reciprocity can be viewed as an African relationship that was the foundation of their amazing accomplishments (libraries, universities, fish farming, brewing, artisanship, architecture, the practice of yoga and meditation, achieving social peace and harmony and so on) that the world emulated.

Differences in cultural thought and female and male imbalance, can account for the belief in and construction of "Race-ism" and the consequential practice of chattel enslavement. Cultural differences can explain the taking of millions of intelligent, brilliant, educated, skilled African women, men and children from all walks of life; to different parts of the world, to carry out the work of the conquerors – Arab and European women and men. The trauma and impacts of these events can be explained over time.

*Mathematics*

The girls and boys in the Study are able to grow, manufacture, create and produce artifacts that they can sell. They understand the value of what they are doing from production to sale and use after sale.

This knowledge can be contextualized in the study of Western Economics, on how the world is divided into rich and poor countries and how it is further divided by class in both the rich countries and the poor countries. It will be a continuation of the earlier teaching on GNP relating to financial wealth, based on the ability of the students to understand.

The idea of materialism and individualism can explain the unequal divisions of money in the world and lay the foundations for understanding capitalism (an economic system built on the private ownership of resources, production, land by some and the exploitation and subjugation or enslavement of others, to create untold amounts of wealth for those in power) which is in complete opposition of ancient African values and beliefs. The African philosopher Ptahhotep wrote 4,500 years ago that, if one seeks to have perfect conduct and be free from evil, then one must above all, guard against the vice of greed, as greed is a grievous sickness with no cure, which divides mothers, fathers, and family, and is the aggregate of all evil (Hilliard, Williams, & Damali, 1987, p.25).

The cultural context of beliefs around the evaluation of wealth will be used to build upon the definition of culture and its role in the lives of people. Examples of what has value and how this value is devised from place of origin to destination can be studied e.g. Coltan; a metallic ore found in rocks in the eastern areas of Congo that when refined, becomes metallic tantalum, a heat-resistant powder that can hold a high electrical charge for mobile phones. Coltan is collected by children (boys) in the Democratic Republic of the Congo (DRC). How much does the child receive after spending all day digging for it, then undertaking the perilous journey to the buyer, during which time the coltan may be taken by bandits (possibly other children)? How much do we pay for the mobile phone across the world? Who gains wealth through this child's labor?

*Geometry*

What is the circumference of the Earth and how far is the Moon? What are the distances and sizes of the planets that we recognize in this solar system? Who are the Dogon people and how did they know about Sirius B? What is their relationship to KMT and other nations in Africa? What is the planet Earth made of? What do we know of our universe?

*Astronomy*

The movement of the stars were recorded and known by the ancient Africans. There are still 4 texts known to exist that explain the Sun, Moon and star movements. The ancients created the zodiac and the 12 divisions of the zodiac relate to the 12 months of the year that relate to today's calendar and the seasons that relate to the plants and their growth. This ancient knowledge teaches the students the significance of time and what wrist watches and clocks are recording. Ancient clocks like the water clock of Karnak/I Sus, provide the foundation of the modern clock.

Images of the architecture can continuously be referred to in order to make the connection between the positions of these buildings and the stars. References can be made to the sun, star and moon Divinities.

*Music*

As Vimbai Chivaura states,

[t]here is no past or future in African dance. The living, the dead, and the unborn, come together to celebrate a common destiny. All are possessed and moved by the spirit of the rhythm of the dance. All respond to the heartbeat of the drum and dance as one. To dance out of rhythm is a sign of one's estrangement from one's people. Thus, in order to experience and preserve their connection to the African tradition, people of African descent in Africa, North America and the African

diaspora as a whole, take part in the rituals and ceremonies and African people in the communities learn to sing the songs and dance the dances of their African ancestors (2015, pp. 349-353).

Drumming should be utilized at the beginning of the day for the students; to signify spiritual unity, the start of the school day, and to center the children in the rhythmic sounds of life. The students should practice drumming to harmonize their own vibrations as a collective and to prepare for learning. Events involving music and drumming, even outside the educational setting, should be planned.

## 9-10 to 15-16 years

For the children older than 9 years, the groundwork has been laid for the next few years during which the deeper development of these Disciplines will be studied. Clearly, hormonal and developmental changes will take place in the children, and Rites of Passage will take on a more critical role in the transition of children through their year groups. By the ages of 15-16 these students will be able to attend university.

CHAPTER 5

# Locations of Afrocentric Schools

While the Afrocentric School has its roots in the urban US, it is recognized that the location of the school is of prime importance to the model that the school will develop. Whether the location is rural or urban will dictate how the development of the school will proceed. A school built in Brazil in a favela will be different from a school built in a township in Soweto South Africa as will a school built in Afram plains in rural Ghana or in a city like St Louis in the US South or Paris in France.

## Model 1: The Community based Afrocentric School

The Afrocentric School as Community Based is guided by the principle of Sankofa – the idea that we take from the past what is important for building for the future. Essentially, there are two types of this model, the rural and urban. Wherever communities have evolved and are intrinsic to the development of their women, men and children, this model may be appropriate. For example, in Brazil and South Africa, racism in urbanization has created levels of impoverishment whereby people exist on the edge of survival. Favelas and Townships are examples of this manifestation. In this light, knowing the needs of the communities is of paramount importance to the education of the children.

The lifestyle of the communities within which the schools will develop will greatly affect what provisions can be made for the scholars and communities. For instance, in greatly impoverished areas where schools may not exist, where the communities do not have their basic needs met and the children are working to help their families survive: The welfare of the community may exceed the need for literacy in the mind of the people. Conversely, literacy may be viewed as a way to change the social conditions. Literacy may also be perceived as of major value, as globally the attainment of literacy is often a privilege that is paid for.

Indigenous Knowledge (IK) may well be the basis for the survival of impoverished communities. Importantly, IK is what Afrocentric educationists seek to disseminate and also learn. This knowledge will play an integral role in the development of this model. The process of Education is learning, teaching and becoming. The learning of IK will be necessary in the creation of the Community Based Afrocentric Model whether it is in Africa, South America, Central America or Australia.

In reality these communities of women, men and children affected by domination and alienated from access to any of its amenities and wealth, may still hold some of the ancient truths and principles that the Afrocentric school and Afrocentric theory, for that matter, seek to build upon and impart.

In the social arena, there must be agreement with the communities, their local leaders (elders) and families that such a school can be accommodated. In some cases, the knowledge of the Nations of people will play a great role. As a result of conquest and domination, inequalities among people who are the same color may manifest as class or Nation inequalities which can be seen in Europe for example, and subsequently across colonial Africa. This hierarchy has been important to orchestrate disagreement and disquiet among Nations who have historically lived together in peace like the Hutu and the Tutsi Nations. At the same time, knowledge of the mixed communities of African and First Nations people as in the favelas and communities in the Americas, will be important. The children, who attend the Community Based Afrocentric School, will have to have their absence from work/survival replaced with a remuneration that will bring the family something of value for the attendance, like appropriate foods. In the situation where the child is a babysitter, accommodation should be made; for example, the babies may come with their carers.

The language is an important consideration as the colonial language may be the one necessary to teach the children. There is the recognition that indigenous languages may be spoken. Ideally, the teachers should be able to speak these languages. However, the reality is that much academic knowledge of the Ancients/Ancestors although researched and developed by the descendants of those with IK, has been translated into European and Arabic writings. There is the continuous need to learn Indigenous Knowledge and respect the language of IK at the same time as imparting what is currently known. There is also the vision that in time, the knowledge translated into these foreign languages will be translated back into indigenous languages.

The school site and building will be negotiated between the community and the Afrocentric School Educators. The building may be planned as a new building or repaired as an old building or may begin in the home of a person or family with space to accommodate some children. In a village in Ghana, a school was built by the community of the Bikpakpaam (Konkomba) Nation that was in keeping with the sunbaked earth brick (clay), round design of the houses with thatched roofs. In this way, the school was cool for the children during the hot part of the day and in the cooler part, the children could learn outside. The school was built within sight of the community.

## Model 2: Urban-based Afrocentric School as US Charter

The model of this type of school is based on the urban city type developed in the US. It is the state/public school that has become a Charter school bound by the rules of the state in testing, hours held, and the teaching of literacy. These schools are allowed to cater to the cultural needs of their populations/students. Thus, schools in Black communities of people of African descent have been able to teach Afrocentric curriculum alongside Eurocentric curriculum. These schools are predominantly situated in the poorer disenfranchised areas of the cities.

Because the Afrocentric idea and curriculum is added to the Eurocentric belief and curriculum that has been traditional to the US and the development of Eurocentrism and white supremacy, there is always a tension. To a degree, a school of this kind can plant new ideas about who the African person is. However, there is always the contradiction between the Eurocentric belief in the inferiority and debasement of the African woman, man, girl and boy to contend with. It is more often the case that after years of psychological abuse, African people will believe that positive information about their history and achievement is a lie, or a fantasy or a feel-good program of no substance.

Importantly, any positive information about the history of African people will not be totally lost. Poor results in literacy in these schools, does not mean that Afrocentric ideas will not be embedded. To associate the level of literacy attainment with the level of Afrocentric understanding in these schools when testing is based on Eurocentric ideas and is not logical. Thus, one cannot dismiss this model, as it is no different in many cases than some offers of African American Studies and Programs in University that do little to challenge the Eurocentric paradigm. There will always be some students and even professors who begin to understand. This type of school, no matter how fragmentary the teaching, has its uses.

## Model 3: The Independent Urban-based Afrocentric School

This school is an independent institution that is grounded on the principles of Afrocentricity. It is a private or charity run organization that teaches the children Afrocentric curriculum. It can be placed in any city location where there is a preponderance of African descended people who believe that their children should learn the history of humanity from an Afrocentric perspective. Its existence can only be based on the perceived need for the installation of this cultural-based institution.

The lifestyle of the people will determine what resources are available for starting the Urban Based Afrocentric School. As in the case of the Community-based Afrocentric School, the Urban Model will require the community or members of the community to see the need. The imposition of this independent school in a community cannot sustain without the acquiescence of the mothers and fathers and carers of the children who will attend.

Local knowledge will be important to find out the general feelings of the area regarding the development of the independent model. At the same time this knowledge will be important for evaluating the strength and weakness of Eurocentrism and Afrocentrism in the minds and experiences of the people. There are areas of African descended people which may hold refugees running away from African despots, descendants of enslaved African people who are seeking new lives in new countries, and African people escaping from chaos and wars etc.

<u>Social conditions</u> will certainly have a role in determining the needs of the people. In older historical settings where communities have developed over time, there will be a certain understanding of what has transpired over years of neglect and the desire for change will be fundamental to the possibility of setting up the school. In this case, the local leaders, elders and persons of respect will be known. It is likely that there are already Afrocentric thinkers there. Where more recent communities are still in a fragmented stage and living in disarray as a result of more recent trauma from other places; there is less likelihood of planting an Afrocentric school.

<u>Language</u> will be important as the older the urban community, the more the imposed language will be learned. In developing communities there may be many languages still being used by people of differing countries and nations who might still be making the transition to the dominant language. The language of the school will be determined by the dominant language, although as said before, most of the teaching materials will have been translated into the languages of the colonizers or those languages that dominate the colonized. For example, in an African country, there may be 10 languages relating to 10 nations within, and the colonial language will either be European or Arabic, in this case, the most powerful nation's language will be the next indigenous language that will be spoken. For example, in Ghana the colonial language is English and Twi is the dominant African language. However, in order to be sensitive to the current situations, it must be recognized that although the dominant language might be the language of the largest nation, there will need to be some historical and herstorical awareness of how this came about. In other words, it is incumbent on the schools' designers to recognize that invasion and colonization have changed the power relationships within these allocations. The Afrocentric position is that ultimately, indigenous ancestral lands will return to the rightful keepers. Like the Islamic influence which focuses

on the Quranic teachings and Arabic writing, the Christians focus on Bible teachings and European languages. Both of which debase the African as we earlier read.

The site of the Urban Afrocentric School will be linked to the permission of the City planners. However, as has been the history of educational institutions, city communities can offer sites in places like community centers or closed school buildings etc. It is always possible to begin a school in the home of a person or family who understands the significance of the Afrocentric School. Again, it will be about negotiating the area of the site with the locals who wish to have the school embedded in their community. At the same time, it is feasible to build an Afrocentric school, create a profile of the school, and then inform the community of what the school will teach. The school could ideally begin with the entry of young children who are just at the age to start school. Although slightly more complex, it is also possible to begin the work with slightly older disenfranchised girls and boys. The school can determine the hours, days or evenings of operation suitable to the resources and areas.

Afrocentricity supports the economic, cultural and educational elevation of African people in an effort to create cultural consciousness. Its method is Afrocentric and Pan African, participating at the national and international levels in the creation of an advanced cadre of individuals whose aim is to bring into existence an African renaissance. Its members are committed to do all that they can to encourage the awakening of African consciousness, and the creation of the United States of Africa, in order to give back to Africa its greatness and sacredness. May each Afrocentric school in the world be free from oppression and free to exist, develop and thrive, in order to build a greater future for Africa, her Diaspora, and therefore humanity; grounded in ancient cultural unity.

# PART II

# Lesson Plans

## LESSON PLANS
## FOR AGES 3-5 YEARS

# Overview

The 7 disciplines of Grammar, Rhetoric, Logic, Mathematics, Geometry, Astronomy and Music, will overlap throughout the educational process, as none can exist without the other. It is their recognition and utility that we strive to apply.

The idea of the educational process at this age is to familiarize the children with symbols of writing and reading (letters) to prepare the children for literacy. At the same time, the children will be learning literacy in relation to their community understanding, as well as the development of their global knowledge. In this way, they will be locating themselves in the world and forming a cultural identity of who they are. It is imperative that the girls and boys are learning the positive aspects of themselves as human beings.

Expectations of the children's accomplishments are based on our own expectations as well as the standards used, which are produced by the Traditional children who have achieved their parents' and communities' expectation for each age group.

Familiarizing the children with the 26 letters of the alphabet that they must memorize will be considered the teaching of an Art form to be undertaken repeatedly throughout the year. Counting will be taught throughout.

Every day there should be a time set aside for music and dance and meditative peace and quiet.

Towards the end of the year the students will have achieved a body of work that can be shown to family, community, and students at other Afrocentric schools in conference style presentations.

## Language Arts

### Learning to read and write
Understanding symbols i.e. letters and their sounds
Alphabet practice through drawing (the children are learning how to develop their wrist and hand movements for writing)
Significance of color
Placing letters together as sounds and forming words
Writing words through drawing

## Rhetoric

### Learning the significance of sound and its effect
Communication regarding connection
Pronouncing sounds of letters and words and making speech
Telling and speaking about experiences through stories
Speaking about knowledge of a particular subject

## Logic

### The meaning of logic through discussion and knowledge based on truth
Sound logic can only grow and develop through truth. The concept of history inclusive of herstory must be fundamental in education in order to facilitate the understanding of past and present.

The use of Aesop's stories to understand African morals (and others) is helpful to build a basic foundation for logic and reasoning.

### *The Boy who looked after goats, and the jackal*
A young boy was looking after the goats for his family just outside the village. He thought that it would be amusing to worry the villagers

by pretending that a jackal was attacking the goats. He shouted "jackal, jackal" and the villagers came running to save the goats. The boy laughed at the villagers and tricked them several more times. The villagers were angry as there was no jackal at all. One day the jackal came and the boy called out "jackal" to the villagers but they did not listen to him. The jackal was able to kill and run away with a goat.

The moral of this story is that it is difficult to believe a liar even when s/he tells the truth. Another way to understand this is that it is important to be truthful so that when it is critical that one is believed, people will know your history and that you are an honest person.

The French made film by Michel Ocelot called *Kirikou and the Sorceress* is a useful learning tool for young children, that firmly shows the logic of behaving in a good way and living in truth. It is about a brilliant baby who is born with ancient knowledge and an inquisitive mind, who uses logic to understand people and life. He learns from his mother and grandfather and works to help his community. It is a film that can be shown many times as there is more to learn and teach each time it is shown.

## Basic Mathematics

Learning the number symbols through counting
Counting using fingers, cowrie shells, objects and pictures
Addition and subtraction through fingers and cowrie shells
Multiplication and division with cowrie shells

## Geometry

Measurement, distance and time
Shapes: circles, arcs, squares, triangles as art
Application of shapes to local and global buildings
Materials necessary for building or creating anything

## Astronomy

Space, time and distance in reference to the sky, Sun, Moon, Earth
Learning the days of the week, the months of the year and the seasons
The globe as a reference to the planet Earth
Nature and the importance of humans, animals, fish, birds and plants
The need to care for our environment
Naming local nature
Africa, the birthplace of humans, location of students in the world

## Music

Sounds and their use in relation to music
Recognition of local music, dance and song
Illustrations, DVDs and CDs of local music and African world
Demonstrations

## Language Arts

Teaching the alphabet:

- Write the alphabet on the board or on papers given to the scholars

- They will repeat each letter symbol in the order to make it easy to memorize
- Each child can point out the letters
- The letters can be sung with a simple familiar tune

Next the scholars will learn that each letter symbol makes a sound.

The sound of each letter can then be associated with a simple familiar object or thing.

Since the languages and sites of the schools differ, then the alphabet letters should relate to what is relevant to the children.

Below are some examples in English. The explanation of each "object" or "subject" should include what the children know so that the instructor can be guided. B for beads could be for boy as G could be for girl etc.

### *a is for ant*

What do the children know about ants?

Guide the children to know of the positive aspects of ants (if unaware).

Discuss the nature of ants that live and work together and build cities etc.

## THE AFROCENTRIC SCHOOL

*b is for beads*

These beads are made from glass

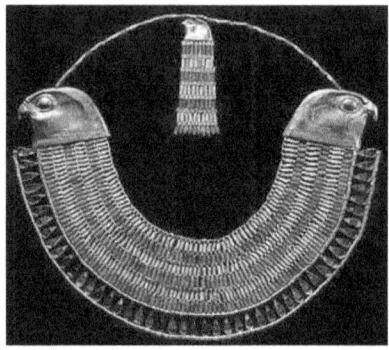

Beads are ancient like these African beads from KMT

This necklace is made from precious stones and glass

## C is for cow

Cows are precious they are considered as wealth and money

## d is for drum

The drum is one of the oldest instruments
It is sometimes called the heart of music as it can beat like the heart

*e is for elephant*

The elephant cares for its family
The elephant can live a long life

**f is for fish**

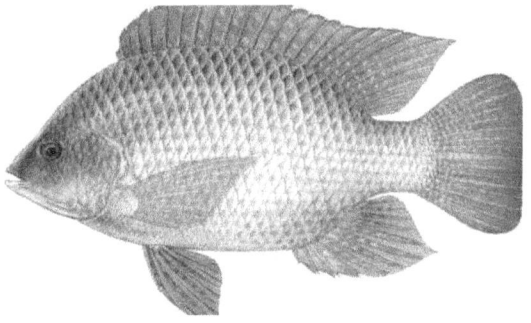

This is the Tilapia fish
It is African and is shown in ancient paintings

## Writing and Reading

Discussion on the importance of reading and writing for:

- Knowledge building
- Learning how to understand what important people are saying
- Recording what has happened

- Recording the tools and measurements that we might need to build
- Instruction
- Reading about the stories and lives of girls and boys
- Copying what is important

Ask the children for examples of how reading and writing might be useful. Show the scholars the words and pictures of stories that you read. They can link the words to the sounds and memorize.

These African people of KMT taught the earliest Reading and Writing

They recorded medicine and how to heal people
They wrote about how to live in peace with others

## Sociocultural Studies

### *The African Origin of Humanity*

The scholars will learn throughout the years, the African origin of civilization and that the mitochondrial DNA of all humans, shows that we are all linked to one African mother. African people settled all over the world. In other words, **we all came from Africa**. Modern humans (we), Homo sapiens sapiens are over 250-300,000 years old. Some left Africa and travelled to other parts of the world and settled for thousands of years.

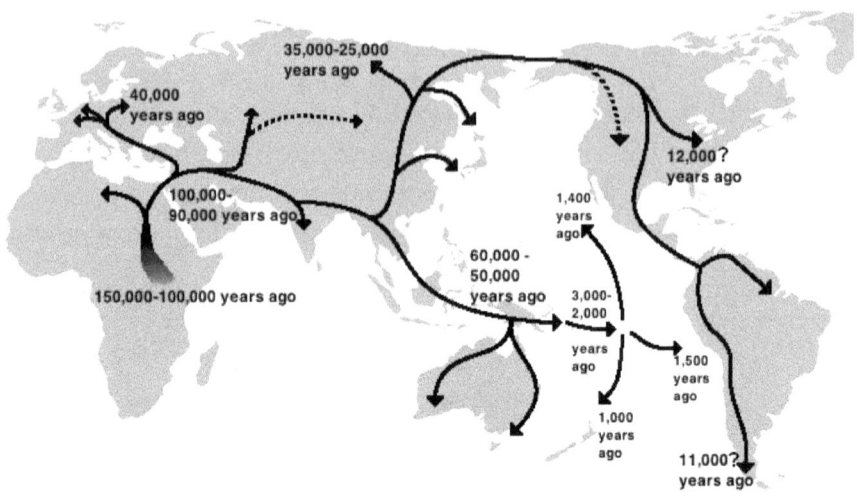

Africa at the center of the world

In understanding human history, it is also imperative that the people who came before us and tried to make a better world for us will be remembered. They are called our Ancestors. We remember them because they were good people. We thank them for all the good things that they did for our family, the community and the world. That is the way that African people and their Diaspora can remember their history and honor those that came before them so that the future generations can exist.

It will be difficult for the children to fully understand the concept of thousands of years ago; however, their own sense of history can be made clearer when they remember being much smaller and younger and accomplishing different things. What they did in the morning before leaving home is history. Measuring their current height and then measuring them throughout the years will be another way of establishing the significance of history; in this case through personal growth.

*Melanin*

Melanin is found in the brain, central nervous system, heart, liver, glands and other organs such as the eyes and skin. Melanin is the pigment responsible for the color of our eyes, hair, and skin. Although, the amount of melanin we have in our skin, hair, and eyes does not define the amount that we have in our brains and other organs.

The more melanin found in our skin, the darker we are. Melanin protects our skin from the sun so that we can produce vitamin D which we need for our bones. Everyone has some amount of melanin in their skin (excluding some people born with a condition called Albinism, whose bodies have great difficulty producing melanin) but some of us have more than others.

Once upon a time, all people had lots of melanin in their skin; they were dark skinned and what we consider today Black. After thousands of years, those African people who settled where there was less sun, began to lose the melanin in their skin. The less melanin they had in their skin, the easier it became to produce vitamin D with much less sunlight. The less melanin a person has in her/his skin, the lighter the color of skin.

*Culture*

As people settled in different parts of the world, they developed their cultures to suit the environments that they lived in.

Cultures can be divided into two main cultures.

Southern cradle, Africa: Female and Male balance–respect for each other
Northern cradle, Europe: Male superior to Female
Mixture of both cradles: Female and Male balance – respect; and Male superiority.

*Ancestors*

Setting up a shrine or sacred special place to remember our Ancestors is important for the children so that they know that they are connected to their historical and cultural past through their family, community and humanity, globally.

The Ancestors are the good people who have passed away and their bodies are no longer with us but their spirit is still around us watching over us, guiding and taking care of us.

The shrine is a special place that we go to remember these good people. These good people are in our families, our communities and all over the world. We remember their names if we can and we thank them for all that they have done. We also ask them for their continued help and guidance.

African people have remembered their Ancestors for thousands of years, this is an important part of our culture.

## Mathematics

*Counting using fingers, words and symbols*

It has been found that children will often be adept at selling and buying at young ages, and using their mental skills in this area of monetary gain and loss, far outreaching children who attend full-time school; yet, when attending school, the transition from real business to written and symbolic mathematics is in many cases a failure.

In part, there is little understanding that if the children can run financial business in the market then their mathematics must be supreme.

The problem lies with the notion of inferiority often attached to these children, not only because they are of African descent but also because they are poor and or not literate.

Explain to the scholars that using mathematics is a way to keep a record of what exists.

Ask the scholars to give examples of how useful counting is.
The children should first learn to count objects with their fingers.
Throughout time, the hand has been a tool for measurement as has the foot and fingers as digits
Associating the digits with the symbols of numbers will come after.

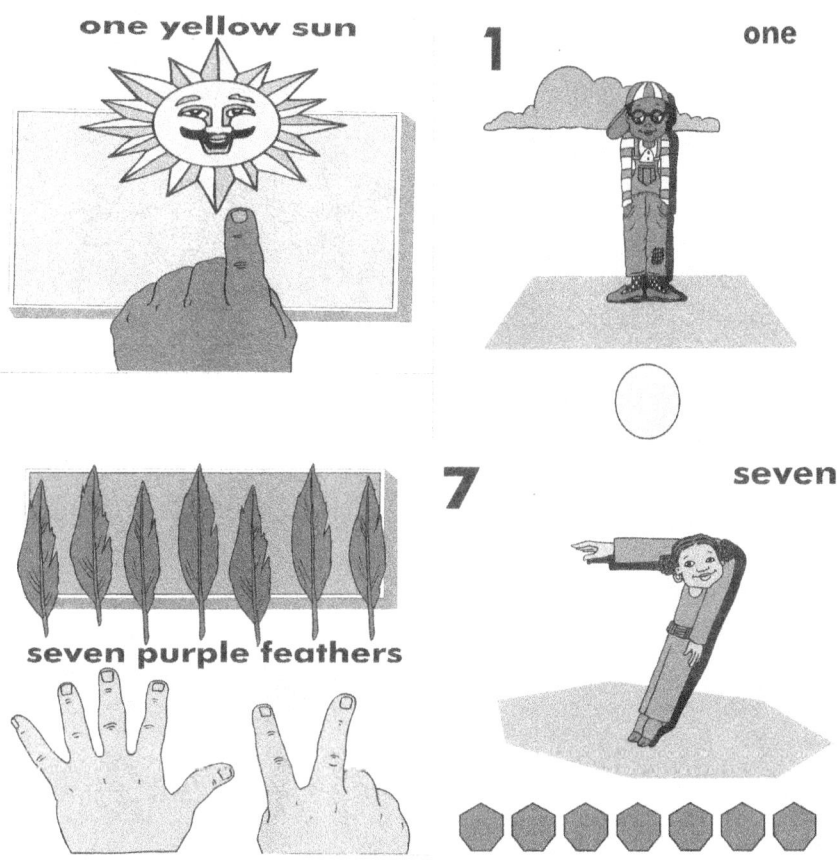

Afro-Bets 123 Book
By Cheryl Willis Hudson
(2002)
Scholastic Inc

Counting with Cowrie Shells

Counting with Cowrie shells will help the scholars learn of the importance that cowrie shells played in African life:

- Spiritual guidance
- Spiritual symbols
- Records
- Computing
- Business
- Jewelry
- Games

Most of this information will come from the book called *Africa Counts: Number and Pattern in African Culture* by Claudia Zaslavsky (1973). Predynastic ancient Egyptian (Kemite) African people used the Cowrie shells, they can be found in jewelry taken from their tombs and exhibited all over the world.

Cowrie shells can be used to count as well as to add, subtract, multiply and divide.

These actions can be transferred to the number symbols and the math symbols of +–x ÷.

It will be useful to count the shells in groups of 10 to familiarize the scholars with the significance of 10.

Most monetary systems currently use 10 in coinage,

- Kilometers, meters and centimeters in distance, depth, width and height
- Weights kilograms and grams
- Degrees of heat from the sun in centigrade
- People in the UK still use hands and feet as measurements
- Feet are used for length and width
- Hands to measure the height of horses

By the end of the year, the scholars will be able to count in hundreds.

## Geometry in Art

Understanding through art work

The Mud Cloth made by the Bambara nation from Mali offers examples of beautiful designs that the scholars might use to inspire them to draw and color their mathematical and geometric patterns.

Squares can be drawn and given to the children to color and design in their own ways.

The Mud cloth itself is made from natural cotton and natural dyes and is in this way environmentally safe and sustainable.

These shapes can be found in buildings and paths between homes and streets. The shapes will familiarize the children with geometry and its use in building.

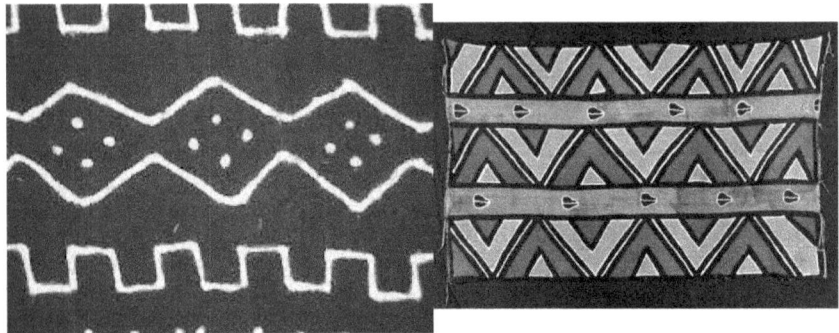

Circles will be seen as critical to geometry.
Ghanaian circular cloth prints that represent water and wells

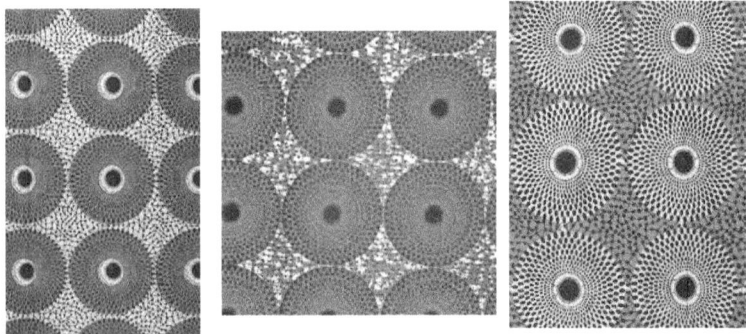

These circular shapes can be found in nature everywhere, like the shapes of trees, stems, and patterns on animals and birds.

*Review*

    Can you name some circular objects in your home?
    Can you name some circular objects that people wear?
    Can you name some circular objects in the education room?

## Geometry in Architecture

The scholars will be shown how basic shapes can be used to build homes and places.

The children will try to draw the shapes and the instructor will provide these shapes to be colored in to make lovely designs. The children can be given the shapes to make patterns.

The significance of the circle in architecture
An Arc is:
Something curved in shape
Part of an unbroken curved line
Astronomy: A circular section of the path of a celestial body
Math: A section of a curve, graph or geometric figure

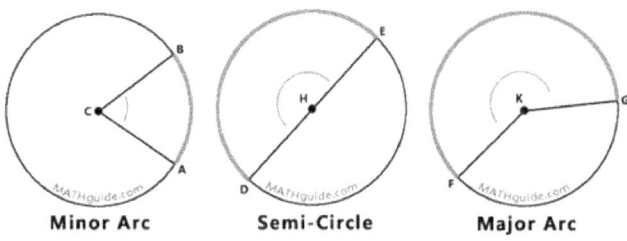

An Arch:
A curved structure that spans an opening
Serves as a gateway
Parts of structures

A Temple in Mali constructed by the Dogon Nation

Architecture of the Dogon Nation of Mali made from sun dried bricks

Architecture of Musgum Nation of Northern Cameroon
A compound built of sun-dried clay

The Bamileke Nation architecture at Bandjoun, Western Cameroon

*Reclaiming African Knowledge* 107

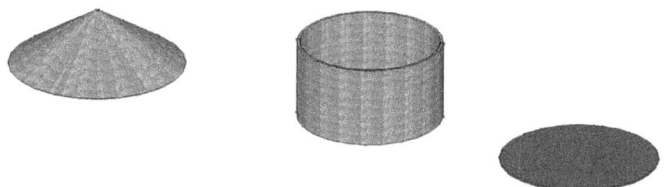

Conical and cylindrical shapes

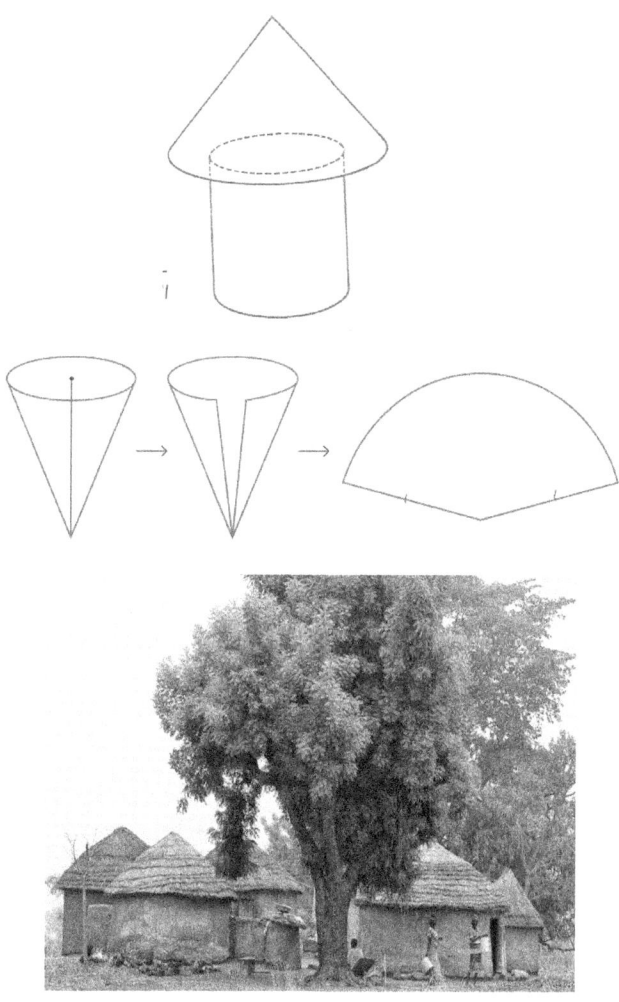

Konkomba Nation homes of Ghana

Triangles and squares

Triangle

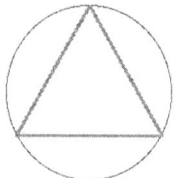

Triangle made from a circle

 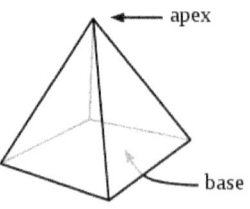

Pyramid complex at Giza   4 Triangles on a square base

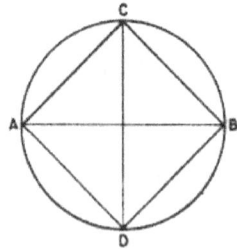

A square made from a circle with triangles

# Science

## *Astronomy*

The Sun, the planet Earth and the Moon

These pictures will familiarize the children with the most immediate aspects and images of where we are in the cosmos.

The scholars will learn that our Earth goes around the Sun which keeps everything on Earth alive with its heat. People cannot live without the Sun. People have always appreciated their connection to the Sun and life.

A pendant in bronze representing the Sun, by the Dogon Nation of Mali

- They will learn that the Moon is lit up by the Sun that helps us see at night.
- From the globe the scholars can see that the Earth has water that we need to live. They can see the many oceans and rivers (and clouds) that keep us alive.
- The children can identify Africa and where they are located.
- The idea of time, day, night, week, month, year and how we know it, will be simply explained through the movements of the Earth and Moon around the Sun, and will be understood in time.

Importantly, it takes time for the children to adapt the sightings of the real spheres in the sky to the models or images displayed in the education room.

The scholars can speak of their experiences to talk about how the Sun, Moon, and rivers affect their lives.

*Botany*

The scholars can name local plants and the instructor can form a garden outside or inside, with pots to plant. The scholars can help with the planting, nurturing and caring for the plants, as well as research and learn all that they can about the properties of the plants that they are growing.

Plants are very sensitive and respond well to respect, care and love, as well as the necessary environment in which they can grow.

The scholars may know about medicinal plants in the locality (they can be knowledgeable at 4 years). These plants should be identified and if there are none locally then the scholars should learn about healing plants like:

**Sutherlandia frutescens** or **Cancer Bush** which grows in South Africa

It is used to remedy illnesses such as tuberculosis, wasting syndrome, bronchitis, indigestion, reflux esophagitis, gastritis, and peptic ulceration.

The **Neem tree** grows in Africa

Neem is used as an insecticide, insect repellent, and oral dentifrice; and in traditional medicine to treat malaria, diabetes, worms, as well as cardiovascular and skin diseases.

## Music

Music is perceived as the living practice of philosophy; the route to harmony with nature and the celestial bodies, the Creator, the unknowable, the mother and the father, all that is, was, and ever shall be; and the Ancestors.

Discuss with the scholars their local music, musicians, and the music that they listen and dance to. A film on music across the world can be shown to highlight the cultural similarities in music throughout the African diaspora.

## 112  THE AFROCENTRIC SCHOOL

African Drummers from Brazil
https://www.youtube.com/watch?v=iZhAxbAx72U
4 years old Djembe drummer
Isaiah Chevrier
https://www.youtube.com/watch?v=iZhAxbAx72U
Abdoulaye Chevrier
https://www.youtube.com/watch?v=lVPLIuBy9CY
FOLI (there is no movement without rhythm) Guinea

By the end of the year, the children should be taking drumming lessons and feel a measure of confidence in their developing skill.

If the school cannot provide the children with drums immediately, then the scholars can bring objects to the education room that can serve as drums like tin cans, boxes, buckets and so on. If the school applies for funding, drums should be on the list of necessary resources.

A drum teacher will be required to teach the scholars about the history and meaning of drumming and how to play together.

The scholars will be able to watch drumming performed by other Afrocentric school scholars at the end of the year to both inspire and be inspired by one another.

Drumming is important because it is a way that the children can learn; through playing and dancing to connect with the rhythm and spirituality of life. This grounding will lay a foundation for other instruments that they might like to play in their lives.

LESSON PLANS

# for Ages 5-6 Years

## Language Arts

The scholars will be reading with a focus on sound and spelling. In particular, comprehension will be important to assure that not only can the children read but they understand what they are reading. Grammar relating to sentences, paragraphs, full stops, capital letters, will be shown through examples on the board. The teacher will explain their significance and always involve the children by encouraging them to show what they know or understand, which can also help other children in the process. Essentially, the education room setting involves everyone learning together.

### *Writing as Recording*

Recording life events, philosophies on leading a good life, medical ways of healing, plants and their properties, and sayings of wisdom as practiced by the ancient Africans are important reasons for writing.

### *History*

History is an important concept for the scholars to understand. Personalizing history by showing the children the importance of growth, their own growth and the growth of their animals and plants, will help. They can remember when they were babies or when plants were seeds etc. In this way it becomes easier to talk about life from a historical perspective. From the age of 3-5 years, the idea of the movement of humans from Africa to the rest of the world thousands of years ago, is solidified by the comprehension of time, through personal growth as time goes on.

In the words of John Henrik Clarke,

"The events which transpired five thousand years ago, five years ago or five minutes ago, have determined what will happen five minutes from now, five years from now or five thousand years from now. All history is a current event."

These words serve as a basis to discuss the nature of the events of history. The scholars should be asked the meaning of this sentiment over time as they come to understand it better.

Below is an illustration of Djehuti of ancient Kemet who is known as the scribe. It is he who is the recorder of events in the life of a person. This particular illustration can be colored in by the scholars.

*Djhuiti*

Djehuti, the male Scribe and Seshat, the female Scribe

## *Daily Life*

Speaking about daily life as well as interests and responsibilities, in the context of chores and roles in which we play in our families, will serve to help with speech. Children in each location in the world will have differing chores and live in differing political and economic conditions. This type of information and discussion can be developed over time and will help the scholars to also learn about children around the world.

What is happening on a local and global scale is of interest, although children are barely brought into the conceptual framework when political and economic decisions are made.

The students can be asked to journal the events that one does from rising to going to bed. This is a record of what one has to do from personal hygiene, chores and studying, to caring for a sibling and eating. These actions can be looked at later to remind the scholar of differences in responsibilities and knowledge as a historical document.

## Languages

Conquest means the control of a place or people by military force.

The conquest of Africa by Arabian people and European people influenced the music of Africa. African people in Africa can speak a few languages; their local <u>indigenous</u> ones as well as the main colonial languages.

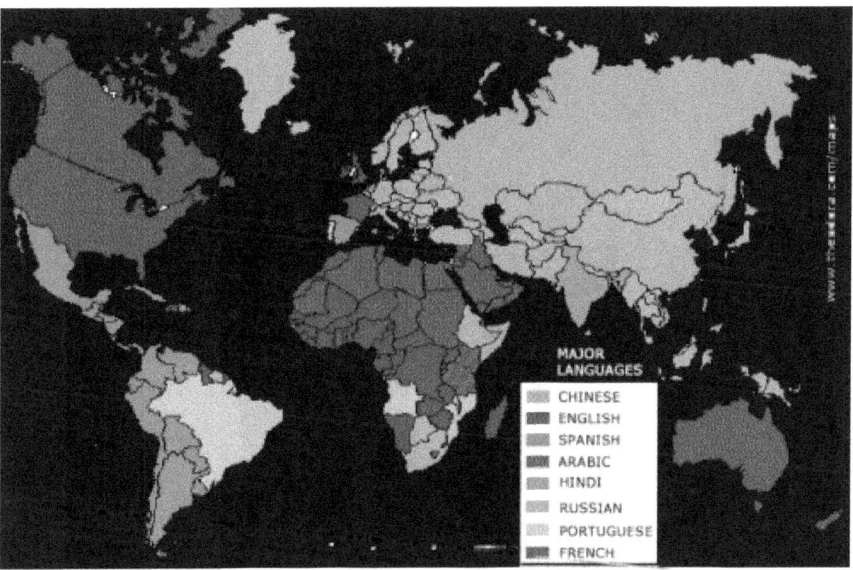

World map of languages

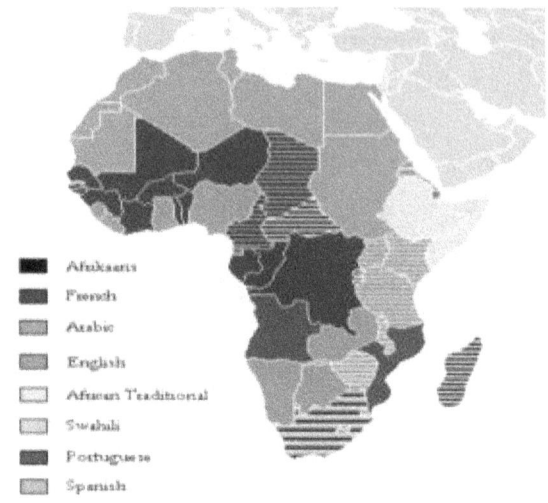

Map of colonial languages in Africa

**Review and Discussion**

What languages do you speak and sing in?

## Wisdom and Ethics

### *Ankh*

The symbol of Life; the Feminine and Masculine balance from which life exists

## Fables

Stories with an African moral basis should continue to be told to bring order to chaotic thinking; to create a foundation of Truth that can guide the scholar. Some examples from Aesop's fables that can be used throughout the years are:

The Tortoise and the Hare

The Goose that Laid the Golden Eggs

The Fox and the Crow

The Lion and the Mouse

The Crow and the pitcher

The North Wind and the Sun

The Wolf in Sheep's Clothing

The Gnat and the Bull

The Fox and the Goat

The Boasting Traveler

The Crab and her Mother

Father and Sons

The Owl and the Birds

Local stories are another source, and books such as *Selections from the Husia: The Sacred Wisdom of Ancient Egypt* by Maulana Karenga can be modified for the scholars of any age to understand throughout the years.

## The Teachings of Maat

Bringing Order to Life

To live in Love

To speak in Truth

To be Just

To have Hope

To live in Harmony

To live in Balance

To uphold Female and Male reciprocity – Empathy

What do these teachings mean? Give examples

- What is respect?
- What happens if one treats others (family, people, animals, plants, the earth) with respect?
- What happens if one treats others with disrespect?

*Reinforcements*

The scholars should visit sites of interest (for example):

- Nature reserves to see local fauna, birds and animals.
- A zoo so that the scholars will learn of captivity and how the animals and creatures that we see are not free to be who they really are. Comparing and contrasting them as free and captured is a project.
- Visiting the homes of people who contributed to local community development.
- A Museum to show historical artifacts and explain their meaning and use, and to discuss the reasons why there are Museums.
- A theatre to see a play or film of meaning.
- A place to see Art work of any kind whether it is in the street or in a gallery.

## Mathematics

At this age the scholars will be able to count at least to 100 and will be working on adding, multiplying, subtraction and division.

### *Two-Dimensional Shapes*

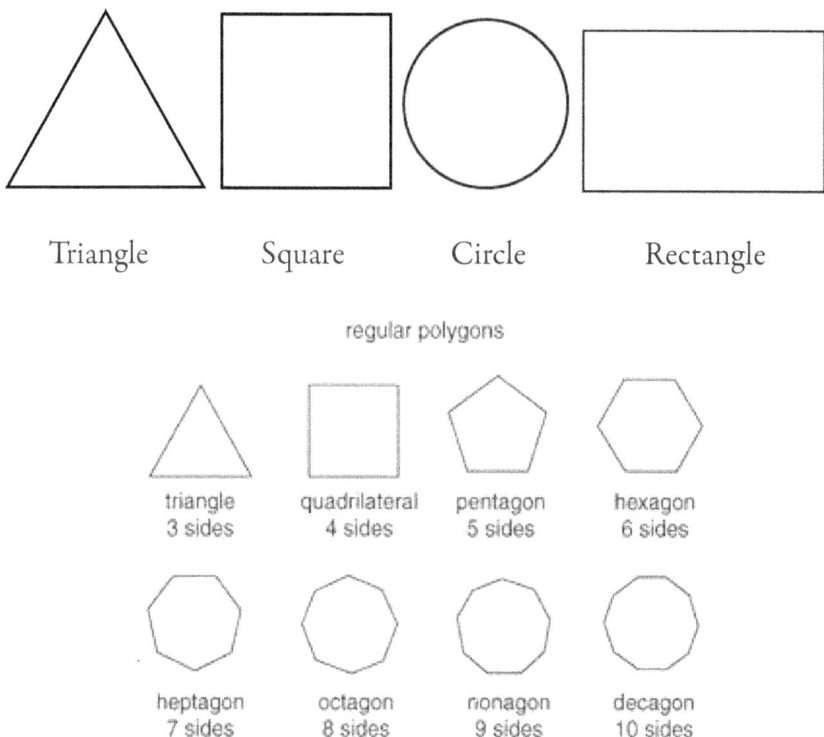

These are important shapes to remember

The sides are all equal. The children can color in and measure such shapes to know that the sides are equal. This is important because later they will be learning the areas of these shapes.

## Three-Dimensional Shapes

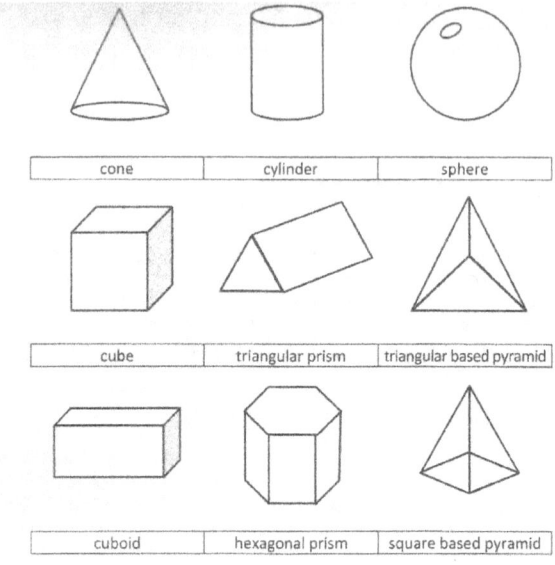

A 3D object has height, width and depth, like any object in the real world. Example: your body is three-dimensional.

**Review and Discussion**

Do you think that the girl or boy who grows the yam must consider the weather and season and the right time to grow the yam?

- If so, why is this important?

What must the young person think about when she sells the yam?

- How much time it took to grow the yams.
- How long it takes to get to the market.
- The potential cost of transport to get to the market e.g. bus fare or petrol.
- What s/he would like to buy after selling the yam.

What might the girl or boy consider so that s/he may grow more yams and perhaps another plant food or something that the family needs?

- The person who buys the yams may get many and then go to the city to sell them.

What should the seller include in the price, to sell it to the customer in the city?

- How much s/he paid for it.
- How long the journey was.
- How much it cost for the transport it took to make the journey.
- What s/he might like to buy after selling the yams.

What is the most important thing to consider before selling the yams?

- The yam grower must consider not selling all of the yams so that s/he retains enough yam cuttings to grow more yams.

## Geography

Prior to the European and Arab conquest of Africa, the continent did not look like this. Many nations lived across Africa.

These countries are all created by the leaders of European and Arab countries.

For this year, the scholars should be learning the names of the currently recognized 54 countries in Africa.

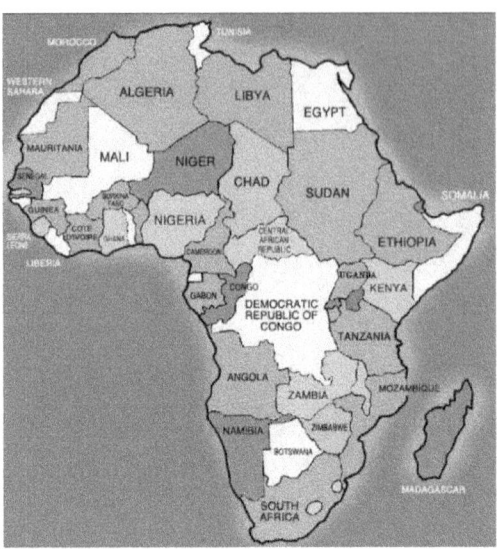

## Science

*Astronomy*

The ancient Africans from KMT developed astronomical knowledge from keeping records of the movements of the planets, thousands of years ago. They are responsible for giving the world the calendar year that we use today, as follows:

- It takes the planet Earth 365 days, one year, to orbit or travel around the Sun.
- There are 12 months in a year.
- The Moon orbits the Earth in around one month.
- The word month is derived from the word moon.
- It takes the planet Earth 24 hours to turn or revolve as it goes around the Sun.
- When the Earth faces the Sun, it is day.
- When the Earth faces away from the Sun, it is night.
- When one side of the Earth is in day and most people are up and busy working, the other side of the Earth is in night and most people are sleeping.

The globe can be used to show the scholars how the Earth turns, the approximation of the Sun and the Moon, and how they turn.

The scholars can learn the names of the planets that we know of and learn of the Dogon people of Mali who located a planet called Sirius B thousands of years ago.

## *Climate and Seasons*

Show illustrations of climates and define the climate and nature of the seasons that the children live in. Look at differences in the nature of the animals, plants and birds that live in these climates.

These are the main climate zones of the world:

- Tropical. Wet (or rainforest) Monsoon. Wet and dry (or savanna)
- Dry. Arid. Semiarid.
- Mild. Mediterranean. Humid subtropical. Marine.
- Continental. Warm summer. Cool summer. Subarctic (or boreal)
- Polar. Freezing most of the time. Tundra. Ice cap.

The types of plants, including trees and animals are greatly affected by these climates.

Pictures of animals and plants associated with these areas can be shown with the use of computer or nature films like David Attenborough's *Planet Earth: The complete series*.

### Review

How many days are there in a year?
What are the names of the 12 months of the year?
What are the seasons of the year?
Which season are we in when we are at the greatest tilt towards the Sun?
Which season are we in when we are at the farthest tilt away from the Sun?
What part of Earth always rotates closest to the Sun?
Can you name some of the differences in the lands and environments of those closer to the Sun and those farther from the Sun?

## *Plant life*

By this time, Traditional African children are growing plants and then taking them to market to sell with their parents.

Learning about the value of a product and selling it and then buying something else needed or wanted.

The African child from a Traditional rural home will learn from a young age the value of what her/his family sells and needs.

The young person grows a yam by planting the cutting, taking care of the plant and then taking it to the market. If the weather is good for the yam to grow well, then the young person will have a good-sized yam.

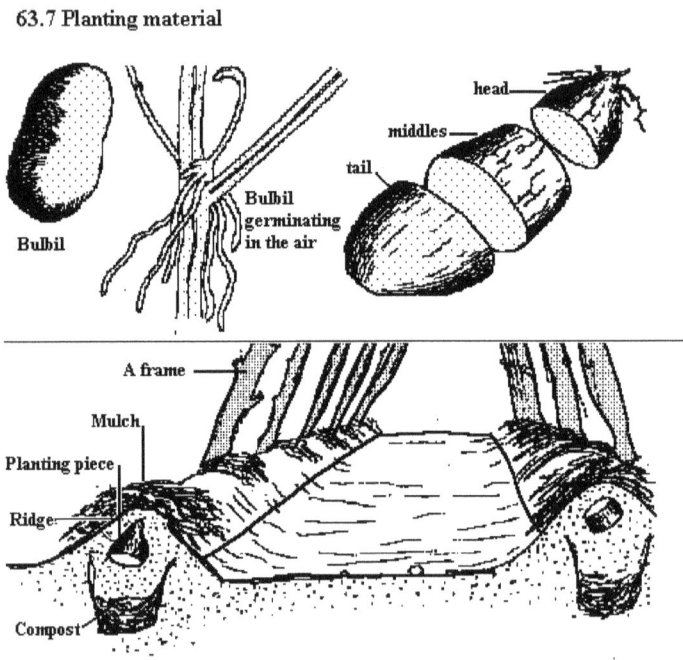

63.7 Planting material

Record the growing of the plant from the planting of the seed and what it took to keep the plant alive i.e. the sun, water and space in the soil as well as forms of love and care.

Reading interesting information every day to the scholars and having the scholars read out loud and to themselves, will help them to develop a love of reading and writing.

## *The Human Body*

Skeletal structures can be introduced as a way of comparing and contrasting similarities and differences in humans, animals, birds, fish and insects. Ideally the education room will have a skeletal structure of a human so that bones and vital organs can be learned over time.

## Reclaiming African Knowledge

The scholars will become familiar with how the body works over the year.

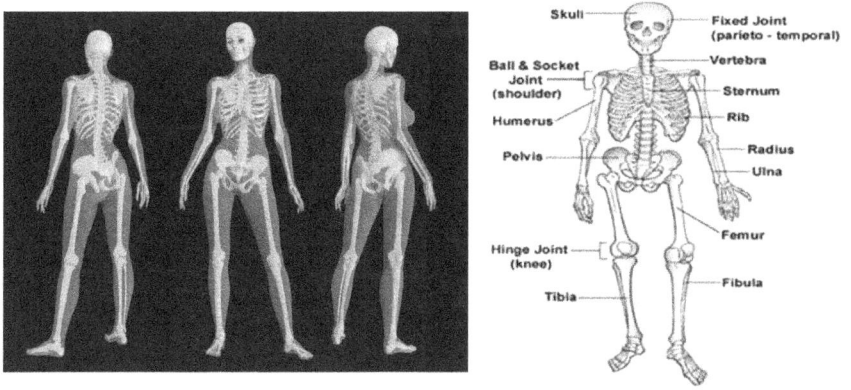

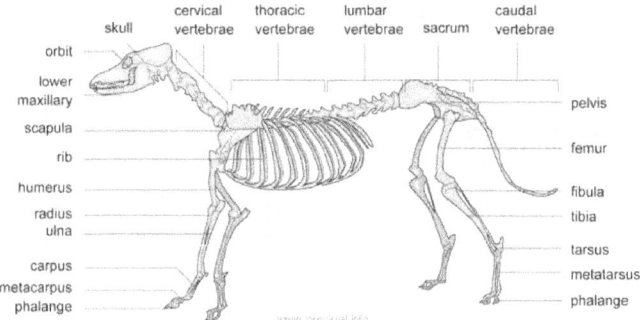

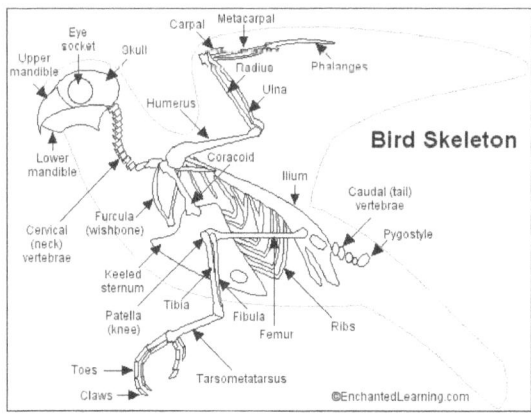

## The Arts

*Weaving*

Weaving is a way of creating something useful. Almost everything material that can be used for covering or clothes is woven.
Kente cloth from Ghana

Kente cloth is silk woven on small looms which make strips of cloth that can be joined to make a much larger piece of cloth. Above you can see the strips joined together.

Weaving can be used for making baskets to carry the shopping.

The scholars can work with strips of colored paper and design a Kente cloth

A woven mat with Palm leaves

Remind the scholars of the use of these shapes used in building

## Song and Dance

What type of dances do you practice?

Use the computer to look at different dances, music and songs from Africa.

https://www.youtube.com/watch?v=W3tKFLafu3s

Plan what type of dance and song the scholars will create for the end of the year when they perform for their parents and scholars from the other Afrocentric schools.

Music and dance are included in the day to day teaching environment of the school. The scholars will be able to drum at the beginning of the circle meeting in the morning when the day begins. This special time is used to focus their thoughts for a blessed day for everyone and to remember the Ancestors.

# LESSON PLANS
# FOR AGES 6-7 YEARS

**B**y this age, sentence structuring should be in place and spelling an ongoing development. The scholars are reading and writing well and they are knowledgeable about the reasoning for the need to read and write. The teaching of writing is considered an Art form and should continue to be taught this way. The wrist and hand movements necessary for smooth writing will be easier for the scholars at this age. They can compare their earlier attempts with their current achievements, recognizing that one can only improve through experience. Often, children believe that if someone is accomplished at a skill, that it took the person a short time to become skilled. Children can also believe that if they cannot attain the same level of skill immediately, then there is something wrong with them or that they will never achieve it. That belief will be understood and overcome in the context of practice.

As a result of the holistic (Afrocentric method) teaching of subject matter so that each discipline is not separated (Eurocentric method) with culture and history as context, the scholars are able to use their logic in understanding the connections. This is reflective of the ways that Traditional African children are taught.

For this year the scholars will be expected to learn about the enslavement of African women, men and children.

They will look at the movement of African people across the world through enslavement. Maps and photographs will be integral to understanding these movements visually.

- The scholars should already be aware that the population of the world began when African people travelled from Africa, the center of the world (see Pangea map below), and settled all over the world.
- The scholars should be aware of some of the knowledge that our ancient African people developed which influenced the world; Grammar through Reading and Writing, Rhetoric through speaking; Mathematics through creating, producing, selling and living; Logic through thinking about Reality and Truth; Geometry, through building and constructing anything; Astronomy as a way of understanding life and nature as parts of the cosmos; Music, as the expression of life and spirit through harmonizing sound for dancing and healing.
- The children should understand a little more fully the meaning of culture and how people differ in their beliefs and ways of acting and thinking. Environmental conditions may be used as a way of understanding how people might look (loss of melanin) and think differently (culture) about the value of life, including nature, animals, humans etc.

## Geography and Sociocultural Studies

For this year the scholars will be expected to learn about the movement of people across the world. Maps and photographs will be integral to understanding these ideas in a visual way.

The scholars should already be aware that the populating of the world began when African people travelled from Africa, the center of the world, and settled all over the world.

The scholars should know some of the knowledge that African people developed which influenced the world. Kemet can be used as an example of ancient Africa and its profound knowledge.

The children should understand a little more fully, the meaning of culture and how people may differ in their beliefs and ways of acting and thinking.

This information sets a context for learning about the capturing and enslavement of African people still living in Africa. They will want to understand why African women, men, girls and boys were captured and enslaved thousands of years later.

Importantly, the knowledge given to the world from Africa will be continuously spoken of, so that cultural beliefs and different values will make sense to the children as to why enslavement took place.

At this point in the scholars' learning, cultural difference will be very important. This information sets a logical context for learning about the capturing and enslavement of African people still living in Africa. They will want to understand why African women, men, girls and boys were captured and enslaved thousands of years after people left Africa.

## *The Continents*

The children should be shown the Pangea, how the world looked 300 million years ago before it divided into what are now known as the seven continents, along with today's countries, with Africa in the center.

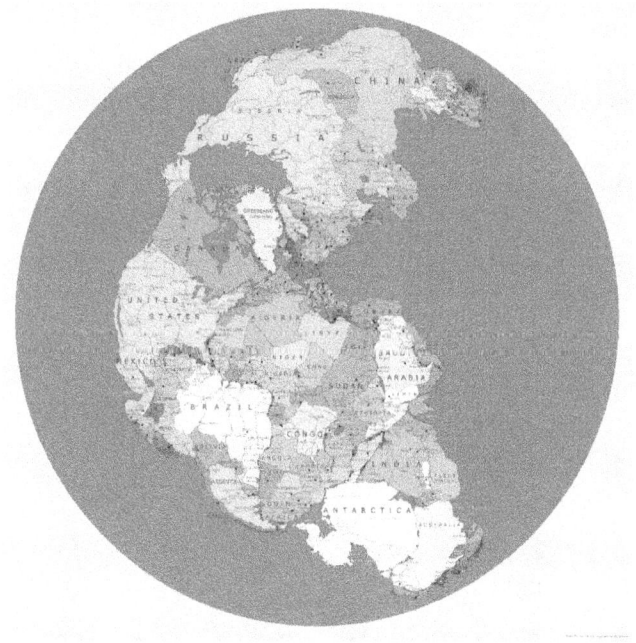

Africa and the surrounding countries in Pangea
Can you see Africa where the first humans came from?

# THE AFROCENTRIC SCHOOL

Of course, it will be important for the children to know that although these are today's countries (so that we are able to see where we are today), these are not like the countries when they were in the Pangea or long after.

Below is a map of Africa from the book *The World and Africa* by W.E.B. Du Bois, that shows Africa about 3,000 years ago when African women, men and children had control of their lands.

This map will be relevant throughout the years as the scholars learn about these ancient civilizations that we know and are still learning about, as new evidence comes to light in Africa.

Africa 1325 BCE until 1850 CE

*Important*

Later, the maps can be sized and shown with transparencies so that the ancient Nation states of the people can be seen with the modern Nation states.

## *The African Diaspora*

Thousands of years after people had travelled and settled all over the world, millions of African women, men, girls and boys were captured and taken from Africa. They were enslaved by Arab and European people. They created a belief in their culture and religion that African people (Black people) were their natural slaves. In reality, African people were their teachers. They knew that African people were very clever, had good ways of living, and worked hard. These people wanted to use African people to do the work that they should do themselves, for nothing.

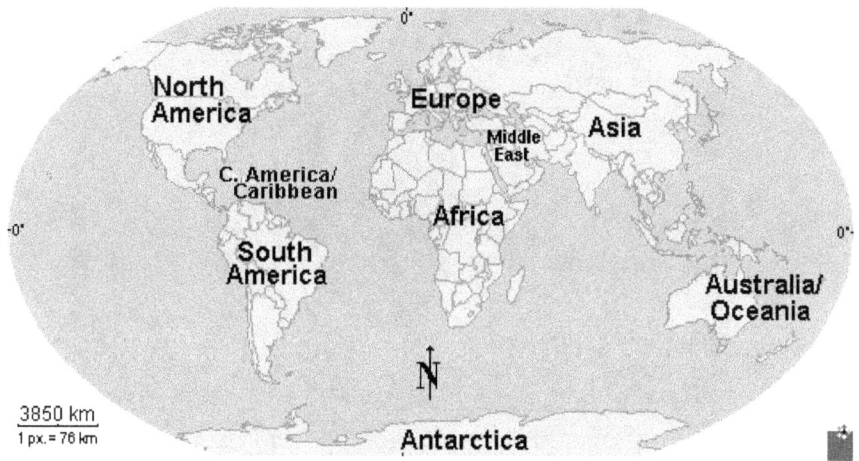

Enslavement meant that African people were forced to work for nothing. It was a cruel system that did not value the lives of African people.

Remember that thousands of years before, African people had said and believed that we must live in Truth and Love in order to live a good life.

The work that African men, women and children were forced to do, made their enslavers extremely rich. It made them so rich that these countries in Europe and Arabia (today's Middle-East) are still wealthy.

For Europe the money from enslavement was invested in making machinery that could do things like weaving cloth faster than a small family or community, and so making more. The money from enslaving African women, men and children was the most important money in the history of Europe and European culture and Arabia and Arab culture.

On the map of Africa below, you will see that all the African countries are created by those Arabian and European people who enslaved African people. We know this by all the major languages that African people speak today.

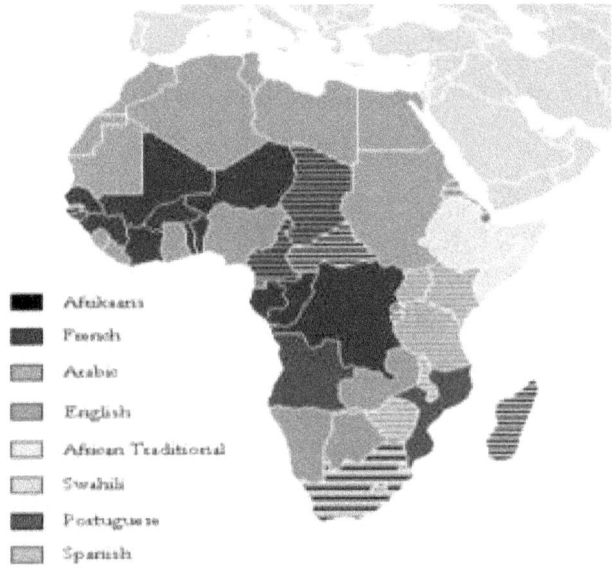

The same European and Arab people who went to Africa to capture and enslave African people, also took over Africa and built their own governments and controlled Africa to make wealth for their own countries.

Before the Europeans and Arabs came to take the whole of the African continent, Africa did not look like this. All the Nations of people who lived across Africa were not separated by borders like those above (See the ancient African map of African nation states). These new Arab and European borders were called colonial borders.

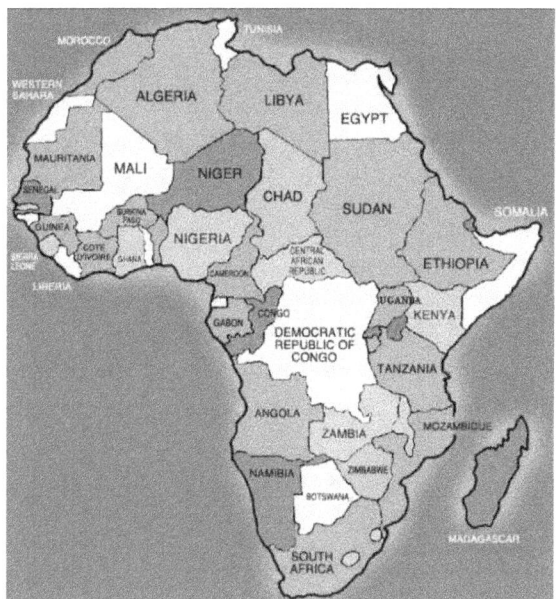

Let us look at the African countries and look again at the map of languages and find out which African countries speak which languages.

Now we shall look at the map below to see the countries that captured African men, women and children were taken to. They were forcibly taken to North and South America, the Caribbean, and the Arabian lands (the Middle East).

The Caribbean is a group of islands sometimes known as Central America, as they are between North and South America. The Caribbean is the home of over 45 million African people.

- The British Europeans controlled Jamaica, Barbados, Guyana, The Virgin Islands, Trinidad and Tobago.
- The French Europeans controlled Haiti, Guadeloupe, Martinique, Guyana.
- The Spanish Europeans controlled Cuba, Santo Domingo, Puerto Rico.
- The Dutch Europeans controlled Surinam and St Eustatius.
- The Danish Europeans controlled the Virgin Islands and so on.

Sometimes there were wars among these Europeans over control of the islands.

Control over these islands and lands meant that they controlled the lives of enslaved African people and had the guns and weapons to force people to work hour after hour, day after day, year after year, with no respite.

Below is a map showing where African people were taken from in Africa and what parts of the world they were taken to.

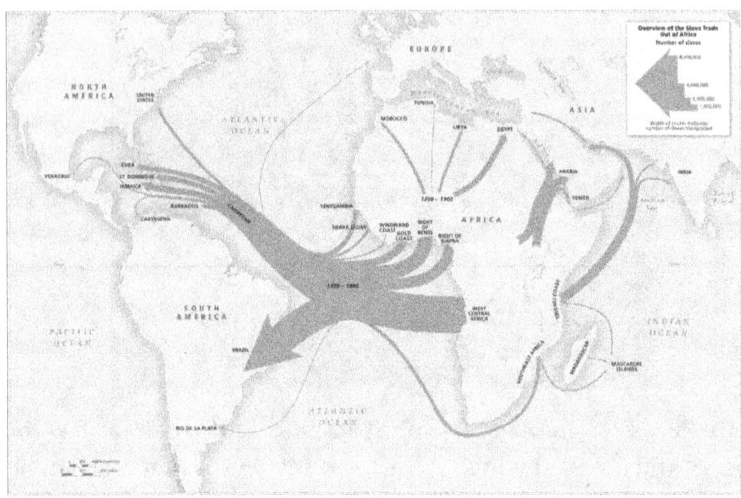

Below is a map of Africa showing the areas in which Arabian people enslaved African people, and where they took them.

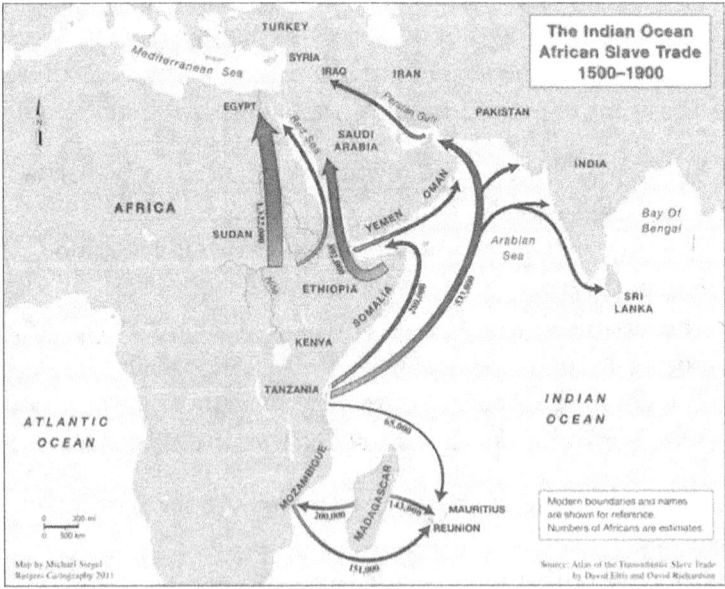

*Lesson Plans for Ages 6-7 Years* 137

Over 1,000 years ago Arab people enslaved African people in Africa and took them to Arabian lands. Over 500 years ago Europeans captured African people from Africa and took them to the Americas and Europe.

The descendants of Africa spread out across the world over hundreds of years are known as the Diaspora. The Diaspora means those people whose Ancestors were captured and forcibly taken from Africa who are people of African descent.

The people of the African Diaspora are often known as Black people of wherever we live, like Black Brazilians, Black Venezuelans, Black French, Black British, Black Germans, Black Americans, Black Canadians, Black Dutch, Black Italian, Black Arabs, Black Libyans and so on.

The percentage of African people in:

Venezuela is 15%

Peru 10%

Colombia 40%

Brazil over 50%

Below are some pictures of African Diasporic children

*Physical similarities*

Brazilian children                                 Venezuelan children

Peruvian children　　　　　　　　　　Columbian children

Libyan children　　　　　　　　　　　Yemen children

These children have in common that they are the African Diaspora which means that they have:

- Common Ancestors
- A recent common geographical origin, Africa
- Common African Cultural ways e.g. in music, beliefs, hairstyles
- Common history of enslavement
- A common history of inequalities and racism

Think of, talk about and write about cultural similarities that you can find in your community.

Do you know where your parents and their parents come from?

Discuss what injustice and racism are as the children perceive them. They will provide a basis for discussing and teaching its complexity as a global enterprise.

### *Indigenous, First Nations People of the Americas*

What is important to know is that before African people were enslaved by European people, Europeans had already travelled to the

Americas and taken the lands of the indigenous people. The original people of the lands of South America, North America and the Caribbean are known as indigenous First Nations people, because they were the First Nations who lived there. However, it is important to remember that when these indigenous people first arrived in the Americas, thousands of years ago, they were African.

These people were conquered before African people were brought to their lands. The lands were divided by European conquerors in the same way as Africa. Today, each made up country (using colonial borders) speaks a European language.

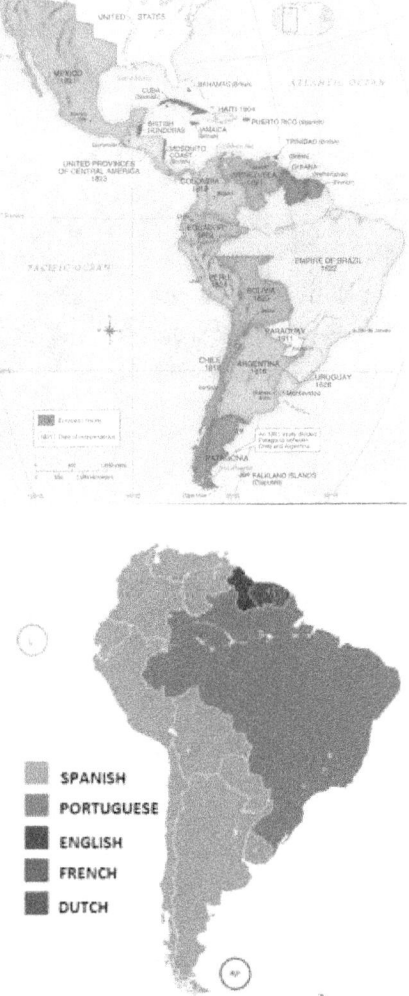

140     THE AFROCENTRIC SCHOOL

Below are some of the children who live in these countries. The children in these pictures are indigenous to South and Central America. They were the first people in their countries. They were African in origin and many of their values and beliefs are still culturally African. They believe in their Ancestors, music and spirituality.

Brazilian children      Venezuelan children         Belize children

Mexican children       Canadian children           American child

Indigenous means:

- The first people who lived in a place before others came.
- The children of the Americas are sometimes known as the First Nations people (Canadian indigenous people created that name to identify themselves). This is a more respectful title.

## Mathematics

This year the scholars will look at objects or products and learn that there is a beginning and end from need (demand), to idea, to creation, to use. The Traditional rural African children in the study, know from an early age what it takes to create an object or product. They have a concept of the production of something, such as growing food and eating it, matting, building a home or making a wooden stool. However, those children in more urban material-based societies, see products in their finished condition, like chicken pie, a carton of juice, a mobile phone or a table. Urban scholars often have little knowledge of how these products are fabricated.

### Benchmarks: Multiplication and Division

Below are some examples of what 6-7-year-old children are expected to know in Western schools that set the pattern globally.

## 7: Division

Today we are baking in Kids Club. I bought a box of 12 eggs. The recipe for a cake needs 3 eggs, so I have put the eggs into groups of 3. I wonder how many cakes we can make?

12 divided by 3 is 4
12 ÷ 3 = 4
There are 4 groups of eggs. We can make 4 cakes.

### Get ready

1. 15 divided by 3 is \_\_\_\_\_
   15 ÷ 3 = \_\_\_\_\_

2. 16 divided by 2 is \_\_\_\_\_
   16 ÷ 2 = \_\_\_\_\_

3. 15 divided by 5 is \_\_\_\_\_
   15 ÷ 5 = \_\_\_\_\_

4. 16 divided by 4 is \_\_\_\_\_
   16 ÷ 4 = \_\_\_\_\_

### Teacher's tips

Division can be represented as sharing and as grouping. Equal grouping is a better model for division as it links to repeated subtraction. 12 grouped into threes to make 4 groups (12 ÷ 3 = 4) can be modelled by repeatedly subtracting groups of 3. The ÷ sign also relates better to division as grouping and reinforces the inverse relationship that division has with multiplication.

## THE AFROCENTRIC SCHOOL

### Let's practise

You can use multiplication facts to help with division.

5 × 2 = 10         10 ÷ 5 = 2
5 multiplied by 2 is 10     10 divided by 5 is 2

Group these and write the answers.

⑤ 5 × 4 = \_\_\_\_\_
   20 ÷ 5 = \_\_\_\_\_

⑥ 2 × 9 = \_\_\_\_\_
   18 ÷ 2 = \_\_\_\_\_

⑦ 5 × 3 = \_\_\_\_\_
   15 ÷ 5 = \_\_\_\_\_

⑧ 2 × 8 = \_\_\_\_\_
   16 ÷ 2 = \_\_\_\_\_

### Have a go

⑨ Join these to the matching answers.

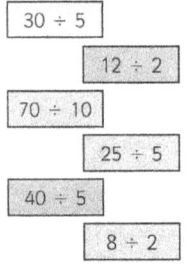 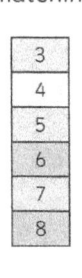 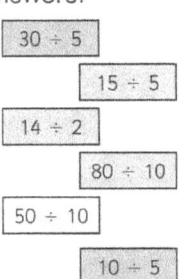

⑩ What division facts do you know with an answer of 9?

\_\_\_ ÷ \_\_\_ = 9      \_\_\_ ÷ \_\_\_ = 9      \_\_\_ ÷ \_\_\_ = 9

*Lesson Plans for Ages 6-7 Years* 143

# 8: Fractions

I have been baking cakes with Charlie and we made one cake in the shape of a circle and two cakes in shape of squares. We need to cut the cakes now to share them between everyone at Kids Club.

Here is the whole of the circle cake.
There is 1 cake.
Fractions are equal parts of a whole.

I cut the cake into two equal parts.
One part is a half or ½.
Two halves make a whole.

I cut the cake again to make 4 equal parts.
One part is a quarter or ¼.
Four quarters make a whole.

Charlie cut one of the square cakes in half and it has 2 equal parts. Alfie cut the other cake, it has two parts but they are not equal. Can you tell which cake it is?

## Get ready

Draw one more line to make quarters.

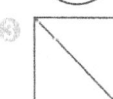
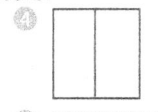
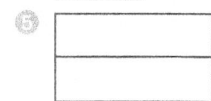

### Teacher's tips

Help your child to understand the representation of fractions as two small numbers separated by a line. Explain that the line means 'divided by', the bottom number (the denominator) is the number of parts the whole is divided into, and the top number (the numerator) is the number of those parts that are taken.

## Let's practise

Each set has been divided into four.
Count one group to find how many in one quarter.

⑦ $\frac{1}{4}$ of 20 is _____

⑨ $\frac{1}{4}$ of 4 is _____

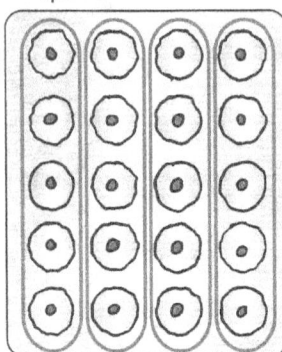

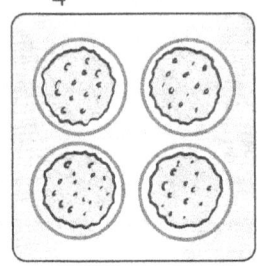

⑧ $\frac{1}{4}$ of 12 is _____

⑩ $\frac{1}{4}$ of 8 is _____

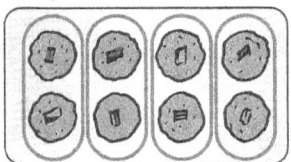

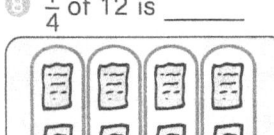

⑪ $\frac{1}{4}$ of 16 is _____

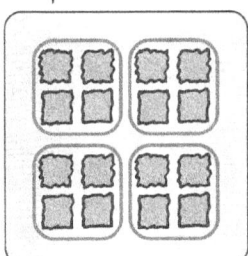

## Have a go

⑫ Write the missing fractions on this number line.

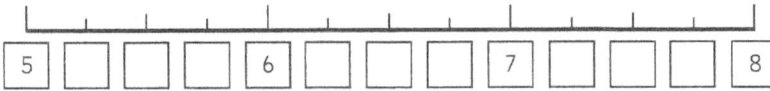

*Lesson Plans for Ages 6-7 Years* 145

## *Applied Mathematics: Making a Wooden Table*

It begins with the tree

This man was a farmer who grew cassava but he could not make enough for his family to live. He was given the chance to chop down hardwood trees in his area of Africa, for more money than he had ever had. He travels 60 kilometers to where the trees are. He can cut down 40 trees per day with his chainsaw that the foreign company lent him. The foreign company pays him an average of $6 per tree.

- How much can he earn in a day?

In the foreign country, hardwood is worth 100 times more.

In this African country, more than half the population earn 8c per month.

- How much can a person who earns 8c per month earn in 1 year?

Soon, there will be no more hardwood trees left in this country.

- What happens to the climate when trees are cut down (deforestation)?

Next the trunks are taken to a depot and are sawn into planks.

146  THE AFROCENTRIC SCHOOL

The example below is to show how to work out how much the cost of making planks is.

Sample Calculation: It costs roughly $6 per tree to cut. The journey to the mill with the driver, truck, and petrol costs $1.00. To get the log to the mill costs $1.00. It costs $6.00 per log to cut. The mill charges $2.00 to cut the tree into planks. The planks travel by ship in containers to the country that you live in. The costs to ship planks to the country must take into account how many planks are being shipped, how long it takes, and how much fuel the ship uses.

The planks will then be sent by train or truck to the destination of shops that sell wood. The shops will charge a certain amount for the wood to cover the cost to get the planks to the shop. The more planks the shops buy, the cheaper the plank becomes.

There are some people who want to make their own tables for home and some people who want to make many tables to sell.

- A design for a table has to be made. What type of table would you design? It can be a circle, oblong, triangle, oval or even a simple square table.
- How many legs will it have?

If you buy your wood to build your table you will pay what that country wants to sell it at. In some countries because hardwood does not grow there, it will be very expensive to buy. The people paying the man in Africa to cut down the trees, sell the wood for 100 times what they pay the man to cut down the tree.

So, when you see a table you will know that a lot of people who need to live helped make that table.

Below are tables designed in Africa.

Please choose an object, item or product, and research where it came from and how it was made.

Whilst the children are learning mathematics, there will be constant tests to make sure that they are becoming skilled at using the mind as well as the written form of symbols.

## *Geometry: Angles*

We are going to look at how circles can be used to make shapes.

We need a pencil, ruler, graph paper, a compass and a protractor.

A protractor is a measuring instrument, usually made of transparent plastic or glass, for measuring angles. It is used to measure and draw angles. They can be semi-circular in shape, 180° and there is also a full-circle protractor of 360°.

The circle has 360° and this formulation is owed to the ancient Egyptians who introduced a 360-day calendar.

For thousands of years, African people had studied the Sun, the planets and Earth's movements. Back then, the year was divided into three seasons, each containing four '30 day' months. Each of these months was then further divided into three ten-day weeks. As a result, a year contained 36 ten-day weeks for a total of 360 days.

As we know, the calendar year is 365 days, so the ancient Africans added the five remaining days to this 360-day period.

We remind ourselves of these days by saying 30 days has September,

## THE AFROCENTRIC SCHOOL

April, June and November, all the rest have 31 except for February alone, which has 28 days clear and 29 in each leap year.

As the Earth moves around the Sun, each day the Earth moves 1/360 which is one day towards its next year. This movement is translated into degrees on the circle or the protractor.

Below is a protractor, the semi-circle type which is 180°, half of the circle that is 360°.

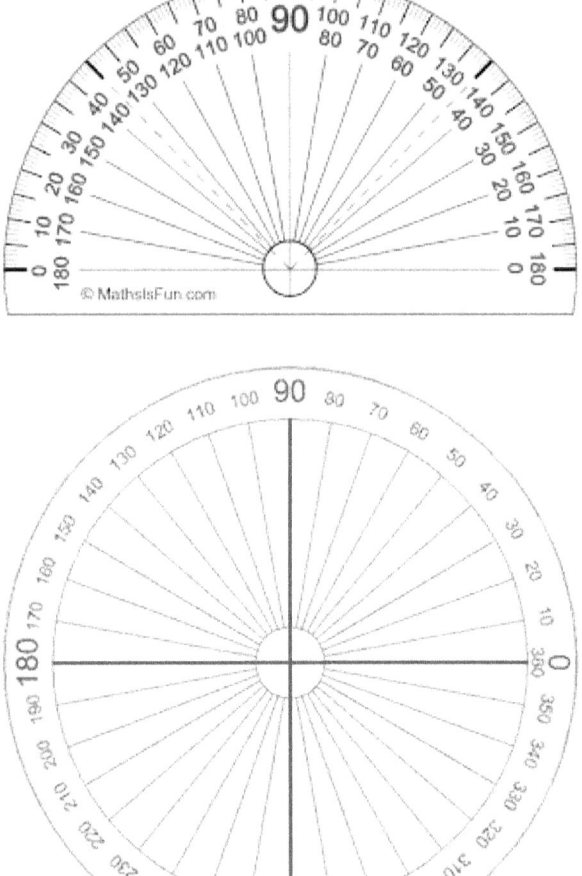

*The circular protractor (360°)*

*Graph paper*

Practice using the angles on the protractor and a ruler to make triangles. The degrees on 3 sides of the triangle add up to 180° which equals a semi-circle.

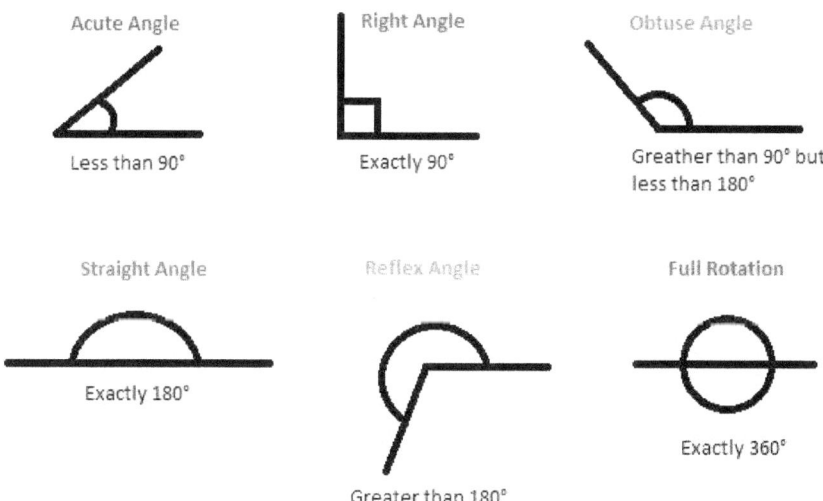

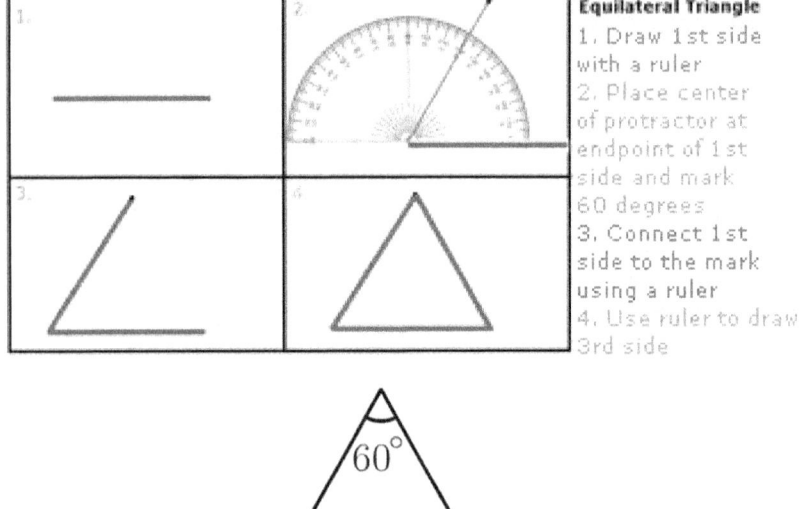

It is from the circle that the squares and triangles are made.

The scholars can study the importance of the circle and its relationship to the movement of the Sun and the Earth and planets.

The calendar, the hours in a day, the days of the week, the months in the year and the number of days in a year will be explained more fully in relation to what the children understand so far.

In time this knowledge will lead to understanding the pyramid.

Later, when the scholars' hands are steadier and stronger, they can become familiar with a compass to make circles, using the ruler to measure the size of the circle they make. The scholars may also use the compass to make patterns with the circles.

# Science

## *Trees: The Lungs of the World*

Research into trees is fascinating and the children should be encouraged to learn about the trees and other plant life in their environments.

Trees are very important for humans, animals and plants. They are sometimes called the lungs of the world.

What does this mean?

Where are the lungs in a human body and what do we use them for?

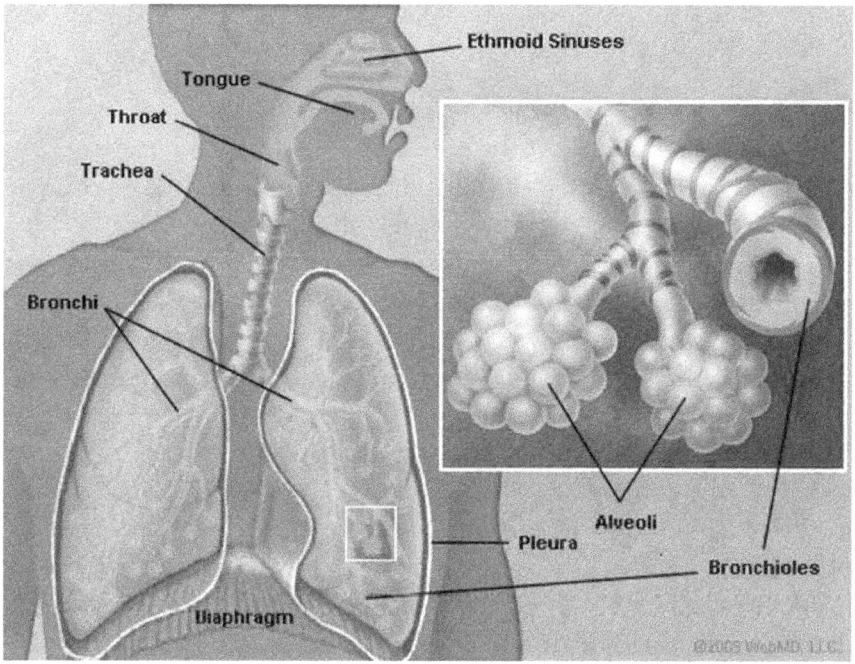

We breathe in Oxygen through the nose and mouth down through the trachea or windpipe, and then into the lungs. The lungs fill with the air through the fine tubes called bronchi. The bronchi divide into smaller tubes called bronchioles and then become so tiny that we need a microscope to see them.

A microscope is a magnifying machine that makes tiny objects look large.

Below are microscopes

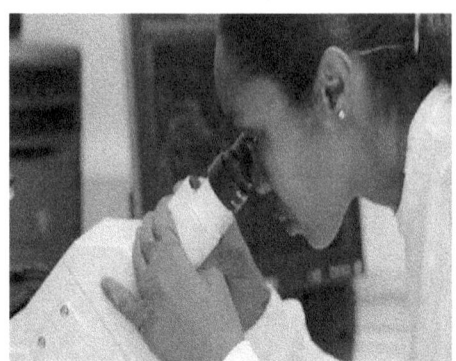

The bronchioles end in clusters called alveoli. Inside the alveoli, the oxygen from the air is absorbed into the blood to keep us alive.

The Carbon Dioxide that we do not need, travels back through the alveoli and we breathe it out through the lungs.

The trees breathe in the Carbon Dioxide and breathe out Oxygen. So, we keep the trees alive and they keep us alive. The more trees that we cut down, the less healthy the air is.

When trees are allowed to grow freely it does not affect them badly to have some chopped down so that we can have things made from trees. It is important though, that we understand that they are living plants, and give respect and thanks to them for the vital part they play in the lives of humans. When millions of trees are cut down to make money for rich people who sometimes do not live in the same countries, then they cannot make enough seeds to replace them. Cutting down too many trees on a massive scale also upsets the ecosystem around the trees, including the animals that live in them and use their wood and branches, and the humans who rely on them for both oxygen and wood.

The hardwood trees from the rainforests have lived for hundreds of years and they live as families. They live together and know each other and they also know when they are under threat. If they do not like some of the animals or insects that try to live on them and harm them, they will send out poisons and smells to make the insects or animals leave them. If one of the trees is ill then because their roots meet each other under the ground they can send healing nutrients to the sick tree to heal it.

- What is happening to the trees near you?
- Are there any trees near you; if so, how close are they (i.e. in your garden, on your road, around the corner)?
- Can you name any of the trees that grow in your neighborhood?
- If there are no trees, try to find out what happened to them.
- It will be healthy to go to visit a place where there are trees.
- Name some of your favorite fruit trees.

Here are some favorite fruits below

Orange tree                                                              Mango tree

Banana trees                                                              Jackfruit tree

Do you know which countries they grow in?

## *Deforestation*

What happens to the environment when trees in rainforests are cut down? We call this Deforestation. More than half of all plant and land animals in the world live in tropical forests.

Deforestation causes:

- Extinction of some plants and animals
- Changes to climatic conditions
- Desertification
- Displacement of populations

Whatever happens in one part of the world affects the other parts of the world.

Perhaps you can plant a tree where you live, in the education setting or somewhere outside.

## *Medicinal Plants*

Throughout the history of Africa and the African Diaspora, there have always been trees and plants that are used to heal. They are medicine trees. In Australia, indigenous First Nations people who migrated from Africa around 75,000 years ago, call the Eucalyptus tree, a medicine tree. Many are being cut down to build highways.

*First Nations children from Australia*

Below is the ancient African goddess, Het Heru (Hathor); she had many titles. She was known as a healer and the Sycamore tree was the healing tree in her time. She was called the goddess of the Sycamore tree. The Sycamore tree grew figs, and its bark and leaves had healing properties.

Do you know of any plants that can heal people?
A list of plants that can heal and what they heal should be built over the next few years.

The idea is that all the schools will create a list that at the end of each year, will be combined to develop their own resource.

*Music and Healing*

Music is used to heal in Africa and places that African people were taken to during enslavement. There are special healing practices all over Africa that include drumming and song. The ways of using music to heal were linked to harmonizing. This is why we owe so much to our African ancestors in ancient Egypt, because they wrote down what they knew.

To begin with, in order for the healer to know what is wrong with the patient, there needs to be information about the history of the patient and family history and how the sickness took place.

What questions does the doctor ask you when you are ill?

What treatments have you had for sickness? Medical healing is not only about using plants or tablets to get better. Healing can include family care and love and calling on the Ancestors to help as well as using music. In Traditional Africa, the medical healer relies on spiritual connection and practice as much as the physical practice of healing. The process of healing is therefore holistic and comprises mind, body, and spirit. They have gone through years of training to learn from the wisest and best doctors how to heal.

The music can help the person to heal by changing the way the person is thinking. Perhaps a sad person can begin to feel happier and this will help in the healing.

https://www.youtube.com/watch?v=9p4LSYKFHxE

This is music from a healing drum played by a Caribbean man living back in the home of his Ancestors; Africa.

How do you feel after hearing his music?

- Find out if people that you know are healers.
- Try to find or learn about a plant that can heal.
- Make a song of poetry or write a healing song that you can sing that can make people feel better.

This is a repeat from the lesson plans of 3-5 years

Sometimes where people have very little money, children make their own drums out of boxes and tin cans with sticks and whatever they can find to beat on.

If the education center cannot provide drums then the scholars can bring to school something that can make a rhythm on (do not bring anything that the children can cut themselves on) and play together.

A drummer or drum teacher should be found first to guide and teach the children the meaning of the drum and its use.

# LESSON PLANS
# FOR AGES 7-8 YEARS

At this age Africology will be an important part of the children's curriculum. Africology takes into account a broad overview of how humans build society and how institutions are an important part of living in society no matter how small or how large.

It is vital for the children to understand that all over the world where African people were enslaved or colonized, there were countless African women and men who fought for their freedom and the freedom of others.

At this age, there should be a focus on *comprehension*. Comprehension in this context is the reading of material and the ability to understand what the material is about, as well as answer questions about the content of the text. The children should read and discuss their comprehension of each of these African persons, and the effects that they had on the lives of people of African descent all over the world.

It is essential for the Educator to know how much the scholars are able to remember and understand. In this way, the Educator is constantly monitoring her/his teaching with the knowledge of how much individual scholars know and need to know, so that all the scholars are being brought along together. This way, unnecessary hierarchies do not arise. The children will help each other to learn, as it is an African cultural concept to understand that '*I am because we are*'. As in the Traditional rural setting, the children are both learners and teachers and this should be encouraged in the classroom setting. They will learn to respect each other for their special skills.

Presenting their knowledge in front of the classroom will prepare the students for later presentations as they get ready for the year end, to meet other Afrocentric school scholars either in person at the conferences or via screen. Throughout the scholars' educational experience and knowledge gain, they are learning to apply their logic to understand the story of humanity. In this way, they can begin to look outside the fabrication of the story that dehumanizes the African woman, man, girl and boy and debases nature.

## Sociocultural Studies

### *What is Culture?*

The major institutions like family, education, spiritual, entertainment and economic systems (whether fair exchange or exploitation) are all important to living in a society. These institutions are shaped and influenced by culture.

What is culture? Culture is based upon the values and beliefs of a society of people. These people use culture to direct them. They build their institutions according to what they believe is best for the continuation of the family, community and nation.

If the people are living in a society where they cannot live safely, and do not have basic needs like water, healthy food, a proper home to shelter them, enough money or things to exchange for what they need; then they are not living as they would want to live. Their human rights are not being met; in other words, they do not have the human rights that all people are entitled to. The men, women, girls and boys of the African Diaspora, whose ancestors were enslaved or colonized, live in a culture that has been developed to impede their human rights to a healthy life.

Culture should be explained clearly for the rest of the lesson plans. Some African Matriarchal cultural beliefs laid out by Cheikh Anta Diop can be used as a guide for the children:

- Importance of agricultural lifestyles
- Land is communal in the main
- Egalitarian society is necessary
- Family is the center of social organization
- Community is highly regarded

- Respect for the Ancestors
- Mothering is the most important job in society and should be valued, respected and honored (Mothering can be carried out by the biological mother or any person who steps into that role)
- All children are looked after, respected, cared for by parents and extended family/community
- Matriarchal culture is optimistic and peace loving

*African Rural and Urban Lives*

In order to understand other societies on a personal level, the children can write to each other to enquire about where they live and the personal and social issues that affect their lives. The scholars can write about how they would change things. For instance, life in South African townships, Brazilian favelas, cities in the U.S.:

- What was the history?
- How were these societies created?
- What is life like here for women, men, girls and boys?

The scholars can gain important knowledge of the realities of African people who were enslaved and colonized centuries ago. The scholars can gain knowledge of African rural and urban lives and how these countries were made, who made them and what language/s they speak.

*Sankofa*

The children should become familiar with the symbol of the Sankofa bird, which represents the significance of learning our history in order to prepare for the future. The concept of Sankofa means '*go back and fetch it*' to signify that we must reclaim our past and what is needed from it, in order to build a strong and stable future, based in Truth.

African people believe that one must look at history and find the best of achievements on which to build a future.

The Sankofa bird

The Sankofa bird carries the egg that represents the world
It shows us the responsibility that we have for understanding history to know those who came before us and how we became who we are today

## Rhetoric and Writing

The scholars can discuss their findings and decide the topic which they will speak on at the end of year Afrocentric school conference, which can be arranged through a developed network of Afrocentric schools.

Rhetoric which should be grounded in Truth, provides the sounds that can heal as well as fortify in war.

The history of writing can begin at this age. The idea of history is making sense to the scholars. They are seeing that through time, events happen and changes take place. Writing is the expression of sound that is changed into a symbol. The image of the symbols for writing in ancient times, could feed the mind with meaning. The earliest writing that we know of was considered sacred. Words had to be written that were special. Words were written to remember the laws of how we should treat each other and live good lives. Writing was used to tell stories to help explain and understand certain concepts, ideas or experiences. Writing recorded the events that took place and reminded us of events that needed to take place in the future. Writing was used to record what people needed to live. Writing was used to record what we bought and sold. It was used to record who died and who was born.

Below is Mdw Ntr for young children, published by Ayi Kwei Armah and Aboubacry Moussa Lam. Per Ankh. It provides examples of the ancient alphabet using the Mdw Ntr and explains the meaning of the symbols that represent the letters.

The scholars can use it to learn the ancient letters and sounds that existed before the writing and speech that we use today.

They can learn that this African writing was the foundation of writing all over the world.

At a later age the scholars can study the complexity of the Mdw Ntr in order to translate for us work that has so far not been translated, as well as to go over translations to see if they are culturally accurate.

## Lesson Plans for Ages 7-8 Years

### Hieroglyphics for Babies

from being quintessentially unlettered, it was Africa that first achieved the crucial shift from illiteracy to literacy, from prehistory to history; that over 5000 years ago, Africans created the world's first great civilization, Kemet; and that all humanity gained, and still continues to gain, from that indelible achievement.

Unlike the old racist historiography loaded with clumsy bigotry, the new historical

### Les Hiéroglyphes dès le berceau

n'étaient que des mensonges, que loin d'être un continent sans écriture, l'Afrique a, la première, dépassé l'analphabétisme pour inaugurer l'ère de l'écriture, abandonné la préhistoire pour entrer dans l'histoire. Ils ont aussi démontré qu'il y a de cela plus de 5000 ans, les Africains ont créé la première grande civilisation, Kemet ; et que l'humanité tout entière a tiré et continue de tirer profit de cette réalisation indélébile.

Contrairement à l'historiographie raciste et désuète inspirée par un parti pris de mauvais

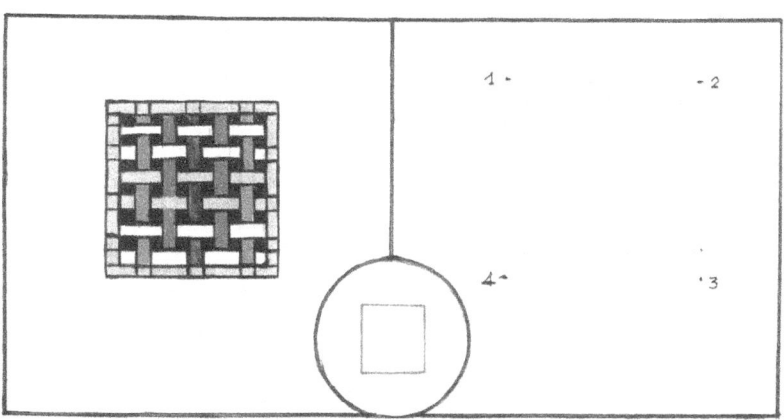

### The Letter p

### La Lettre p

Ancient Egyptian scribes used the image of a stool made of reed matting to represent the sound p. That kind of stool was called *p* in their language. Hence the decision to use the image to represent the sound p.

Les scribes de l'Egypte ancienne utilisaient l'image d'un tabouret en roseaux tressés pour représenter le son p. Ce genre de tabouret était appelé *p* dans lour langue, d'où la décision d'utiliser son image pour représenter le son p.

12

## Hieroglyphics for Babies

scholarship is based on documents, oral and written, retrieved from the forgotten millennia. Among these the most significant are the hieroglyphic writings of ancient Egypt.

The writing system of ancient Egypt was the first writing system we know and understand to this date. Five thousand years ago the signs were already well developed.

## Les Hiéroglyphes dès le berceau

aloi, la nouvelle école de pensée historique s'appuie sur des documents, tant oraux qu'écrits, parvenus de millénaires enfouis dans la nuit des temps. Parmi ces documents, les plus significatifs sont les hiéroglyphes de l'Egypte ancienne.

Le système d'écriture de l'Egypte ancienne est le premier que nous connaissions et comprenions à ce jour. Il y a de cela 5000 ans, les signes étaient déjà bien au point.

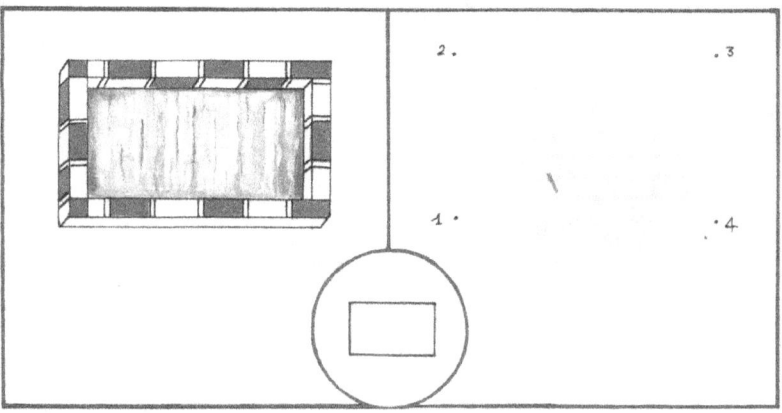

### The Letter sh

Homes and public buildings in ancient Egypt often had a pool of water in the garden or courtyard. Such a pool was called a *sh*. Scribes adopted the image of a pool to represent the sound sh.

### La Lettre ch

Les maisons et édifices publics de l'Egypte ancienne avaient souvent une pièce d'eau dans leur jardin ou cour. Une telle pièce d'eau était appelée š/*ch*. Les scribes ont, pour cela, adopté l'image d'une pièce d'eau pour représenter le son š (ch).

13

## History

With the idea that speech should be used carefully and correctly, the scholars can study and speak (with great respect) about a person in African history who tried to change the lives of African people.

These are our Ancestors.

Here are some examples of the many men and women who fought against enslavement (Freedom fighters).

### Yanga in Mexico

Gaspar Yanga or Nyanga (c.1545) was an African leader of a maroon colony of enslaved African people near Veracruz, Mexico during Spanish colonial rule.

Yanga was a great warrior. He successfully fought against a Spanish attack on the maroon colony in 1609.

The maroons continued to try to free African people from their enslavers. In 1618, Yanga achieved an agreement with the colonial government for self-rule of the settlement, later called San Lorenzo de los Negros and also San Lorenzo de Cerralvo.

People said that Yanga was a prince stolen from a royal family of **Gabon, Africa**. The word "Yanga" is used in many regions of West and central Africa. In the Yoruba language in Nigeria the word means "pride".

In the late 19th century, Yanga was named as a National hero of Mexico and El Primer Libertador de las Américas. In 1932 the Maroon settlement he formed was renamed as Yanga in his honor.

## Zumbi in Brazil

Zumbi (1655 – 1695) was also known as Zumbi dos Palmares. He was an important Maroon warrior in Brazilian history. Zumbi was one of the pioneers of African resistance to enslavement. He was also the last of the kings of the Quilombo dos Palmares, a city in the mountains of runaway Afro-Brazilian slaves in the present-day state of Alagoas, Brazil.

Quilombo dos Palmares was an independent kingdom of Maroons, who escaped from the Portuguese enslavers in Brazil. It was a region the size of Portugal in Bahia. Palmares had a population of over 30,000 people, some of whom were First Nation indigenous people.

Zumbi was descended from a royal family from **Angola, West Africa.**

## Toussaint L'Ouverture in Haiti

Toussaint L'Ouverture was born in 1743. He was a former enslaved man who led the Haitian independence movement (The Haitian Revolution) in 1791 during the French Revolution. Under his leadership,

Haiti became the first independent African Diasporic state to free itself from enslavement. The Haitian Revolution is the only successful slave revolt in modern history, in which the enslaved people overthrew their oppressor and took over governance of the land.

Toussaint L'Ouverture was born enslaved. He was the son of an African man who was captured. It is believed that his mother's name was Pauline and his father's name was Hippolyte, who was an aristocrat from the Allada Kingdom and the grandson of the King of Allada in **Benin, West Africa**.

Toussaint had knowledge about medicinal plants and herbs. He was a warrior and General.

## Nanny in Jamaica

Maroon is a term used to refer to African descended peoples in the Americas who escaped from slavery and set up their own communities. Many of the Maroon people in Jamaica, joined in marriage with the First nations Arawak people of the island and lived in the communities together. In 1739 the first Maroon war in Jamaica ended with a peace treaty with the British, who were defeated and had to accept the Maroons' freedom. Nanny of the Maroons, was an African priestess and powerful Obeah from **Ghana, West Africa**. She was a prolific leader and freedom fighter; one of many African women who fought against enslavement. She was feared by British enslavers. She inspired and led many African people to a free life away from enslavement and a cruel oppressive life. Nanny was recognized as a great hero by the Jamaican government in 1977. A statue honoring Nanny can be found in Jamaica.

*Nat Turner in the United States*

Nat Turner was born in 1800, enslaved in Virginia in the US. He was taught to read through the use of the bible, which he read and understood so well that people were amazed. In his reading of the bible, within the principles of Truth, Love and Compassion (the ancient African principles of Maat), he found that the enslavers, including those who read and taught the bible, had no understanding of it. This was apparent in their practice of enslaving people as well as their cruel treatment of enslaved African women, men and children. He carefully formed a guerrilla army of free and enslaved men, to free women, men and children from bondage. The white enslavers had many weapons to protect themselves and to harm enslaved people. They were greatly enraged that a Black man would rebel against them and free other enslaved people.

Nat Turner is greatly respected amongst African Americans especially, for his incredible bravery and efforts for freedom.

*Queen Anna Nzinga in Angola*

Born in 1583, Queen Nzinga ruled the Ndongo and Matamba Kingdoms of the Mbundu people in **Angola, West Africa**. She successfully led an army against the Portuguese who came to enslave African people. She was a powerful voice in the peace negotiations with nearby countries. She is remembered in Angola for her political and diplomatic skills, as well as her brilliant military tactics. A statue of her was placed in Kinaxixi, Luanda, Angola in 2002 in recognition of her fight against the Portuguese enslavers.

### *Harriet Tubman in the United States*

Harriet Tubman was born Araminta Harriet Ross in the 1820's in

Maryland, U.S. She was one of nine children. Her parents were both descendants of the Ashanti warrior people of **Ghana, West Africa,** and had been enslaved in America. Although born into slavery, she had escaped and fled from the South and enslavement by 1849. She eventually reached the North where she was legally free. Instead of beginning a new life in freedom and never looking back; she decided that she must return, knowing that freedom was possible, and bring her family and others North to freedom as well. Harriet returned to the South thirteen times freeing over seventy men, women, girls and boys. She was part of an organization that set up a secret system of routes leading from the South to North in which people along the route would provide a place to hide and food for those fleeing enslavement; this system was called *The Underground Railroad* and Harriet was known as *The Conductor.* She was both a heroic leader and a warrior. She risked her life for others and remarkably, never lost a passenger on her missions of freedom along the Underground Railroad. Harriet gave all that she had to the struggle for freedom and humanity, later serving as a nurse and a spy for the North, during the American Civil War. In 1913 she died of pneumonia, after having created a home for orphans and the elderly which continued for years beyond her passing. Harriet Tubman is remembered as one of the greatest freedom fighters in American history.

Look at the map of the world and discuss where these brave leaders came from.

Describe what these brave African women and men did.

What does Liberation mean?

What is a Maroon?

These women and men who helped their people were healers, what do you think made them healers?

## Mathematics

The latest examples of standardized tests, used in western schools that are globally recognized for 7-11-year-olds, can be found in the **Collins** practice workbooks.

### *History of Geometry*

Looking at the history of mathematics will help to show the scholars how important mathematics has been to Africa and that its use was evident in the building of homes, temples and pyramids. The mathematical genius of African people influenced the world. Much of this is still too complex to reproduce; for example, the pyramids as they were built in Africa, still cannot be replicated even today.

Robin Walker's important work *Blacks and Science* Volumes 1,2,3 (2011-2016), is a compilation of various scholars' works including Cheikh Anta Diop, Ivan Van Sertima, and Anthony Browder. This is an essential teaching book that can be made age appropriate for different year groups.

Another imperative book for teaching about the history of mathematics in Africa is Anthony Browder's, *Nile Valley Contributions to Civilization* (1992).

There is evidence to show that the ancient Egyptians invented the 3:4:5 triangle. This was used in their architecture. This triangle is used all over the world for building. It is a right-angled triangle with a hypotenuse. A hypotenuse is the longest side of a right-angled triangle, which is opposite the right angle. As explained, the vertical side of the right-angle is 3, the base is 4 and the hypotenuse is 5. This is known as the perfect triangle.

Below is the perfect triangle using centimeters to measure the 3:4:5

***Geometric Arts and Architecture***

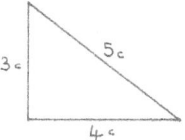

Carpenters create these measurements in all buildings to make sure that the building corners will be square or 90°. These same sizes can be multiplied so that the 3 4 5 rule can become:

- 3:4:5
- 6:8:10
- 9:12:15
- 12:16:20
- 15:20:25 and so on

The side that is three adds 3, the side that is four adds 4, and the side that is five adds 5, so that the same pattern or rule can be used in any size building using these ratios. This will ensure that the foundation and corners are squared, straight and balanced so that the building will remain upright and safe.

Below is an example of a corner using the rule so that it will be a perfect right angle every time.

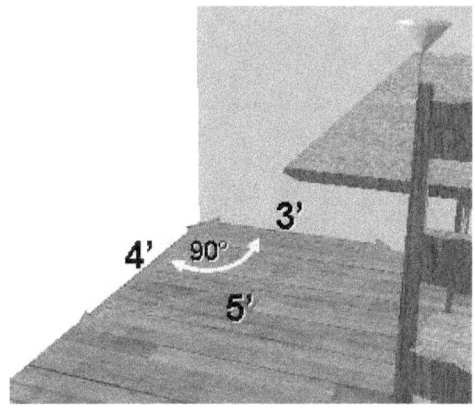

This knowledge formed the basis upon which the pyramids could be built.

This teaching lays the foundation of more complicated mathematics, geometry, and algebra that will be taught when the children are older.

The scholars can use the triangular 3:4:5 shape as a design which can be multiplied into a larger pattern and colored in. The educator may also do the drawing on the board to help guide the scholars. The children can use their rulers and compasses to achieve this. They can also be provided with ready-made drawings in the 3:4:5 pattern, to color in. This will familiarize them with the idea of architecture, and also print design, that can be transposed onto cloth. The designs can be combined to form one whole design.

*Geometric Shapes*

Use the protractor and the compass to create the circles and the angles.

- The circumference is the outside measurement of the circle
- The radius is the line drawn from the middle of the circle to its edge
- The diameter is the line drawn through the middle of the circle from one end of the circle to the other.

Creating an Equilateral Triangle with 2 equal sized circles

Diagram 1

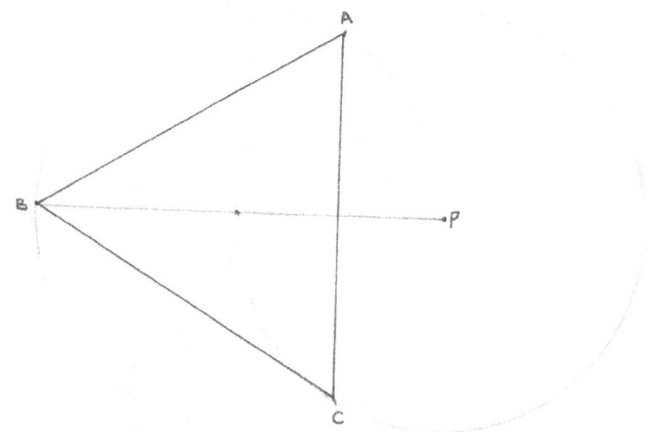

1. Use the compass or protractor to draw a circle.
2. From the outside edge of the circle make a point on the circle. This point is called P. This point will be the center of the next circle.
3. Then, with a ruler, draw a line from point P through the middle point to the other edge of the circle making the diameter. That point is B.
4. Draw another circle the same size using point P as the center point. Use the compass or protractor at the same measurement.
5. At the points A and C where the circles cross, draw a line from A to C as shown in Diagram 1.
6. Join the lines A with B and B with C.

You will have an equilateral triangle. Each side measures the same distance. Use a ruler to show that the lines are equal.

The angles where the lines of the triangle meet will be 60°.

Making an Equilateral Triangle inside 2 equal circles

Diagram 2                                              Diagram 3

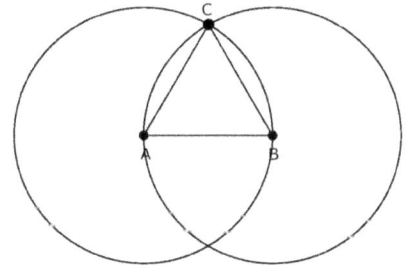

1. Create the first circle using a protractor or compass.
2. Choose a point on the first circle to be the center of the second circle of the same size using.
3. Draw a line between the two center points of the circles A for circle 1 and B for circle 2. The line will be the radius of circle 1 and 2. This line forms the base of the triangle.
4. At the top where the two circles meet call the point C.
5. Make a line from A to C and a line from B to C.

This will be an equilateral triangle as shown in Diagram 3. Measure the length of the lines in your work with a ruler to prove it.

To help the children, draw the circles for them and then ask them to follow the instructions with pencil and ruler and then measure their triangles.

Relate the circle to the Sun and the positions of the Earth moving around the Sun. The children will begin to understand that understanding the movement of the Sun, the Earth, and the Moon along with other planets, is the basis of creating geometry and understanding the science of life.

## Science

By the end of the year, the scholars will be able to understand time and the importance of it to our existence.

Time allows us to know the seasons, how long they last, and how to prepare for them when growing food and plants.

We know how to use time when we need to be at places and leave them.

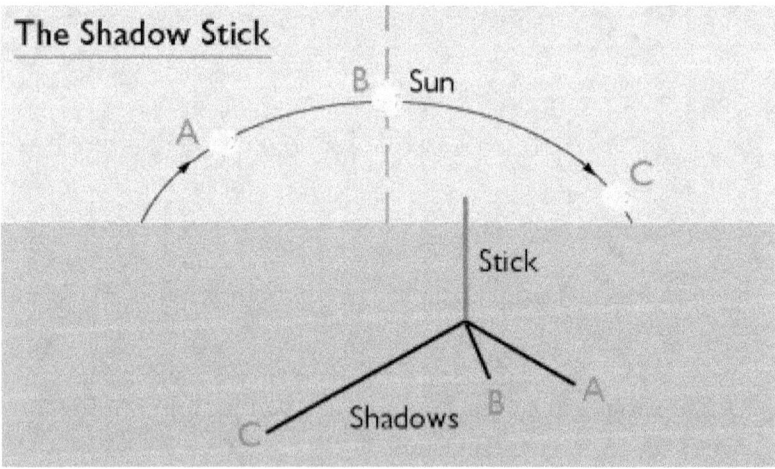

Above is a vertical stick. As the Earth moves around every 24 hours, one part of the Earth moves away from the Sun, and the opposite side faces the Sun. This movement causes the Sun to create a shadow from the stick which is shortest when the Sun is above (B–around noon), and longer as the Earth turns towards the Sun (A–in the morning) or away from the Sun (C–in the evening).

The movement of the Earth around the Sun provides humans and nature with a way to measure time. Everything experiences time, but humans have written of the measurement of time. Our earliest calendar was based on thousands of years of studying the movements of the planets. The findings were written by the ancient African people. Because of their scientific research and study, we know that:

- The Earth takes 365 days to travel around the Sun.
- The Earth turns around facing the Sun every 24 hours.
- In 24 hours, one side of the world is facing the Sun and the other side is not. The side that faces the Sun experiences day. The other side of the Earth experiences night.
- The Earth has its own moon and the Moon travels around the Earth about (just under) 30 days (a month).
- The Moon has its own orbit around the Earth and the Earth and Moon orbit together around the Sun.

# THE AFROCENTRIC SCHOOL

## Astronomy

### The Sun and the Time

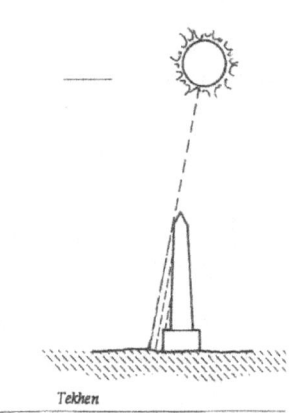
Tekhen

The length of the shadow of the *tekhen* was measured to show the exact moment of the solstice or equinox

The solstice refers to either the longest day or shortest day depending on where you are in the world and how near and far we are from the sun. This happens twice a year. The world is divided into the Southern hemisphere and the Northern hemisphere. Africa is in the Southern hemisphere.

An equinox represents a day where day and night are equal in length.

Clepsydra

The hours of the day or night were shown by measuring the amount of water remaining in the *clepsydra* which was known as the water clock.

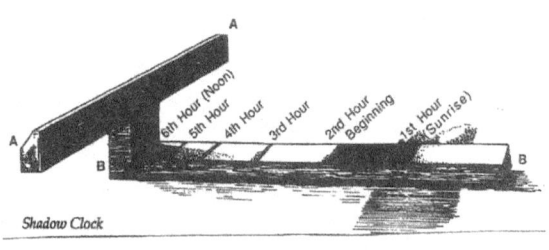
Shadow Clock

The *shadow clock* is considered the oldest in the world. The shadow is used to know the place of the sun in the sky and thus the time. This African clock is about 3,400 years old. The sun rises in the east and sets in the west. The crossbar is turned to face the east for the hours in the day. The shadow falls on the perpendicular bar each hour. At noon, the shadow is the shortest, the crossbar is turned 180% to the west for the last six hours of the day.

From this scientific and astronomical background, the scholars will be able to understand how personal watches and clocks can show us the time.

## Music

African drumming and music will be the basis upon which the scholars will dance and sing and play instruments in the future.

Music and harmony are key to healing as we focused on last year.

Harmony is the coming together of sounds–notes, that when played at the same time, create unity and beauty.

Below is beautiful drumming music from the Dogon nation of Mali. These ancient African people knew of the movements of stars and planets, perhaps thousands of years ago.

https://www.youtube.com/watch?v=s_Ni_gMf_XM

Young Xhosa girl drummers in Walmer township in South Africa.
https://www.youtube.com/watch?v=yG4PLQk0NQY

The same girls from Walmer dancing
https://www.youtube.com/watch?v=2dyVKqq3DCU

LESSON PLANS
FOR AGES 8-9 YEARS

# Language Arts and Sociocultural Studies

**Ancestors**

Giving respect to the Ancestors is particularly important to understand. In this way we are linking ourselves to the Ancestors and history. So many people have forgotten their Ancestors and their history. When African people left Africa in the early migrations, some of them forgot their history and their Ancestors. When African people were taken out of Africa during the enslavement era, they were forced not to respect their Ancestors and are still taught to forget that they had a past before enslavement. The forgetting of the Ancestors and history was no accident. Those people who remained in Africa suffered the colonization of their countries by:

- Arabs
- Belgians
- Dutch
- English
- French

- Germans
- Italians
- Portuguese
- Spanish

They were taught through non-African religions, governments and Arab and European schools and universities that they had no history or ancestors worth remembering.

However, it is important to recognize that there were also many people who did not forget their Ancestors.

Remembering the Ancestors has helped African people to grow strong and remember who they are. Many African people and First Nations people who honor their Ancestors try to find out or research their history to make sure that they can pass it on to the next generations.

What happens if you forget your Ancestors?

You forget your culture.

What happens if you forget your culture?

You forget who you are.

Do you remember what culture is?

Discuss and define culture and its importance (refer to previous chapter).

*Female and Male Reciprocity*

Female and male reciprocity is the foundation of African life.

Make up a story about a boy or girl who lost his/her culture and found it. What happened, why did s/he lose her/his culture? How did s/he get it back?

This will be a written story that will be discussed for some time in the Education room so that everyone is clear about the Ancestors and culture. In this way, the scholars can share their ideas with each other. These ideas will be developed in discussion through the Educator. The scholars should all be clear on their stories. The story can also become a play acted out by the class.

As the scholars become familiar with African culture through information, knowledge, practice and behavior in the Education setting, as well as the practice within their family and home, they can see and identify some of the ways that we still practice African cultural ways.

*Spiritual Systems*

The Hebrew religion; the Christian religion; the Muslim religion; the Buddhist religion; the Hindu religion are all fundamentally based on the cultural beliefs of the ancient African people from Kemet.

KMT

- The first symbol is a piece of burnt wood, charcoal and it means Black; it also stands for the letters KM.
- The second image is an owl that is considered wise and the letter it represents is M.
- The third symbol is a loaf of bread and stands for the letter T. The symbol is also used to show a feminine side.
- The fourth symbol is the circle with a crossway going through it that represents a road plan and this refers to a village, a city or a nation.
- KMT means the country or the land of Black people.

We know this because the Kemites, as these African people called themselves, wrote down their ideas on paper, carved their words in stone and painted their words in pictures. These ideas are very old, much older than when they wrote them down because they had practiced them for thousands of years to make sure that these ideas worked.

The Kemites had ideas on how to live wisely. They believed that:

- People should treat each other with respect.
- Women and men should be equally respected and respectful of each other.
- Children should be cared for because they are the future.
- Elderly people should be cared for because they know about the past.
- The Ancestors should be remembered. Ancestors are the good people.

- People should not think that if they are rich, they are better than the poor.
- People should not be violent to each other.
- People should discuss ideas and issues in order to come to agreements.
- People should not take something that is not theirs.
- People should not lie.

Ideas like these are so important that they are written inside the teaching books of modern religions. The books are:

Judaism – The Torah

Christianity – The Bible

Islam – The Koran or Quran

Buddhism – The Tripitaka

Hinduism–The Vedas

These ideas are guides on how to live a good life. They are standards for good behavior. These standards are part of African culture.

African people understood that everything in life was made from energy including humans, animals, plants, rivers, mountains, deserts, seas, clouds, planets, seasons and the Sun. They worked out how long it took the Earth and Moon to go around the Sun, the Moon to go around the Earth, the movements of the planets, how plants could heal, and how everything is connected.

They recognized that the energies of life were mysterious. Humans created stories all over the world to explain the beginning of life. These stories are called creation stories.

African people believed that there was a powerful energy responsible for all that has ever been, all that is and all that ever will be. The name of the powerful energy from which all energies came from was called many names. For example, in Kemet at one time, this force of life was called Atum: The unknowable, the mysterious, the female and male of all that is. Some people call this energy God, the Creator or the Universe.

This source of life, Atum, produced 4 pairs of female and male energies known as goddesses and gods or Deities. They represent life.

- Tefnut – goddess space and water. Partner Shu – god air

Their children were:

- Nut – goddess sky. Partner Geb – god earth

Their children were:

- Aset – goddess motherhood. Partner Asar god – nature/abundance
- Nebt Het – goddess protector. Partner Set – god chaos.

African women and men taught that there are female and male energies in everything.

Maat is a female energy, she is the Divinity of Truth, Harmony, Reciprocity, Justice and Balance.

The meaning of these words Truth, Harmony, Reciprocity, Justice and Balance should be studied carefully.

Thousands of years ago the judges and lawyers always thought of Maat before they went into court so that they would be wise and make the correct decision.

People would think of Maat when they began their day and they wanted to do the right thing and have a good day.

People tried to live a life of Maat or live in Maat.

*MAAT*

**Review and Discussion**

Name two African cultural ideas that we still practice?
Do you know a creation story?
Find a creation story if you do not know one?
Tell the story to the education group.
Write about the story that you found.
Explain where it comes from.

# Logic

### *The Game of Senet*

Before the game of chess, the ancient African people in KMT played a board game called Senet, more than 3,300 years ago. One person or two people could play it. It had 30 squares. It is not known how to play this board game but it is related to life and death and a possible future of the player or players.

Below is the artisan Sennedjem playing Senet with his wife. Next to this painting is the Queen Nefertari, the wife of Rameses II.

A Senet board found in the tomb of Tutankhamun

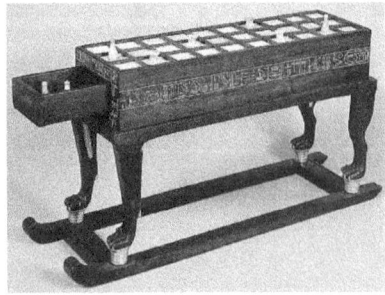

### The Game of Chess

Chess is a mathematical board game played between two opponents on opposite sides of a board containing 64 squares of alternating colors, usually Black and white.

Each player will represent one color or the other; Chess is often played with Black and white squares and pieces but not always. There are also games with frosted glass and clear glass.

The player who gets the lighter color goes first.

Each player has 16 pieces: 1 king, 1 queen, 2 rooks, 2 bishops, 2 knights, and 8 pawns.

The goal of the game is to checkmate the other king – to prevent the king from being able to move on the board – to capture the king.

Each player places her/his pieces in 2 lines.

The first line consists of the King, Queen, Rooks, Bishops and Knights and the second row directly facing the opposing side is made up of only pawns.

The Pawns are like the soldiers. They are the first line of defense for the king, queen, rooks, bishops and knights.

Pawns can only move directly forward one square, with two exceptions.

Pawns can move directly forward two squares on their first move only.

Pawns can move diagonally forward when capturing an opponent's chess piece.

A pawn that reaches the other side of the board can become a Queen.

The Rook, looks like a little castle and moves horizontally or vertically, through any number of unoccupied squares. The rook captures by taking the square on which the enemy piece sits. The Rook can also change places with the King, in a special move to protect the King, called Castling.

The Knight looks like a horse and can move forward, backward, left or right two squares and must then move one square in either perpendicular direction.

The Knight can only move to one of up to eight positions on the board.

The Knight can move to any square that is empty.

The Knight can skip over any other pieces to reach its destination position.

The Bishop looks like the KMT crown of the South and can move in any direction diagonally, as long as the path of movement is clear.

The Bishop cannot move past any piece that is on its path.

The Bishop can take any other piece that is in its path of movement.

The Queen begins on the square of her own color. She sits next to the king and can move around the board more freely than any other piece. She is therefore more dangerous and more vulnerable. She can move forwards, backwards and diagonally to position herself to take the other pieces and capture the opposing king.

The Queen cannot "jump" over any piece on the board, so her movements are restricted to any direction of unoccupied squares.

The queen can be used to capture any of the opponent's pieces on the board.

To lose a Queen is a great loss to a player.

The King can move one space in any direction. He can never move into the position of checkmating, that means he cannot move into a position where he is threatened by his opposition.

All the pieces, the Queen, Rook, Bishop, Knights and Pawns protect the king from capture, sacrificing themselves for his safety, if necessary.

Chess is a mathematical game.

Chess develops memory.
Chess improves concentration.
Chess develops logical thinking.
Chess promotes imagination and creativity.
Chess teaches independence.
Chess develops the capability to predict and foresee consequences of actions.
Chess inspires self-motivation.
There are scholars all over Africa who are playing Chess. When the Afrocentric school scholars are getting skilled in the game, they can contact other Afrocentric schools, and schools throughout the Diaspora where scholars are playing Chess, and have tournaments to help increase their skills.

## Science

### *The Solar System*

The planets

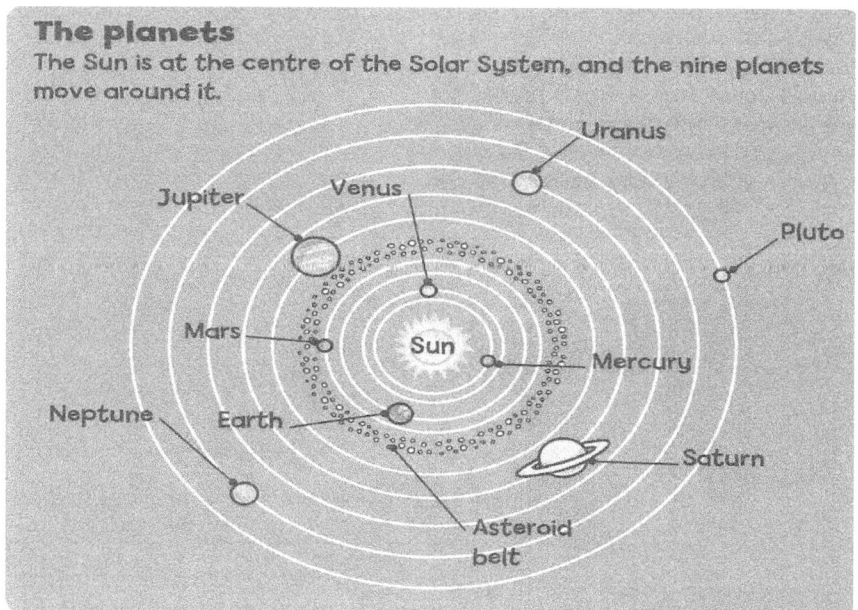

Our universe is called the solar system. The Sun is in the center and the nine planets orbit the Sun. The Sun is a star. These planets, like the Earth orbit the Sun with their moons as do the asteroids and comets.

Asteroids are rocks that may be bits of planets that come together and form a ring or belt between Jupiter and Mars as they orbit around the Sun.

Comets are made of rock, dust and ice which orbit the Sun. Comets have an icy center (nucleus) surrounded by a large cloud of gas and dust (called the coma).

The Moon is sometimes considered a planet. Earth and Pluto each have one moon and Mars has two moons, Neptune 13, Uranus 27, Saturn 34, and Jupiter has 63 moons.

Sizes of the nine most famous planets in our Solar system are:

- Jupiter (69,911 km / 43,441 miles) – 1,120% the size of Earth
- Saturn (58,232 km / 36,184 miles) – 945% the size of Earth
- Uranus (25,362 km / 15,759 miles) – 400% the size of Earth
- Neptune (24,622 km / 15,299 miles) – 388% the size of Earth
- Earth (6,371 km / 3,959 miles)
- Venus (6,052 km / 3,761 miles) – 95% the size of Earth
- Mars (3,390 km / 2,460 miles) – 53% the size of Earth
- Mercury (2,440 km / 1,516 miles) – 38% the size of Earth

Below is a picture of the planets next to each other to show their sizes in relation to each other

Can you name the planets?

The Dogon Nation of Mali has an ancient history of knowledge of the solar system. They know about 3 stars; Sirius, Sirius B and Sirius C.

Sirius C has still not been seen by modern astronomers. Sirius B orbits Sirius every 50 years. The Dogon people know about the planet Venus and its movements.

#### Earth's Moon

Sometimes the Moon looks like a silver ball and sometimes it looks like a thin slice of a silver ball. It looks as if the Moon's size changes, but it does not.

The Moon is always the same size; how it looks to us depends on the position of the Moon as it goes around (orbits) the Earth.

It is the Sun that makes the Moon shine. As the Moon passes around the Earth, the Sun shines on half of the Moon.

Below is a diagram of the Earth, and the Moon going round the Earth. The Sun is shining on the right side of the Earth and Moon. The inner circle of the Moon shows how the Sun shines on the Moon. One side of the Earth and one side of the Moon has the Sun shining on it. On the left side of the Earth it is night time. The Moon always looks the same in space, with one side facing the Sun.

The outer circle of the Moon moving around the Earth, shows the 8 phases of the Moon as we see it from the Earth. Gibbous is a Latin word that means hump or bump. The gibbous means that over half of the Moon is shining.

Waxing refers to the Moon any time after the new Moon and before the full Moon.

Waning refers to the Moon any time after it has been full and before the Moon is new.

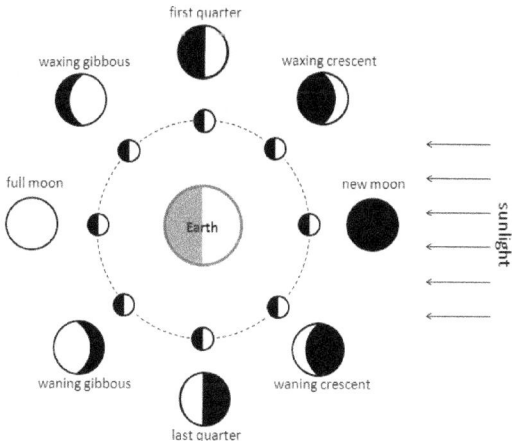

From the Earth we sometimes see only part of the sunlit areas. The sunlit areas seen from the Earth are called the phases of the Moon. They happen during a Month.

There are 8 phases of the Moon. The Moon goes from no sunlight on it, the new Moon to full sunlight, the full Moon and then back to no sunlight on it.

These phases are known as:

- New Moon
- Waxing Crescent
- First Quarter
- Waxing (Gibbous) *Gibbous means over half the moon is shining*
- Full Moon
- Waning (Gibbous)
- Last Quarter
- Waning Crescent

The journey of the Moon through 8 phases lasts almost a month. The Moon orbits the Earth in almost 30 days. The ancient African people used the Moon to create the month.

When the Moon passes between Sun and Earth, the Moon's shadow (lunar shadow) is seen as a solar eclipse on Earth. Eclipse means the covering of the light from one celestial body by another.

When Earth passes directly between the Sun and Moon, its shadow creates a lunar eclipse.

Lesson plans for Ages 8-9 Years 189

Below is a geometric design of the positions of the Sun, Earth and Moon during the solar and lunar eclipses.

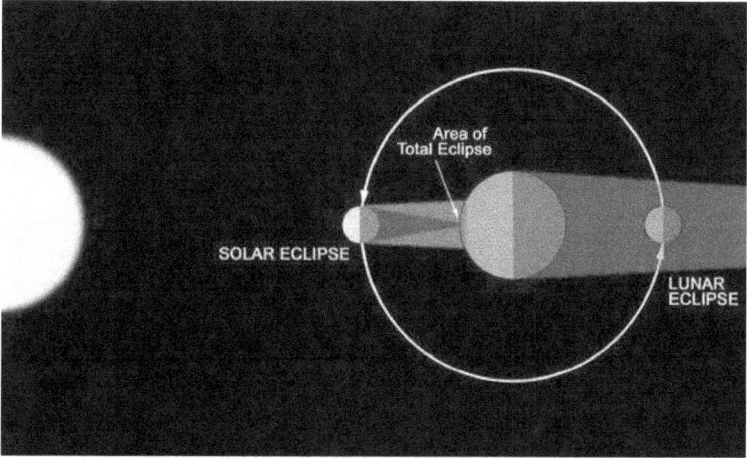

You can use your protractor, compass and ruler to draw this arrangement of the Sun, Moon and Earth to explain both the solar and lunar eclipses.

*Solar Power*

Solar power is the future of Africa. With the amount of sun available, the move towards solar energy has become the way forward in supplying electricity. Electricity is used for electrical appliances from lighting to charging batteries and mobile phones, as well as running vehicles. Solar energy is becoming more popular around the world.

Below are 2 forms of solar ovens that simply use the sun to bake. Sunlight is converted to heat energy. A solar cooker needs an outdoor location that is sunny for several hours, protected from strong wind, and where food will be safe.

In the first picture, the young lady uses the solar energy to cook her stew and meal. The silver panels heat up from the Sun and the heat cooks the food.

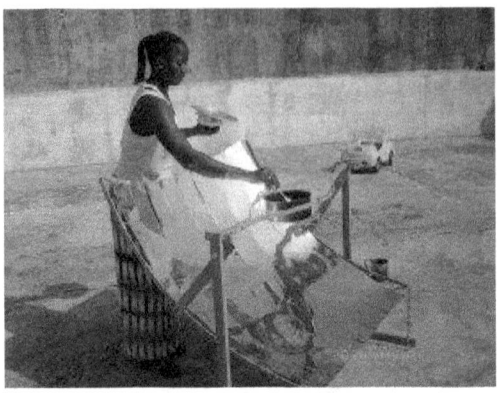

The solar oven below is made from a box and lined with silver foil, with a glass on the top of the box that the food is in. The card around the box is also lined with silver foil, so that the heat from the Sun is reflected onto the box through the glass.

This box can be made by the education group and used if there is sun or solar energy where the Afrocentric school is located.

Solar energy can change Africa today. The Sun is a continuous source of energy in Africa. Some parts of the world have very little heat from the Sun. All humans, plants and animals need the Sun to survive. Africa

*Lesson plans for Ages 8-9 Years* 191

has plenty of it. The first use of solar energy that there is evidence of, was in KMT where homes stored solar energy to use on cold nights.

The ancient African people of KMT were familiar with electricity too. The Sun can produce electricity.

Electricity is a form of energy. It is in the air. Electricity is in particles called electrons or protons which are found in all atoms. Atoms are in everything that exists. Atoms are made up of electrons, protons and neutrons. Atoms join together to form molecules which form everything including humans. Electrons have a negative charge and protons a positive charge.

These protons and electrons can be captured, accumulated and stored. They can also move as a force called a current. Electrical energy can supply heating, cooling, lighting or running computers and appliances.

All over Africa there are plans being made to provide solar panels to store solar energy, which will provide electricity.

Below is a diagram of a solar cell (PV solar cell). This can produce electricity.

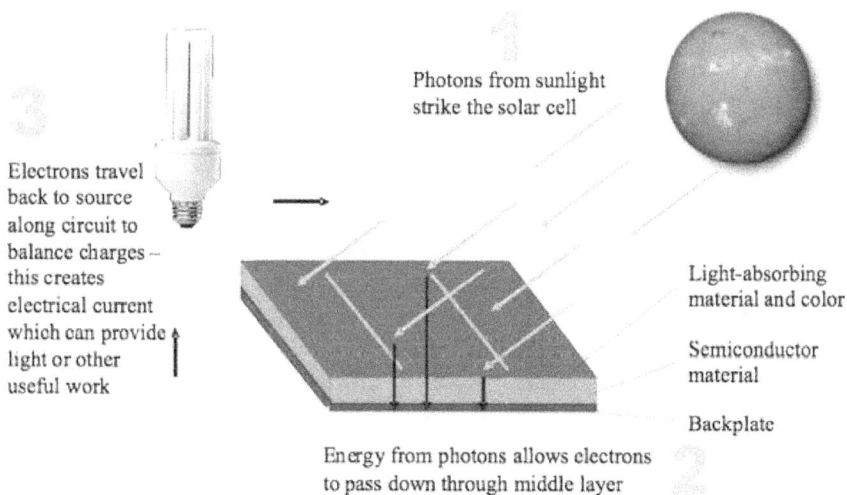

- Photo means light e.g. photons
- Voltaic means electricity.

This cell can convert/change sunlight into electricity.

Photovoltaic cells are made of special materials called semiconductors, such as silicon which is mainly used. Scientists are trying to find new semiconductor materials.

When light shines on the cell, a certain amount of it is absorbed into the semiconductor material.

The energy knocks electrons loose, allowing them to flow freely.

Energy from photons makes the electrons flow in a certain direction. This flow of electrons is called a current.

By placing metal contacts on the top and bottom of the PV cell, that current can be taken and used to power a calculator or lightbulb.

This current, together with the cell's voltage (which is a level of power), defines how much the solar cell can produce.

It is important to learn about solar energy and how it can be used. Solar power technology can help people who cannot afford to use the supply of electricity offered by energy companies, that make huge profits from exploiting human needs.

## Music and Dance

At this age the scholars of life in the rural Traditional African setting, know how to be responsible and carry out the skills required of them. They look after their farms, go to market, create items of need, manufacture and run their homes in the absence of their parents. The children are educated. They play an active part in the music and celebrations of their important festivals.

Drumming provides a fundamental basis for learning any instrument that the scholars might be interested in playing.

There are countless examples of wonderful musicians, singers, music writers who are African or Diasporic across the world.

### Review and Discussion

Who are some of these Artists where you live?

What instrument do they play? What songs do they sing? What type of dance do they perform? What words do they (or did they if they have passed) write?

How has their music influenced you?

What instruments do you love to hear?

### Martial Arts

Below is a painting from KMT; it is a form of what is called today *Martial Art*.

Lesson plans for Ages 8-9 Years 193

A similar Martial Art still practiced today by African Brazilians is called Capoeira. The discipline and training, combined music using the Berimbau, an ancient African instrument that guided the moves, much like the drum guides' dance. This was a way to practice, so that the discipline would be perceived as a dance, rather than the art of combat and defense against the cruelty of the owners of enslaved African people. The berimbau itself could also be used as a weapon.

Berimbau     Haitian children after the earthquake of 2010 are being taught Capoeira by Brazilian teachers

An Educator of a form of Martial Arts will come to the Education center to give lessons to the scholars. In this way they will learn the history and the discipline of self-defense and personal development.

LESSON PLANS
FOR AGES 9-10 YEARS

# Language Arts and Sociocultural Studies

During this year, the scholars will become more aware of the nature of the history of African women, men and children, as they go into more detail regarding culture and enslavement. The important role of mind in culture will be touched upon. In this light, it will be about the students locating themselves in their own history, culture and identity.

As part of the learning, the Afrocentric Sociological perspective will continue to be used for understanding the structures of human societies. This knowledge can help the scholars make sense of the similarity of human needs as well as their own cultural differences.

## Culture

Culture holds the values and beliefs of people in society. It will shape or form the way that each one of these institutions work.

The culture of any people includes their:

- History
- Language

- Psychology
- Spirituality

*History*

The history of a people is based on their experience over time. History tells the story of the people. People make up creation stories of how they came to be. It helps people to identify who they are and what they might become in the future.

The Sankofa bird

Can you remember the importance of the Sankofa bird and what it represents?

*Language*

The original language of all people was an African language.
Can you explain how that is possible?
Language is used as a way to communicate.
Language helps people to communicate with each other. It assists people to pass on their knowledge to help them to have a good life. Language also passes on the people's hopes and beliefs, sometimes in music, art and literature. It can heal people.

*Psychology*

The psychology of people is based on their mind and thoughts. The psyche, where the word psychology comes from, is known as the life and spirit of a person. The psyche, the mind, is influenced by its treatment. If a person is treated badly then a person will become ill. If a person is treated well, the person will be happy. If a person is taught lies, they will become confused. If a person is taught Truth, they will gain clarity.

*Spirituality*

This is the life force or energy that makes us alive. People give this life force many names. Without it, humans, plants and animals cannot live. Humans decide how to use the energy of life. Some people respect this energy of life and some people do not.

**Review**

The history – what people have done
The language – the way people communicate
The psychology – how people think
The spirituality – the life force of people

They are important to culture and will influence the way that humans think and build their institutions that keep their societies going.
*Speak about culture and explain what you know to the education group.*

*Social institutions*

The major institutions of any human society are:

Family – producing and caring for children
Spiritual system – guiding the spirit
Education system – teaching necessary skills
Political system – decisions of development
Legal system – creating and developing laws
Economic system – methods of production and exchange

How these institutions work is decided by the people. The way that is chosen is kept in the cultural memory, for people to practice generation after generation. A generation is about 25 – 30 years, during the time a human child grows to have her/his children.
Look at the institutions of society:

Family – producing and caring for children

Spiritual system – guiding the spirit
Education system – teaching necessary skills
Political system – decisions of development
Legal system – creating, developing and using laws
Economic system – methods of production and exchange

and discuss:

- What is the difference between a non-violent culture and a violent culture?
- How does the culture of a society affect the outcomes?
- How would institutions be run in a violent culture?
- How would institutions be run in a non-violent culture?
- What would society be like in a non-violent culture?
- What are the things that violent societies care about?
- What are the things that non-violent societies care about?

After explaining to the other scholars, take notes on points that other scholars raise, and then write an essay on the differences in the way that you think that violent cultures and non-violent cultures work.

## History

### Africa: The Cradle of Humanity

The ancient history has not always been remembered and is often hidden and difficult to find. The history of Africa is also the history of humanity.

All humans who populate the world today came from Africa. The oldest human ancestors lived in Africa around 250-300 thousand years ago but Africans began to migrate around the globe between 80-50 thousand years ago. Humans are called Homo sapiens sapiens. This is a scientific name given to define humans in 1759.

Groups of people travelled from Africa, all over the world, and settled. Some settled where there was not much sun, and some in places where there was a lot of sun. Over thousands of years, these environmental differences changed the features (phenotypes) of people and the amount of melanin needed in the skin. Melanin in the skin is very important to help protect humans from a lot of sun. The high amount of melanin in the skin allows us to produce Vitamin D under large amounts of sun, without our skin getting very burnt and sore. Melanin in the skin is not needed as much in cold weather; in fact, if you live in a place without much sun, it is useful to have less melanin in the skin so that you can produce Vitamin D from very little sun exposure. Melanin is needed for all humans to live. It is everywhere; it is inside our brains, heart, liver, eyes, hair follicles, glands and other places.

The way that humans lived, helped to create their cultures and beliefs. Those humans in very difficult places to survive, created different cultures from those humans who had plenty of sun, water, plants, animals and very importantly, food.

This difference in climate, developed different ways to live and different cultures. Cheikh Anta Diop studied cultures and found that there were differences between cultures in the northern part of the world, where it was cold and the southern part of the world, where it was much warmer. The northern culture was more aggressive and the southern more peaceful. There were places that these cultures mixed and some chose their aggressive culture and some their peaceful culture.

Remember the Pangea, the one continent in the world 300 million years ago? All the Earth's lands were joined and became separated over time. As you see below, Africa was in the center. These lands were divided into what are known (since the 1950s) as the 7 continents.

What are the names of the 7 continents? What are islands? What are peninsulas?

*The Pangea*

Those people who remained in Africa developed a culture that they wrote on paper, on stone, and in paintings. They also displayed their culture through carvings, artifacts, and on their shrines and buildings. This is how we have learned about what they thought and believed within their culture.

As African people travelled across the world and settled, they painted on rocks and made carvings, along with metal, wood and stone artifacts. These paintings document (record, make evidence of) the history of the people, animals and lands around them. These beautiful art works managed to keep their pigments (natural coloring) over thousands of years.

The painting of the people hunting antelope is from France. The horse is around 20,000 years old from the same cave. The bull is from Spain and was painted 14-20,000 years ago.

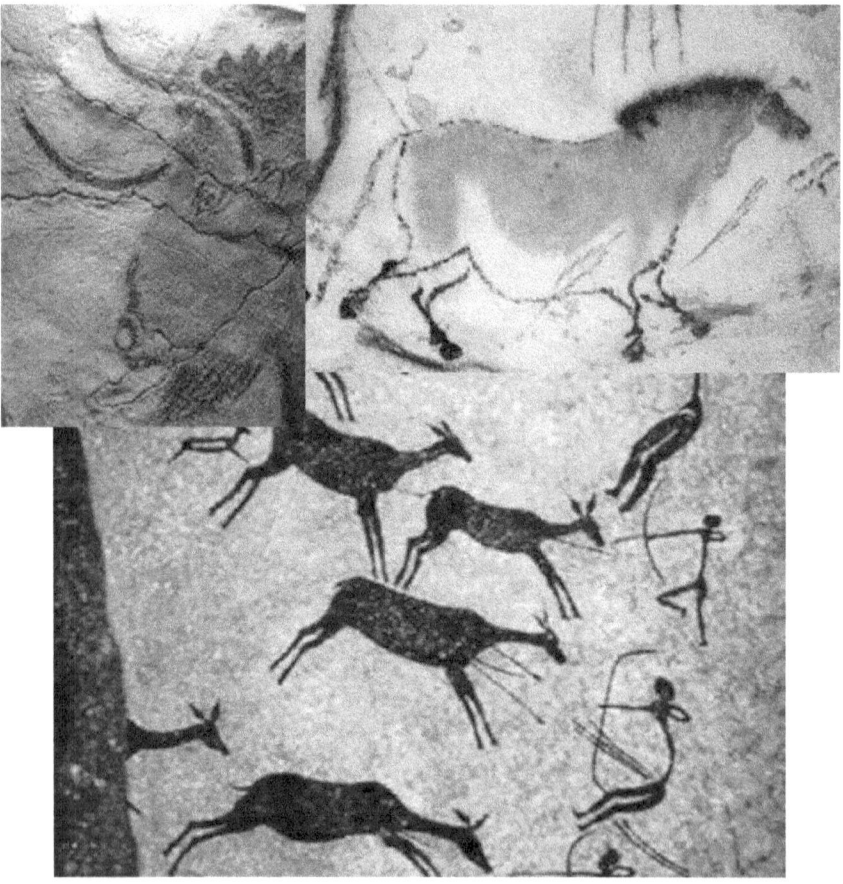

San families
The San people, whose Ancestors painted and documented their lives

An ancient rock painting by the San people of South Africa, in a place called ukhahlamba

Children from Chad

An ancient rock painting by people from the Ennedi Mountains in Chad. Some people are riding white camels in the painting.

These ancient African people not only purposely left evidence of their existence but they also left their descendants. We are the descendants. They are our Ancestors.

The people of KMT left paintings, jewelry, pottery, all manner of artifacts as well as buildings and writing. Their work survived for thousands of years. We can look at it and see what they did. In KMT they wrote in Mdw Ntr. The Mdw Ntr has been translated by many. African people trained to study the Mdw Ntr, have translated some of the writings in new ways based on the culture of Africa. African culture is not always understood by those European translators who do not practice it.

This writing is evidence of how these African people lived. What they wrote, told us their history – what they had done, their language – how they communicated, their psychology – how they thought, and their spirituality – the life force of their people. They always remembered their Ancestors and did not think that they had achieved great things without the help of those that went before.

These dark-skinned African people wrote that they tried to be kind and generous and live a good life. They gave people across the world the idea of what is good and what is not. There are similar ideas among other people in the world that followed in this way of thinking and living.

The oldest of these ideas found written are from Africa. There are 42 laws and standards which to live by. They are used to produce good behavior. They are laws and standards of Maat.

Maat is Truth, Balance, Peace, Reciprocity, Justice and Love. To live this way is to bring order to chaos.

The cultural beliefs of these ancient African women, men and children, who called themselves Kemites, were like the cultural beliefs all over Africa.

*The Conquest and Colonization of Africa*

People came to KMT to conquer it and take its knowledge, ideas and wealth. The people of KMT were able to win back their lands at various times in their history. Later conquerors were the Greek and Roman Europeans. Today the last conquerors, the Arabs, still have the land which they now call Egypt.

The descendants of the European and Arab people who conquered KMT, were the same people who enslaved African people and colonized those in Africa who they did not enslave.

Enslavement changed the whole world. Those who enslaved African people, became extremely wealthy and powerful under a system that they developed called capitalism. They used this power to rule the world. This is the same economic system that most of the world is ruled under today.

African people of KMT taught the conquerors:

- Spiritual and moral values
- Mathematics
- Science
- Architecture
- Medicine
- Writing
- Biology
- Logic
- Geometry
- Astronomy
- Rhetoric

They improved the institutions in their societies.

European and Arab people decided that they wanted African people to work for them for nothing, to improve (make better) their societies and to build wealth in great amounts by not paying for labor. They forced African women, men and children to do what they commanded.

In these places African people were forced, under threat of death, not to practice their cultural beliefs.

The new culture that was imposed/forced was a violent one. The life of an enslaved woman, man, girl and boy was a violent one. Enslavement was an institution and it was cruel and inhuman. Inhuman means that the system was without heart and compassion and was merciless. No human should be treated like this.

The people who made massive wealth from this system and institution of enslavement, tried to make others believe that it was a good system. They wrote newspapers, stories, books, even holy books, and gave speeches to support the view that this was how things were supposed to be, in order that they could feel justified in their behavior.

It became an important belief in their culture. That means that the history, language, psychology and spirituality of the culture supported the enslavement of African people.

It meant that the enslavers had to lie. They said that the life of an African person was worth less than the life of other humans.

This lie was taught in all the institutions.

*Review and Discussion*

What are the institutions that all societies have?

When did African enslavement begin by Arab people?

When did African enslavement begin by European people?

Do you remember where African people who were enslaved were taken?

Do you remember what languages African women, men and children were forced to speak in these places?

Write and prepare a lecture about enslavement to present in front of the class.

Listen to each other's lectures and take notes.

Add the things that you learnt from other scholars' lectures and write an essay.

# Mathematics

## *The Mdw Ntr in Numbers*

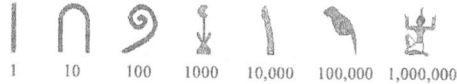

| 1 | 10 | 100 | 1000 | 10,000 | 100,000 | 1,000,000 |

Using the Mdw Ntr write 32
Using the Mdw Ntr write 78
Using the Mdw Ntr write 1,023
Using the Mdw Ntr write 5,360
Using the Mdw Ntr write 1,000,590
Using the Mdw Ntr write 7,777
Using the Mdw Ntr write 100,939
Using the Mdw Ntr write 500,372,081
Using the Mdw Ntr write 4,350,822,164
The people of KMT wrote either left to right or up and down. Read these Mdw Ntr symbols from the left.

The above images are based on *examples from African Mathematics, History, Textbook and Classroom Lessons (Walker & Matthews, 2014)*

## Calculating the Perimeter

The perimeter is the length of the outline of a shape.

To find the perimeter of a rectangle, which is the distance around all four sides, you have to add the lengths of all the four sides.

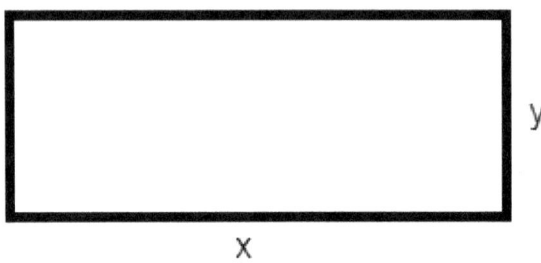

In this rectangle X is the length and Y is the width of the rectangle.
The perimeter is called P
The formula for finding the Perimeter of the rectangle is:
$P = X+X+Y+Y$
$P = 2X+2Y$
$P = 2(X+Y)$ this means 2 x X+Y
If X is 5cm and Y is 3cm then using P =
What is the value of P?
A square has four equal sides and all four angles are 90°.

The formula for finding the Perimeter of a square is:
Perimeter = P and Sides = S
$P = 4 \times S$
If the side of the square is 10cm
$P = (4)(10)$
What is the perimeter of this square?

The formula for finding the Perimeter of a Triangle is:
The left side is *a*, the base is *b*, and the right side is *c*
P = a+b+c
Below is an equilateral triangle so all three sides are the same and all the angles are the same.

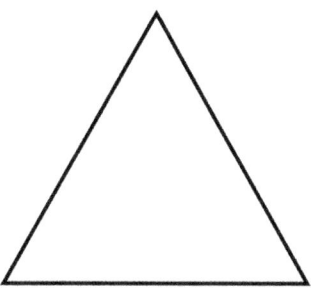

If the sides of the triangle are 8 cm in length
P = a+b+c
P = 8+8+8
What is the perimeter of this equilateral triangle?
Remember the angles should add up to 180°
What are the three angles?
Below is an Isosceles triangle. Two sides are the same and 2 angles are the same. The sides are 13.5cm and the base is 7cm.

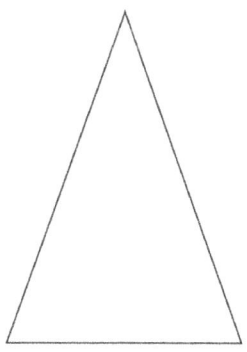

P = a+b+c  P = 13.5+7+13.5
What is the value of P?

## *Calculating the Area*

The area of a rectangle is width times length
A = w x l
The width of the rectangle below is 3cm and the length is 5cm
The Area is 3x5
A = 15 cm² (the little 2 is a power number that means that the number in front is multiplied by itself or is *squared*)
The triangle below also has 4 right angles or 90° angles like a square.

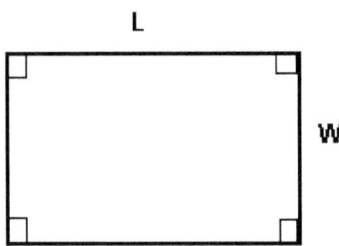

Calculating the area of a triangle. Area is A
Base is b
Height is h.
Because a triangle is half a rectangle, the formula is half of a rectangle. Remember that the Area of a rectangle is width times length (w x l). There are two ways to find the Area of a triangle. There is half of the base x height or the base x height ÷ 2.
Formula

a. A = ½ bh
b. A = bh ÷ 2

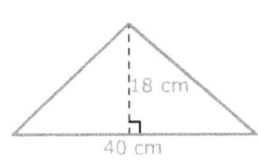

Solution:
In this problem, the height is not a side of the triangle. Instead, it is drawn at a right angle to the base to the tallest point of the triangle.

$$A = \frac{bh}{2}$$

$$A = \frac{(40 \text{ cm})(18 \text{ cm})}{2}$$

$$A = 360 \text{ cm}^2$$

As you see the height of the triangle is in the middle. The line is drawn to the highest point. As the diagram shows the line in the middle of the triangle is a right angle. The formula above shows that:

A = 40 x 18 = 720 ÷ 2 = 360cm²

Below is some useful instruction on finding the area of a square.

https://www.youtube.com/watch?v=CJiSTAuGCmk

Decimals

Using the decimal point is important. It will help to understand how to find the area of a circle.

Working with decimals is an easy way to use whole numbers and fractions using 10s. The decimal point is to separate whole numbers from numbers less than one.

All numbers before the decimal point are whole numbers and those after the decimal point or those on the right of the decimal point are less than one.

For whole numbers we divide them into hundreds, tens and ones etc.

3 hundreds, 4 tens and 7 ones = 347

It can be written as 300+40+7

We will put a decimal point after the whole number 347.

Each number after the decimal point or to the right of the decimal point is a fraction of the whole number

Numbers after the decimal point are divided into ten<u>ths</u>, hundred<u>ths</u> and thousand<u>ths</u>.

Everything after the point is a fraction so that .5 means 5/10<u>ths</u>

.55 means 5/10<u>ths</u> and 5/100<u>ths</u>

It can be written like this, 0 numbers 5 ten<u>ths</u> and 5 hundred<u>ths</u>

.555 would be 5/10<u>ths</u> 5/100<u>ths</u> and 5/1000<u>ths</u>

It would be written like this, 5 ten<u>ths</u>, 5 hundred<u>ths</u> and 5 thousand<u>ths</u>

347.555 could be written as 3 hundreds, 4 tens, 7 ones and 5 tenths, 5 hundredths and 5 thousandths

210.001 would be 2 hundreds 1 ten and zero ones decimal point 0 tenths, 0 hundredths and 1 thousandth

Write in words 502.01 and 728.39

To <u>multiply</u> 502.01 by 10 then move the decimal point one position to the <u>right</u>. The number becomes 5020.1

To <u>divide</u> 502.01 by 10 then move the decimal point one position to the <u>left</u>. The number becomes 50.201

Always move the decimal point the same number of zeros as in the dividing number. If the number is divided by 100, then the decimal point will move two positions to the left.

If the number is multiplied by 100 the decimal point moves two positions to the right.

Multiply 500.28 by 10
Divide 500.28 by 10
Multiply 433.29 by 10
Divide 999.33 by 10
Multiply 2874.52 by 100
Divide 3562.5 by 100
Multiply 500.50 by 10 then write the answer in words as above.

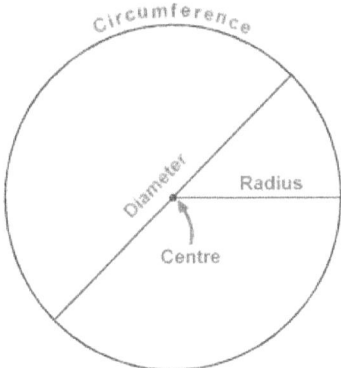

The area of a circle is measured differently from other areas. The equation or method for measuring the area of a circle is based on the equation of the ancient African people. It was created in KMT and learned by many visitors to KMT. In order to learn mathematics, geometry and astronomy, the students were trained by priests. After many years, these scholars became priests.

The pyramids could not have been built without this knowledge.

Today, the formula used to find the area of the circle is called Pi.

Pi is a number that is approximately equal to 3.14. It is the number you get if you <u>divide the circumference</u> of any circle by its <u>diameter</u>. It's the same for all circles whether they are large or small.

The area (that is the space inside of the circle) can be found if Pi is used to measure it.

Pi is written like this . The symbol of Pi is borrowed from the Greek letter p. It was not used as the symbol until the 1700s, around 400 years ago.

The area of a circle is which equals 3.14

A = area

A = $r^2$ this means that area is pi x radius. The $^2$ symbolizes that the radius must be multiplied by itself.

A circle with a radius of 4 will be $r^2$ which is 4x4=16

A=$r^2$ which is 3.14x16

The answer is A=50.24

What is the area of a circle that has a diameter of 12?

A=$r^2$

The radius is half the diameter so the radius = 6

$r^2$ is 6x6 = 36

A=3.14x36

Answer is A=113.04

Find the area of a circle that has a diameter of 6

# Science

### Thinking and the Brain

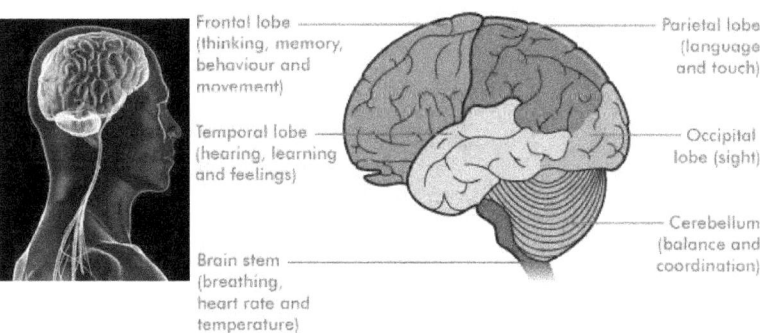

The brain sits in our skulls. The skull is hard and bony. The brain, which is soft and delicate, lies in fluid and membranes to protect it. The brain is very necessary to life and existing. It is where we do our thinking. It is influenced by culture and influences culture.

The senses such as sight, hearing, taste, smell and touch are controlled by the brain. Humans can walk and talk, have memories, and feel happy and sad. These experiences are called emotions and are also controlled by the brain. The brain can solve problems using logic. Humans can dream about things in the future and in the past, as well as things that may happen or may not happen.

The human body is controlled by the brain. Humans tell the brain what they want to do. Culture guides the human in deciding what s/he will do. The brain is part of the nervous system. It is joined to the spinal cord inside the bony spine. This is called the central nervous system.

### *The Brain and the Body*

The spinal cord runs all the way down to the bottom of the spine or vertebral column. The spine holds up the body.

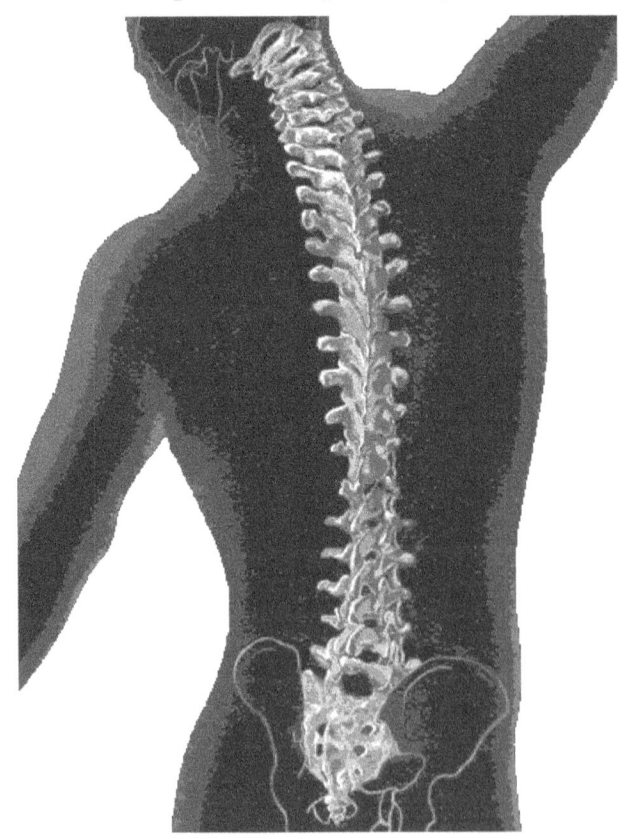

The vertebrae, which are the bones that make up the spine, run from the skull to the waist where the hip bone is. Each bone or vertebra in the vertebral column, has a hole in it so that the nerves can run down through the spine and connect all over the body.

Look at a diagram of the human skeleton and find out where the organs sit.

A diagram of the nerves running through the body

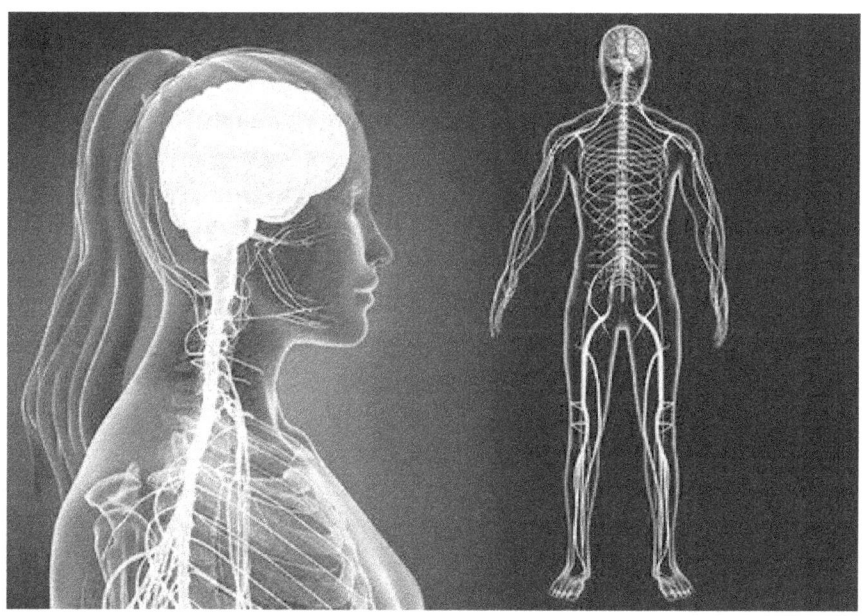

The spinal cord receives all the messages from the nerves that run throughout the body.

Nerves send out electrical messages between the brain and the body. The brain sends messages to the hand to tell you to hold the pencil. If the hand touches fire, a message goes to the spinal cord and back to your hand to tell you to move your hand away quickly. The brain sends messages to your legs and feet to get you moving.

The cerebrum is the largest part of the brain. It is the grey wrinkled part. The surface of the cerebrum is called the cerebral cortex. Different parts of the cerebrum work with different parts of the body. List the parts from the diagram and what they do.

The Cerebellum is at the back and base of the brain. It is involved with movement. It gathers information from the nerves and works out what to do with the information. The cerebellum learns movements which are called "motor". As a child grows physically, their motor skills develop. With practice using the cerebellum, a person can learn to do something like riding a bicycle or typing, so that the body remembers what to do.

The brainstem connects with the spinal cord, and the body is able to keep breathing, digesting food and keep the heart beating.

Memory The brain has two kinds of memory, short term memory and long-term memory.

Scientists are still continually learning about the brain.

There are lots of blood vessels and blood flowing through the brain at all times. The brain uses around twenty percent of the body's energy.

The Brain has two halves. The left side of our brain controls the right half of the body and the right side controls the left half of the body.

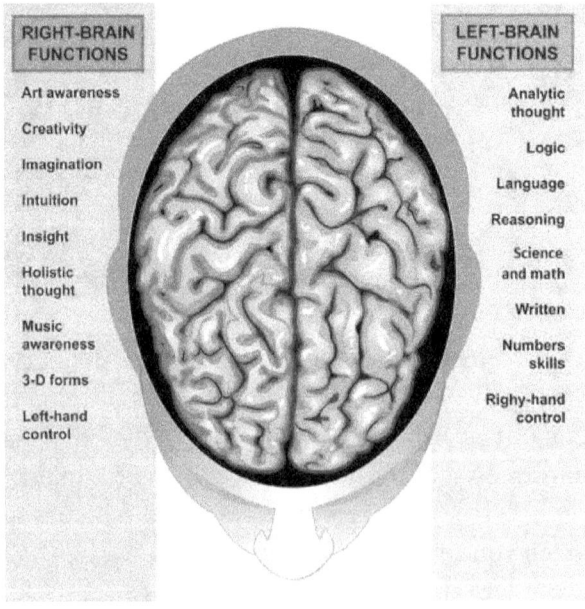

## African Medical Knowledge

The ancient African women and men knew about the brain, the body, the blood, the nervous system and organs like the heart and lungs, as well as how to perform operations and treat illness. We know this because some ancient African medical books still exist. Many others have been lost, destroyed and stolen.

One of the oldest medical books that we know about was written by the African people of KMT. It was written over 3,500 years ago. It is an anatomical book. Anatomical means relating to the human body and how it works.

This important medical book is now named after Edwin Smith, who was an American dealer who bought it from an Egyptian dealer, Mustapha Aga, in 1862.

The brain is responsible for the way that we think and what we do. We use it to learn. If humans learn things that are not true, then they get confused.

We are trying to learn things that are true about ourselves so that we can know who we are and not be confused.

The mind is so important to life. It is the seat of thought. What we learn will affect how we live.

## The Arts

The Capoeira, the drumming and the dancing should continue so that the scholars become more and more skilled. The scholars will have a sense of accomplishment and achievement which they can perform for the school.

Filming their arts like Capoeira will enable the scholars to learn the art of film as a critical art form. The documentation of the process will be in the hands of the Educators, until the time for the teaching of the scholars.

Education on film making, particularly documentary, will require an expert to teach the basic requirements. Documentation is a legacy. It will continue the work of African people who have documented their history so that we can know the Ancestors. In the future when you become an elder, the documentary will show others some of the art that you created.

A documentary film is a nonfictional motion picture, based on truth and reality. A documentary film will document some aspect of reality. Mostly, it is used for educational purposes and or creating a historical record. In this case it may be used to show the artistic work of the scholars.

The documentary will be a short film, for example from 2 minutes to 25 minutes.

Choose a subject that you want to make a film about.

Write a story.

Plan how you would create the story on film based on what you have learned about documentaries that you have watched.

After you have written your story, speak about your ideas to the whole education group. Include the music in the background that gives meaning to your documentary. Let the group and educator choose which documentary to make.

Your documentary will be shown to the other Afrocentric schools to inspire them and to learn from them.

# LESSON PLANS
# FOR AGES 10-11 YEARS

Traditional rural children were able to run a home including planting and harvesting foods, for home use or selling and buying, by the age of 10-11 years old. They are knowledgeable about their Ancestors and Divinities and know how to respect the Shrine and visit it regularly. The majority of girls and boys know about plant use and healing, which they have been learning from the age of 4-10 years old. Those who are selected, will go into training as Traditional Medical Practitioners when they are young women and men.

The lesson plan for 10-11 years, will focus on the colonization of Africa by people from Europe and Arabia. In this way, the cultural imposition of different and oppositional values and their effect on Africa will become clearer. The colonial situation in the Americas with the First Nations people, will also be looked at. The heart will be considered in its biological and astronomical aspects. Mathematics is contextualized by its ancient antecedents. Music incorporates the scholar's need for meditative peace.

## Language Arts and Sociocultural Studies

*The Colonization of Africa*

Arab and European colonization was the making of new countries. Their colonial plan was to rebuild Africa so that its resources, the lands and the people, would work for them. European and Arab people had already colonized KMT at different times in its history. The Greeks took African knowledge, wealth and skills in 332 BCE. The Romans did the same in 30 BCE. The Arabs arrived in 651 CE and are still there.

As well as colonizing Egypt, the Arabs also colonized the rest of North Africa. They fought the Romans for North Africa. These areas became Tunisia, Libya, Algeria and Morocco and what is now called Western Sahara and Mauritania.

Below in green is a map of the African lands that Arabs colonized.

After Arab people colonized the northern part of Africa, European people decided to colonize the rest of Africa.

They wanted African people to farm the lands to grow the foods, to mine gold and other precious metals, as well as to extract diamonds and oil. They wanted this wealth for themselves.

Colonization was violent and cruel. It began when Europeans enslaved African women, men and children.

African Nations had their own lands and boundaries for thousands of years.

The Nations had their own institutions:

Family – producing and caring for children
Spiritual system – guiding the spirit
Education system – teaching necessary skills
Political system – decisions of development
Legal system – creating and developing laws
Economic system – methods of production and exchange

In the map below are the real lands of the Nations as well as the colonial divisions. The white lines are the colonial borders, the new countries that were created at the Berlin conference of 1884-5.

In 1884-5, European leaders met in Berlin, Germany, and attended what is known as the Berlin Conference, to decide how to divide Africa among themselves.

The leaders of 14 countries were invited to the conference. These countries were Great Britain, Austria-Hungary, France, Germany, Russia, USA, Portugal, Denmark, Spain, Italy, the Netherlands, Sweden, Belgium, and Turkey.

Great Britain, France, Germany, USA, Portugal, Denmark, Spain, Italy, Netherlands and Sweden were already involved with African enslavement.

The 14 leaders sat down with pens and rulers and divided Africa up like a cake. They decided which country would take each part of Africa by drawing lines with a ruler. It was in that conference that they carved up the African continent into the countries that we see today on the map.

The picture below is of the Berlin conference in 1884-5 where the colonial plan was made. See the large map of Africa on the wall.

When the European leaders looked at Africa, this is what they saw in their minds and plans.

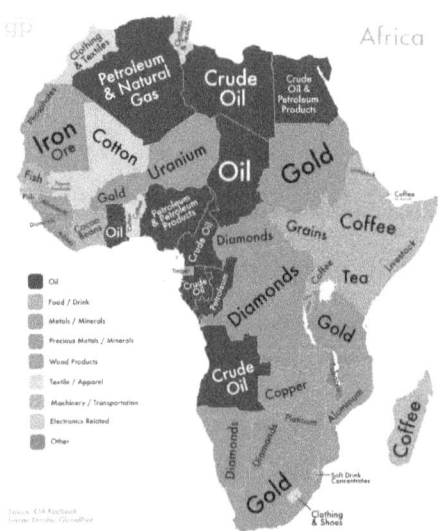

Below is the divided Africa (notice the straight lines of the ruler)

Germany fought 20 years later with the other European colonizers and lost its part of Africa; Namibia. The British took it in 1915 during the European World War 1.

The difference between enslavement and colonization was that the people enslaved were taken out of Africa and the people colonized remained in Africa.

African women and men worked to mine and farm and look after the people who took their lands. Their work kept them away from their own responsibilities. They had to neglect their own societies and cultural institutions:

Family – producing and caring for children
Spiritual system – guiding the spirit
Education system – teaching necessary skills
Political system – decisions of development
Legal system – creating and developing laws
Economic system – methods of production and exchange

The colonizers forced African women, men and children to respect their people and their cultures and to disrespect African women, men and children and African culture.

The colonizers built their own institutions using African wealth and African work. People had to speak the colonial languages. The European colonizers sent some African men to train in Europe to learn to speak the languages well to politically control the countries. Arab colonizers used mainly Arabs to maintain political control.

The new countries had to use the governments that Arabs and Europeans created. The culture of the institutions was no longer African.

African people were forced to believe that colonization was a good thing. The first people colonized did not believe this lie. The descendants came to believe it after generations. Not all African people believed in colonization. Many fought against it.

These colonizers, like the enslavers, became extremely and incredibly wealthy. They sent much of this wealth to enrich their own countries.

**Questions**

When did Arab people colonize Egypt, the land of ancient KMT?

When did the Greeks and Romans conquer KMT?

Can you name the lands where the enslavers came from?

Can you name the lands where the colonizers came from?

Can you name the languages that the new countries in Africa now use?

Can you name any of the countries that enslaved African people were taken to?

Can you name any of the minerals and material wealth the colonizers took?

What happened to colonized African people?

They lost their:

- Lives
- Lands–What grew on those lands went to other countries to make money for the colonizers. People became poor farmers who could not feed their families
- Families and Nations were divided by different countries
- Mines and precious minerals in the earth that people had used for thousands of years for healing and rituals
- Precious artwork and artifacts–They are in museums
- Languages–Forced to adopt colonial languages
- History–New distorted history was made up to support the colonizers and justify their behaviors

- Spiritual systems–New religions were forced
- Ancient knowledge
- Culture
- Identities–New cultural identities were imposed

Colonization was a cruel system of control. In order for it to work, violence was necessary. Guns were used to enslave and colonize. The Gatling gun from the USA (invented in 1861 by Richard Gatling) was used against African people who fought against colonization.

## *African independence*

In the 20th century many African leaders, some trained in Europe, fought wars to control these new countries. They wanted these countries to become independent from Europe.

What does independence mean?

Why did the African leaders fight for independence?

Discuss this important topic of independence looking at the maps and remember culture and society.

What institutions do all cultures need to develop their societies?

How did African institutions change?

When you stand up and speak in front of the class, remember that you are teaching others. You do not know everything. Other scholars can help.

Take notes during the discussions and presentations.

You are learning how to lecture for the future.

## *The Colonization of the Americas*

Colonization happened to First Nations people in North, South and Central America.

In ancient times, First Nations people built pyramids like African people. The Olmec, Maya, Aztec and Inca, all built pyramids.

Below is a pyramid in Mexico built by the Maya

Before African people arrived as enslaved people in the Americas,

Europeans had already divided up the Americas. The first European groups to divide the lands were the Portuguese and the Spanish.

Below are the names of some of the First Nations people in South America

Below are some of the original names of the Caribbean islands named by the Taino people who were of the Arawak Nation:

Lesson Plans for Ages 10-11 Years 225

Below are some of the colonial languages of the Caribbean

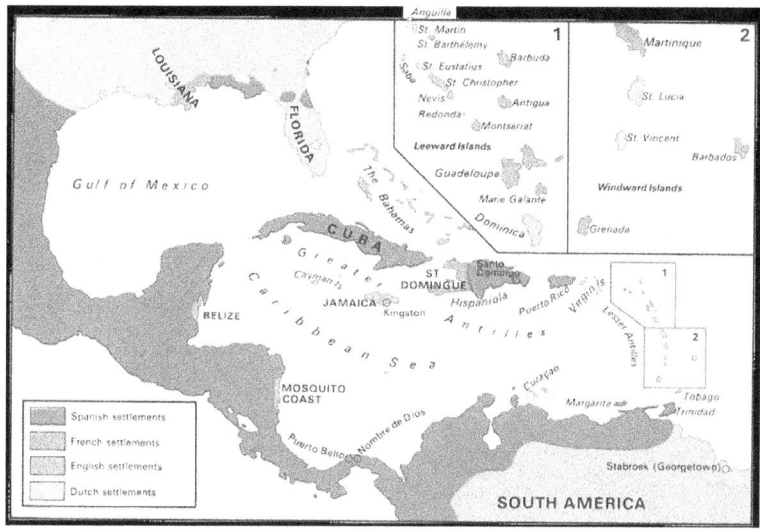

Below are some names of First Nations people in North America before colonization

Colonization began in the 15th and 16th centuries (the 1400s and the 1500s). The Dutch, the English and the French arrived later. The European countries fought wars against each other for these lands.

These Europeans, then enslaved African people and brought them to these First Nations lands.

The colonizers tried to enslave the First Nations people too. Colonization was/is violent. Guns were used to succeed in conquest. First Nations people lost their:

- Lives
- Lands and all that grew on those lands. People became landless. Lands were used to make money for the enslavers and colonizers
- Families were divided in different countries
- Their mines and precious minerals in the earth that people had used for thousands of years for healing and rituals
- Precious artwork and artifacts–Now in museums
- Languages
- History–New distorted history
- Spiritual systems–New religions were imposed
- Their ancient knowledge
- Culture–European culture forced
- Identities

Before the Caribbean was conquered, African people and the Taino people from the Caribbean, traded. The Taino lived on the islands that are now called Cuba, Jamaica, Haiti, the Dominican Republic, Puerto Rico, the Virgin Islands and the Bahamas.

Around 1492, the Taino women, men and children from Ayiti (Haiti) were enslaved on their island by a European called Christopher Columbus. First Nations people could be enslaved on their own lands. Columbus sent hundreds of enslaved Taino to Spain. This is shortly before African people were enslaved and brought to the Americas.

During enslavement, First Nations people and African people often fought together against the colonists and enslavers.

The Quilombos in South America, the Caribbean and North America were towns and cities that African people built after escaping enslavement. The Quilombos were usually built in the mountains. Living in the mountains helped African people see their enemy trying to capture them. First Nations people knew the lands well. They often lived with and helped African people.

The map below shows South America and what it provides to the world.

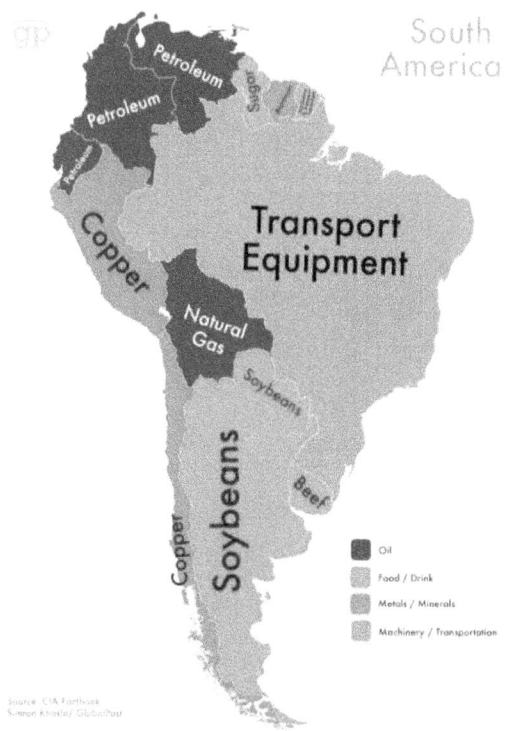

Colonization made the colonizers and enslavers wealthy. The First Nations people and African people that were colonized and enslaved, had most of their lands and wealth stolen. The effects of this history are still present today.

*Review and Discussion*

Why is it important to remember African history?
Why is it important to remember the First Nations history?
What is the African symbol of history?
Find Mexico on the map of the world and find out what is happening in Mexico today.

What is colonization?
Write about colonization and then present a paper on colonization to the class.
Listen to each presentation and take notes to write an essay.
Film the presentations to keep a record of your works.

## Science

### *The Heart*

The Ancient African people from KMT knew about the heart and wrote about it in the Medical book known today as the Ebers Papyrus. It was written 1,557 BCE. It was based on thousands of years of knowledge. The Medical book was bought by George Ebers in 1874.

Below is a diagram of the human body to show where the heart is in the body.

It shows part of:

- The skeleton
- The muscles
- The blood circulation system
- The stomach and the intestines
- The kidneys
- The liver
- The brain

The blood reaches all the parts of the body to keep them alive.

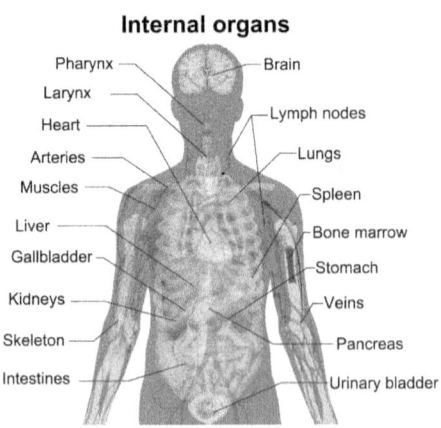

The diagram below shows the heart and blood circulation system. It is known as the Cardiovascular system. Cardiovascular means the heart and blood system.

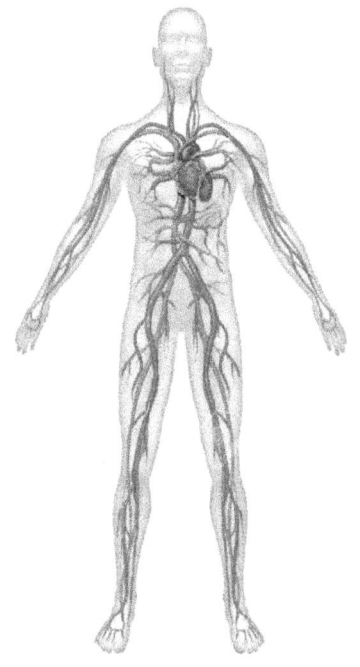

The role of the heart is to pump the blood around the body, including the brain. The brain cannot live for long without oxygen.

Oxygen and Carbon Dioxide are gases that we cannot see. They are in the air that we breathe.

Blood is mostly water with nutrients (food that keeps the body alive) and red blood cells that carry oxygen.

The heart is about the size of a medium sized avocado or prickly pear. It is more on the left side of the body. The heart is made of strong muscles that squeeze and relax to pump blood around the body. The heart has two pumps. There is one pump on the right side and one pump on the left side.

The role of the heart is to take blood from the body that needs oxygen and send it to the lungs to get oxygen. The blood needs oxygen to keep us alive. We breathe out carbon dioxide that we do not need, and the lungs take in oxygen from the air when we breathe in.

Remember that trees take in carbon dioxide and send out oxygen. That is why humans need them. We should respect trees.

Below is a diagram of the heart (the diagram is of a heart facing us)

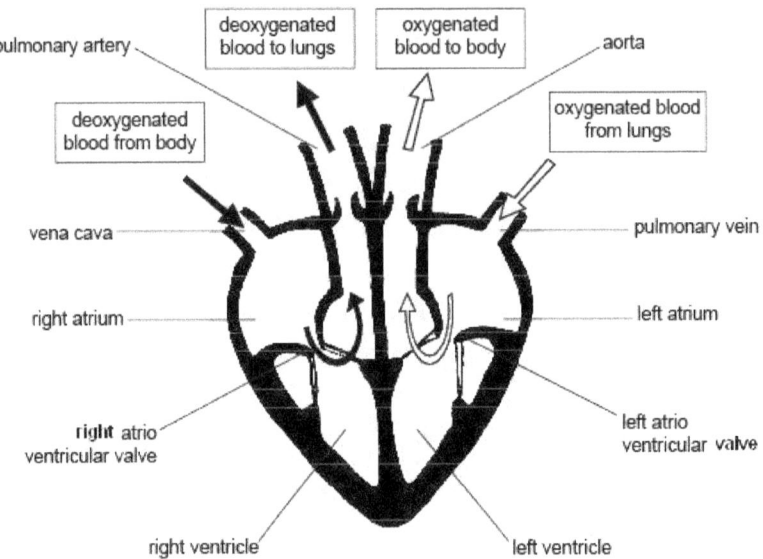

The heart pumps the blood all around the body through our blood vessels. These blood vessels are tubes that carry the blood in and out of the heart. The large ones at the top are called arteries. On the left side of our heart is the Aorta artery. On the right is the Pulmonary artery. The smaller blood vessels are called veins. On the left is the pulmonary vein and on the right is the vena cava vein.

The two pumps in the heart each have two parts. The right side has the right atrium at the top and the right ventricle at the bottom. The left side has a left atrium at the top and a left ventricle at the bottom.

The left side carries the oxygenated blood (blood that contains oxygen) from the lungs to the body. The right side takes the deoxygenated blood (blood that has used the oxygen) from the body to the lungs.

The blood enters each side of the heart from the veins. The blood goes into the atriums and into the ventricles and up through a valve to the arteries.

The atrioventricular valves control the amount of blood coming into the heart. The valves control the amount of blood going into the arteries. They move to the beat of the heart.

The heart beats through electrical impulses. It takes about a minute for the blood to travel around the body. A child's heart beats faster than an adult's. It beats slower when a person is asleep or laying down and faster when a person is running or worried and upset.

The Importance of the Heart in KMT

The oldest medical book on the heart shows that it is crucially important to life. The heart became the symbol of the soul.

A symbol is like a letter of the Mdw Ntr.

Each letter has a meaning in Africa. In Europe the letter makes a sound that has meaning when put together with other letters and sounds.

In mathematics the + symbol means plus or add; the − symbol means minus or take away; the x symbol means multiply; the ÷ symbol means divide.

The symbol of the black fist means African power, Black power or power to the people. It is a symbol of resistance to oppression.

The symbol of the Ankh means life.

The symbol of the heart in KMT means the soul. The soul is the spiritual record of the life of a person. The heart was seen as the force of life.

The symbol of the feather means Truth. It is the feather of Maat, the Divinity of Truth. She wears it on her head.

The ancient African people created the idea that there was good and bad. People tried to live in Truth or Maat.

If a person lives a good life then her/his spirit or life energy would go to a wonderful place.

This means the person tries to be:

- Kind to her/his family.
- Kind to other people.
- Make her/his society better.
- Caring for and helping others.
- Truthful and Honest and Just.

The people of KMT believed that the heart was the spiritual record of the life that the person lived.

The heart was weighed against the feather of Truth.

The feather is very light so the heart had to be as light. If the person was good then the heart was light.

If the heart was light, then the person's spirit went to a beautiful place.

The heart was the symbol of the Soul.

The feather was a symbol of Truth.

Below is a painting that showed the heart (Soul) being weighed against the feather (Truth).

This painting is a copy of the painting from 1250 BCE. It is called the Weighing of the Heart.

This painting is from a book about the journey of the souls of the Priest Ani and his wife Priestess Tutu.

The heart is weighed on the scale on the left side and the feather is on the right side. The rest of the book shows that the Priest Ani and the Priestess Tutu lived a good life.

In the painting above, the jackal headed god Anpu is kneeling to make sure that the scale is balanced. Anpu takes the soul to the beautiful place if it is good.

The Ibis headed god Djehuti is writing down the result of the test.

The goddess behind him is Ammut. She is part crocodile, hippopotamus and lion or cheetah. Ammut will eat the heart if it is bad. She removes the bad from the world.

On the seats above are 12 judges who are watching the weighing.

When we remember the Ancestors, we are remembering the spirits of those who came before us.

We remember the Ancestors because they were good.

*Review and discussion*

What does the heart do for the body?
Why is oxygen important?
Where does oxygen come from?
What part of the body brings oxygen into the body?
What is the name of the gas that our body makes and does not need?
What are the names of the 2 types of blood vessels in the heart?
What do the valves do in the heart?
Which blood vessels carry the blood away from the heart?
What does it mean that blood is oxygenated?
What does it mean that blood is deoxygenated?
What gas do trees give us?
What gas do we give the trees?
What happens to the heart if a person is worried?

How old is the oldest Medical book on cardiovascular knowledge that we know about?
Why does this Medical book not have an African name?
What symbol is the heart?
What symbol is the feather?
What are the weighing scales for?
How old is the painting?
When a person lives in Maat what is a person trying to do?
Why are the physical heart and symbolic heart so important?
Why is it important to remember the Ancestors?

## Mathematics

### *The Lebombo Bone*

Long before the nation-state of KMT, there were people in Africa using mathematical instruments made from animal bone. A mathematical bone was found in the Lebombo Mountains between South Africa and Swaziland. This is where the San people have lived for thousands of years.

Below is South Africa and Swaziland

The Lebombo bone is about 35,000 years old. It is made from a baboon fibula. The fibula is the thinner of the two bones in the leg below the knee. The Lebombo bone is a fragment of bone around 7.7 cm in length.

This ancient piece of bone is said to be like the calendar stick used today by the San people. The bone is believed to be a lunar calendar. It has 29 notches on it with 30 spaces in between and one on the side.

The time in nights represents the phases of the moon. The lunar phase of the moon is how long it takes to go from full moon to new moon. This is called a lunation.

A lunation is the average time of a lunar phase. The length of a lunar month is just over 29 to almost 30 days.

Scholar Robin Walker says that this lunar calendar should be read as 30 spaces followed by 29 notches plus 30 spaces plus 29 notches plus 30 spaces and on and on. These figures represent 30 29 30 29 30... nights. Using these 2 figures 29 and 30, gives a more accurate time of the moon's phases.

These numbers could be added to represent the months in this way:
30  59  89  118  148  177  207  236  266  295  325  354 nights which represent
1 2 3 4 5 6 7 8 9 10 11 12 lunations or months.

The calculations allow for the difference in the 29-30 nights in each month over the year. Add 29 to 30 (29+30) so that we get 59, which is two lunations, then add 30 to 59 to get 89, which is three lunations etc.

This bone is a calculator.

Without using an electric or battery calculator, work out the questions below.

How many nights occur in 3 lunations?
How many nights occur in 8 lunations?
How many nights occur in 7 lunations?
How many nights occur in 5 lunations?
How many nights occur in 1 lunar year and 6 lunations?
How many nights occur in 2 lunar years and 3 lunations?
How many nights occur in 4 lunar years?
How many nights occur in 5 lunar years and 4 lunations?
How many nights occur in 2 lunar years and 8 lunations?
How many nights occur in 6 lunar years and 8 lunations?

### The Ishango Bone

The Ishango bone is a tool handle with notches carved into it. It was found in the Congo near Lake Edward.

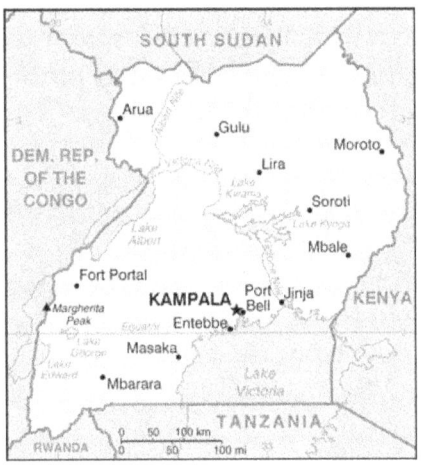

See above, the ruler lines from the 1884-5 Berlin Conference, and how the lakes and lands have been divided.

The Ishango bone below is photographed from 3 different angles. It is 25,000 years old, and like the Lebombo, is a baboon fibula bone. It is about 10 centimeters long. At one end is a piece of quartz stone.

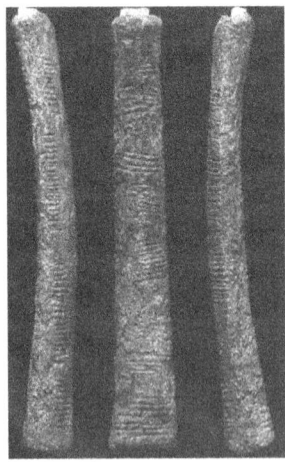

The Ishango bone markings shown in columns

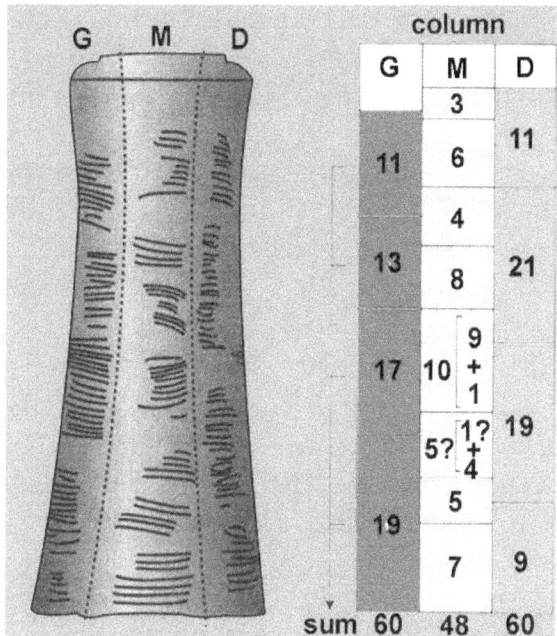

The Ishango bone is a calculator like the Lebombo bone. Some scientists believe that the Ishango bone is a record of movements of the moon and was used as a calendar for special occasions.

As you see above it has a number pattern of 3 6 4 8 10 5 5 7. This is interpreted as:

I. 3+6 = 9 which is 12-3
II. 4+8 = 12
III. 10+5 = 15 which is 12+3
IV. 5+7 = 12

The central number is 12.
The third and fourth numbers always add up to the central number. The seventh and eighth numbers also add up to the central number.

If there was a bone with the numbers 4 8 8 8 17 3 5 11, use the above pattern to show the central number as 16.

If the bone numbers were 7 7 10 11 21 7 9 12 use the above pattern to show that the central number is 21.

If a bone had the numbers 8 16 12 24 40 8 5 31 show that the central number is 36.

If a bone had the numbers 1 4 6 4 10 5 5 5 show that the central number is 10.

If a bone had the numbers 2 8 13 7 20 10 8 12 show that the central number is 20.

If a bone had the numbers 9 16 20 30 39 36 5 45 what do you think is the central number?

If a bone had the numbers 17 39 24 40 49 23 5 59 suggest the central number.

## *Calculating the Mean*

Finding the MEAN (average) or the central number with two numbers go half way between or add the two numbers and divide by 2.

The central number of 3 and 7 is 5.

Calculate it by adding 3+7 and divide the result by 2.

(3+7)÷2 = 10÷2 = 5.

What is the central (value) number of 3, 7 and 8. Calculate by adding the 3 numbers and divide by 3 because there are 3 numbers.

(3+7+8)÷3 = 18÷3 = 6.

We are looking at the MEAN, which is the result of adding the numbers and dividing by the number of numbers. For example, if you add the four numbers: 2,9,12,21

2+9+12+21 = 44 so 44 ÷ 4 = 11. The MEAN is 11.

If we look at the MEAN of the above Ishango bone answers (i) and (iii), we add the two answers. Then divide by 2 and that is the central number.

See below add answers (i) to (iii) which are 9 and 15 they add up to 24 so divide 24 by 2 and the answer is 12, the central number.

I. 3+6 = 9 which is 12-3
II. 4+8 = 12
III. 10+5 = 15 which is 12+3
IV. 5+7 = 12

## *Review*

What is important to know is that African people knew Mathematical and Astronomical calculations thousands of years before KMT. By the time of the beginning of KMT, possibly 10,000 years ago, the precise calculations of the movements of the planets, in particular the Sun, the Moon, and the Earth had been studied thousands of years before. It would not have been possible to know such precise movements and measurements without the study and research of the African people who came before. The San people came from the Lebombo Mountains where the Lebombo bone was found. Ishango was the name of an ancient village where the Ishango bone was found. The Huku-Walegga people live in that area and use a similar calculation system. The bone was found in the area near Lake Edward which empties into the Semliki river. The Semliki river is a source of the Nile River. It is not too difficult to think that the people and their knowledge went down the Nile to KMT.

## Music

The scholars should be fully aware of the importance of drumming. In the US, enslaved African people were not allowed to drum. In the Caribbean and South America, drumming was allowed. The drumming was the language that all African people understood. Messages were sent to the people this way. Uprisings and challenges to the enslavers were able to take place as a result of the messages through drums. Messages of joy and celebration as well as sadness were sent. During colonization in Africa drumming was allowed and messages were sent and are still sent. First Nations people also used drums to send messages for the same reasons.

Can you think of messages that could be sent now?
The scholars are at this time in their education:

- Drumming
- Dancing
- Playing instruments
- Practicing a Martial Art like Capoeira
- Filming, recording these events

## Kemetic Yoga

Kemetic Yoga will be a calming meditation, incorporating movement and discipline practice, at any particular time when it seems appropriate that the scholars need to have a quiet time to reflect. Scholars today are under incredible stress to survive.

Below is a two-minute explanation of the meaning of Kemetic yoga. It is an introduction to Smai Tawi (Kemetic yoga).
https://www.youtube.com/watch?v=Ok9BS6ZgNUM

The site below is a 23-minute exercise of Kemetic yoga for children.
https://www.youtube.com/watch?v=qqzYt8sYHco&feature=youtu.be

# LESSON PLANS FOR AGES 11-12 YEARS

At this age, many scholars are making assumptions about female and male relations from the images and ideas that they pick up. For this year, the scholars will gain a more in-depth understanding of social structures and the potential of ancient African values to today's life.

There will be a focus on Divinities and their importance in social and human development. Female and male balance and reciprocity, as an African and Maatic cultural concept and reality, is defined as a belief and way of life. Cultural difference and its influence on society are described. The culturally constructed concept of "race" is looked at. The ancient African screw pump and its importance to modern technology are explained. The eye is viewed in its biological and astronomical aspects. Mathematics and Art are linked to the use value of the eye.

## Language Arts and Sociocultural Studies

### Social Institutions

The major institutions of any human society are:

- Family – producing and caring for children

- Spiritual system – guiding the spirit
- Education system – teaching necessary skills
- Political system – decisions of development
- Legal system – creating and developing laws
- Economic system – methods of production and exchange

In Ancient Africa, the idea of female and male reciprocity was based on giving and receiving love and respect equally. The belief was that women and men celebrated their difference. They worked together to create a society.

This female and male relationship was the origin of family and society. It was the origin of culture. This relationship needed to be balanced to create the institutions of society. The female and male relationship was considered to be sacred in the spirit and in the physical. This loving, respectful partnership could produce a loving respectful:

- Family – equal treatment of girls and boys and adult carers.
- Spiritual system - guided by women and men to live good lives and respect their Ancestors.
- Educational system – that honors the skills, knowledge and creativity of women and men equally.
- Political system - uses the knowledge and guidance of women and men to create a balanced society that respects, cares for, shelters and feeds all its people.
- Legal system - that creates Maat's laws based on Truth and Justice.
- Economic system - that could produce what is necessary for the people. A way to exchange fairly what family and society can share. To invest in the future.

*African Philosophy and Spirituality*

In order to do the best that they could, African people remembered the source of their energy of life. They called this energy spiritual. The people knew that women and men were spiritual and existed on Earth for a good reason. It was to make the world a better place.

They gave names to the *source of life*. This source was feminine and masculine in one. The Mother and the Father in one. There were different names for this spiritual life force all over Africa such as the Creator,

All Knowing, Comforter, Great One, Great Spirit, the Unknowable, the Mysterious, Grand Ancestor, the Eternal and many other names. This life energy was considered to be a good and powerful force. It was in everything and it was everything.

African people showed their respect to this unknowable force. They knew how powerful this energy was. They believed that it was good. They believed that they could live good lives if they respected what was around them, the lands, the nature, the seasons, the oceans and rivers, the planets, the animals and life.

African women and men looked at the energy of life and realized how complex this energy was. There were different types of energy that were all part of the source. They believed that they could use the energies in different ways to improve life. They worked out scientifically that the energies were feminine and masculine. In KMT they named the energies Ntr or Ntrw for more than one. Ntr is a word that means *of nature* and *the Divine*.

These powerful feminine and masculine Ntrw were symbolized in human forms. They looked like women and men and animals in symbols. African people created feminine and masculine names for the Ntrw. This was done all over Africa, thousands of years before KMT.

In stone carvings, Mdw Ntr, and paintings and drawings, Ntrw often hold the *Ankh*, the symbol of life or *Was Scepter* (a scepter is a special staff or stick), the symbol of power.

Below is the *Was*, the symbol of sacred power.

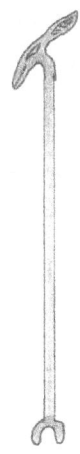

In today's languages, Ntrw has been translated to mean Divinities or deities. The Ntrw had Priestesses and Priests who trained to understand how to use these energies. They used the powers for the good of their societies.

All over Africa, people tried to be like Priests and Priestesses in their everyday lives. There are still women, men and girls and boys all over Africa and the African Diaspora who try to live in this way. In Traditional Africa, you cannot become a Medical Practitioner (doctor) without becoming a Priestess or Priest to a Ntr. That is how it has always been. All the scientists were Priestesses and Priests. Priestesses and Priests trained for years to learn.

African people gave names to the different female and male energies. Each Ntr had different energies. Many of the female Ntrw were Mothers, protectors and healers. The Ntrw had partners.

Below, Djehuti is male and Seshat is female.

Djehuti was the power for knowledge, learning, writing and recording events (history). Seshat's power was through writing as well as building and science (e.g. knowing how to measure the perfect triangle for right angles).

Builders, mathematicians, and those who wanted to be knowledgeable, trained as Priestesses and Priests. They loved and respected the power and energies of these Ntrw.

Aset was a Mother Ntr and was important for showing the protection and love of children and family. Asar her husband or partner was the Ntr for loving nature, growth, abundance (plenty) and life. Those who wanted to have children and or be successful farmers and care for the land, nature, and animals, respected and loved these Ntrw.

This is a statuette of Asar and Aset with their son Heru (Heritage Museum Russia).

Asar has the crown on his head with the feathers of Maat on the side. Aset is holding their son Heru. She is breastfeeding Heru (giving Heru the milk of life).

Below, is a page from a book that is over 4,300 years old. The book is called *The Book of Coming Forth by Day*. It is a symbolic story of what happens to the spirit after a person's body dies.

Hunefer is a Priest who has died. He is having the actions of his life judged. His heart is being weighed against the feather of Truth, symbolizing Maat the Ntr or Divinity. Maat is also the center balance of the scales. If he has tried to live a good life, his spirit will go to a beautiful place. The spirit would return to the *source of life*.

Anpu the jackal headed Ntr is taking Hunefer to have his heart weighed. Anpu is also weighing Hunefer's heart. Anpu's sacred work is to carry the spirit of Hunefer (and everyone) to the Creator.

Djehuti the Ibis headed Ntr is writing down the event. After Hunefer has his heart weighed, Heru, the hawk headed Ntr, is taking Hunefer to the Ntr Asar.

Behind Asar is his wife Aset and her sister Net Heb. The 14 Ntrw above are the judges of the weighing of Hunefer's heart.

*Review and discussion*

Which Ntrw in the weighing of the heart painting are holding the ankh?
What are the special energies and powers of Seshat and Djehuti?
When you want to grow food, and hunt and fish for food, which Ntr's power will you pay your respect to?
If you want to be a good Mother, which Ntr's power will you pay your respect to?
If we want a balanced society, what type of relationship should there be between female and male?
What is the name of the jackal headed Ntr?
What special sacred work does the jackal headed Ntr do?
What are the main institutions that culture and society are built on?
What does Djehuti do in the weighing of the heart painting?
What are some of the symbols that show who is a Ntr?
Why is it important for women and men to respect each other?
What is a priest or priestess?
How old is The Book of Coming Forth by Day?
Can you give 3 names that people have given to the "source of Life"?
What work did Hunefer do before he died?

## Hierarchies

The Ancient African women and men learned that there were good energies and powers in the spiritual world. They learned about the feminine and masculine powers. They used symbols to define them. They gave them names. The people tried to live a good life so that they could work with these powers. Their ideas were copied by people all over the world.

Since the times when women and men were equal, most of the world's societies have been developed to place greater importance on men than women; this is called patriarchy.

When colonization and enslavement happened, it changed the societies that practiced female and male equality.

Today, the main institutions of society and culture are run by men. This is reflected in the following ways:

- Family - when a woman is on her own raising a family, she is the head of the home. When there is a woman and man running the home, the man is usually the head of the home.
- Spiritual systems - the <u>source of life</u> is masculine - male. Most systems do not believe in the Ancestors.
- Educational system – Scholars are taught to believe that inequality is normal.
- Political systems – There are hardly any women politicians and leaders. There are problems of inequality.
- Legal systems - most lawyers, legal trained persons, Judges in the world are men. There is a lot of injustice.
- Economic systems - these economies disrespect the lives, the lands, and the work of ordinary people.

When society and culture is run like this, it is corrupt (not honest).

When a culture believes that a man is superior to (better than) a woman, that is called hierarchy. A hierarchy places one above the other. Patriarchy is a hierarchical system in which men hold the power and women are largely excluded from holding power.

The Truth is:

- A man is not superior to a woman.
- A European man and woman are not superior to an African

woman and man or a First Nations woman and man, or an Indian woman and man or a Chinese woman and man.
- A white woman and man are not superior to the Black woman and man, the brown woman and man, the red woman and man, or the yellow woman and man.
- A light skinned woman and man are not superior to a dark-skinned woman and man.
- A rich woman and man are not superior to a poor woman and man.
- A young woman and man are not superior to an old woman and man.
- An adult is not superior to a child.

*Review and discussion*

Culture guides and influences our minds and our thinking.

If a culture believes in this human hierarchy then it does not believe in Truth, Honesty, Justice, Peace and Reciprocity. It is not a Just culture. It is an Un-Just culture and society.

What is the difference between a Just culture and an Un-Just culture based on hierarchy?

How does a Just culture affect the lives of people?

How does an Un-Just culture affect the major institutions of society?

Discuss the differences in institutions between a Just culture and society and an Un-Just society and culture.

Take notes on this very important discussion and present your talk to the other scholars. Write a paper on the differences between these types of cultures and societies. Remember the history. History will guide you.

## Science

*The Myth of Race*

Race has been used to try and show biological differences among humans. The idea was very popular in the 18$^{th}$ and 19$^{th}$ centuries, and the beginning of the 20$^{th}$ century (1700s, 1800s, and 1900s).

During these times, African women, men and children were being enslaved and colonized. First Nations people were as well.

Biological race was a theory (idea) that European-Western biologists used to try to prove that there were different races of humans. This is called *pseudoscience*. Pseudoscience is a collection of ideas or beliefs, falsely deemed as being scientific. It was believed and taught that some humans were better than others or "more human". Some humans could be masters and mistresses. Some humans needed to be enslaved and colonized.

African and European Scientists studying the research of these biological scientists, found no evidence that there were different human races. In fact, they found that these ideas were not based in science at all and were merely ideas used to justify the enslavement and colonization of people who looked different to themselves. The pseudoscientists claimed that humans had originated separately and were genetically different groups, meaning that they each had different origins.

All humans today are descended from an African mother from thousands of years ago.

All humans came from Africa.

The human type that we are today is called Homo sapiens sapiens. It is a biological word. The Latin word Homo means human and Sapiens Sapiens means wise and sensible.

What scientists know so far is that Homo sapiens sapiens began in Africa about 250,000 to 300,000 years ago. They had plenty of Melanin in their skin. Those who left Africa between 80,000 to 50,000 years ago, travelled to different climates and over thousands of years, their phenotypes (features) changed to suit their new environments as well as some groups losing much of their melanin in order to survive with substantially less sunlight.

Wherever you go in the world, the people that you see are Homo sapiens sapiens.

## *Genes*

The study of *genes* is a biological and scientific way of learning what special <u>traits</u> that your families pass on to you. For example, if both your parents had black or brown eyes, then you are likely to get black or brown eyes. If your mother has long legs, you might get them too. If your parents are dark skinned or light skinned, this will affect a person's skin color.

# THE AFROCENTRIC SCHOOL

The scientists believe that genes are in all plants and animals too. Genes are handed on to the descendants. It makes them similar.

Genes are found in cells. All things that exist are made of cells. A human body is made up of trillions of cells. One trillion is a million, million or 1,000,000,000,000.

In every cell there is a center called a nucleus. The nucleus is like the brain of the cell. It knows what type of cell it is. It knows that if it is an ear cell that it is not a toe cell.

The cell can divide into two, making an exact copy of itself. It can repair the tissue or organ that it is a part of.

A cell is so tiny that it can only be seen under a strong microscope.

Inside the cell nucleus are threadlike (long and thin) chromosomes that the genes live on. There are hundreds or thousands of genes on each chromosome.

The chromosome is a long DNA (Deoxyribonucleic acid) molecule. The DNA molecule is made up of 2 strands, coiled in what is called a double helix. The helix means anything that coils or spirals.

Below is the chromosome or DNA molecule. It is in the shape of the double helix[1].

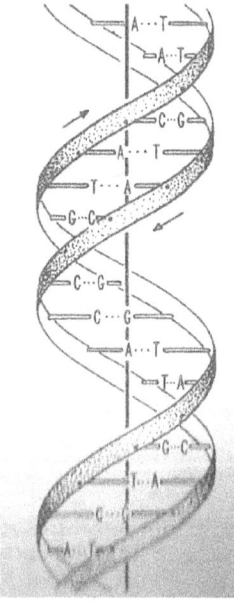

---

[1] From *Ancient Future* (1999) Wayne Chandler, Black Classic Press: U.S.A

There are 46 chromosomes in a human cell. They come in twos or pairs. There are 23 pairs. Twenty-three chromosomes come from one parent and 23 from the other parent. They will influence how we all look. They will influence whether we are girls or boys.

Not all living things have the same number of chromosomes. The fruit fly cell has 4.

DNA (Deoxyribonucleic Acid) is the material in cells that passes on the trait in humans and other life forms. The DNA is responsible for the way that cells develop. Most DNA is found in the cell nucleus. A small amount of DNA is also found in the mitochondria. The mitochondria are in the cells. Mitochondria make food for the cells out of energy. They have their own DNA.

Scientists looked at the human mitochondrial DNA and found a mother-maternal link to ancient humans. That is how the scientists know that all humans are connected to the same African mother.

**The Eye**

The eye is round like a ball. Everything on the outside of the eye is rounded or convex. It bends outward like this (.

The lens refracts (bends) light. The lens is convex. This bend causes light to come together to a focus point.

The cornea is a transparent (clear) window with a convex shape like the lens. The cornea does most of the eye's focusing.

The lens is behind the cornea and changes shape to focus light on different objects near or far.

The iris is the colored part of the eye. It controls the amount of light coming into the eye. The darker eye has more melanin and it protects the eye against too much light.

Because of the light, images form on the retina at the back of the eye. Cells in the retina are photosensitive (sensitive to light).

The retina is part of the brain. It is attached to the optic nerve which is attached to the brain. What the eye sees sends messages to the brain. The brain is then connected to sight.

Some scientists say that when the pattern of light reflected off objects enters the eye, the image is turned upside-down.

Whatever is the truth, the brain lets us see the images the correct way.

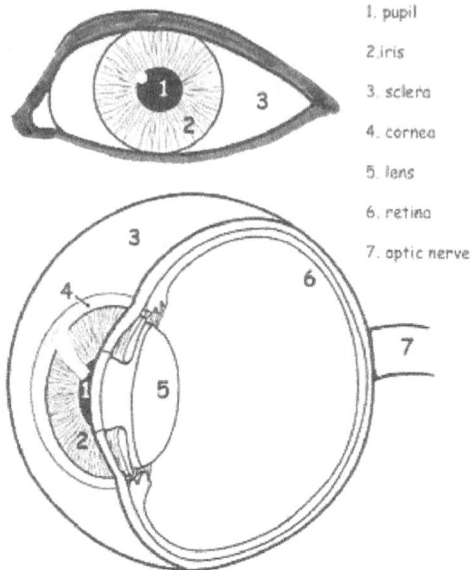

We see things because light reflects into our eyes.

Light is a wave that transfers energy; remember the solar energy that can be used to make electricity. The Sun's light travels through space to reach Earth.

Light is a wave that always travels in a straight line. The light waves from the Sun travel so quickly that it takes 8.3 minutes to reach the Earth. The Sun is 150,000,000 kilometers away. The eye can see the speed of light so it seems instant.

Light is produced by luminous objects like the Sun, Moon, candles, flames, light bulbs and fireflies.

*firefly*

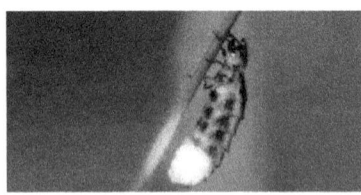

When light is produced, it reflects off non-luminous objects like humans, books, cattle, furniture, trees, fish etc. Some of the reflected light goes into our eyes and that is how we see.

We have two eyes seeing the same image but a little differently. The brain brings the two retina images together as one. The brain has a left side and a right side. The brain knows that it has a right view and a left view.

Diagram of the top of a brain with the eyes inside

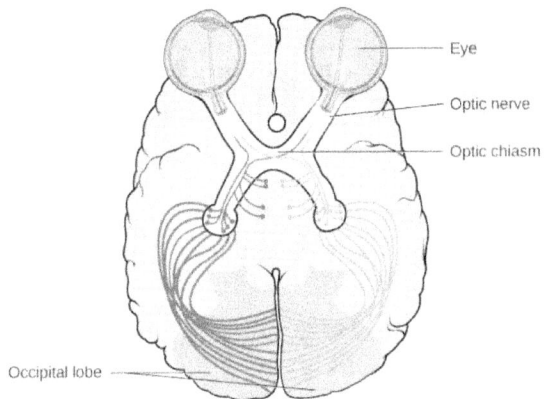

The optic nerves of both eyes join inside the brain. They are joined to the occipital lobe at the back of the brain. This lobe is responsible for seeing.

*Spirals*

Spirals are important to life's movement. They exist everywhere in nature, not only inside the human cell.

The planets turn and spiral in their own orbits around the sun. Tornadoes and hurricanes spiral.

This is a spiral galaxy in the sky. A galaxy is a star system.[2]

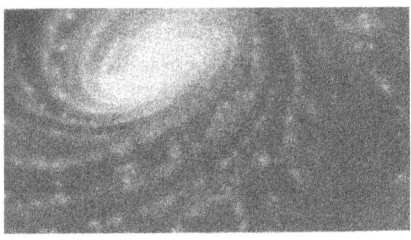

---
[2]From *Ancient Future* (1999) Wayne Chandler, Black Classic Press: U.S.A

The tower screw shell is a spiral or helix. It is the home of a sea snail.

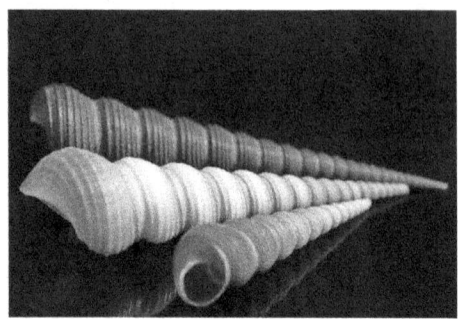

A good example of a manmade helix or spiral is the continuous screw that was invented in KMT. It was used in mining when ancient miners had problems with flooding. Mining had been going on in Africa for thousands of years. Mining was going on in Swaziland, South Africa at least 43,200 years ago. In KMT the miners drilled some deep mines; some over 250 meters below the ground. The screw was used to pump water out of the mines.

The continuous screw was also used in irrigation. Irrigation is the taking of water out of an area of land that has too much water so that food plants can be grown. It was used to lift water to a higher level. The larger ones were generally powered by oxen. Humans powered the smaller versions using the handle. If the area was deep, like a mine, then many of these screw pumps could be put together.

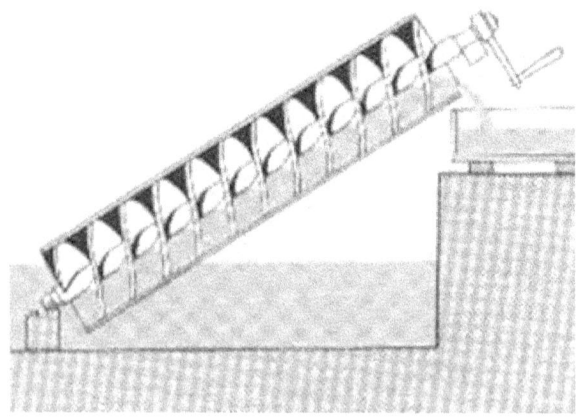

The basic principle of the continuous screw pump is shown in the diagram above. If the handle at the top was turned in an anti-clockwise direction it would draw the water up from the lower level to the top. The screw is held in a shaft or tube. The lower end is placed in the water at a 45-degree angle to the horizontal. The rotation causes the water to go up from the bottom to the top.

The screw is used today to pump sewage into waste water treatment plants. The garbage in the sewer water does not block the screw. It can pump water out of leaking ships, irrigate land, take out water from mines and many other things.

The ancient Greeks borrowed this idea from KMT hundreds of years after it had been invented. Sometimes the screw pump is called the Archimedes screw. Archimedes was an ancient Greek mathematician and astronomer, who was educated in KMT.

More recently, this African model screw pump was used as a hydro turbine to pump water. When used as a hydro turbine water pump it works in reverse to the normal screw pump. The water enters the screw at the top. The weight of the water pushes on the screws. The screws rotate (turn round). This rotation creates energy. This rotational energy can then be used to generate electricity. The screw can now run a generator attached to its shaft. It becomes the generator. The amount of electricity generated is based on how large the screw is and how much water goes through it.

If there are fish in the water, the fish can pass through the helix safely.

It is possible to use this form of power to generate electricity from a source of water like a river. So, an ancient mechanical invention can be used thousands of years later to generate electricity.

*Energy Sources*

Hydro (water) energy is known as <u>clean energy</u>, like solar (sun) and wind energy. They are <u>renewable</u> energy because they can be used over and over again.

Coal, oil and gas are <u>non-renewable</u> sources of energy because we can only use what is available and once they have been used up, there is no more. They pollute the air so they are known as <u>non-clean energy</u>.

Although it is a non-renewable and non-clean energy, wars are fought every day over oil. To move forward, we have to move back to ancient forms of clean energy as the air gets polluted.

*Review and Discussion*

Why is the energy from the hydro screw pump generator considered clean energy?
How does the African screw pump work?
How long ago was it invented?
What did the screw pump do in KMT and what does it do today?
What is renewable energy?
Give examples of non-renewable energy?
What is clean energy?
What energy can the whole of Africa use to generate electricity?
What is another name for the shape of a screw?
Where can you find the helix in a cell?
What are genes responsible for?
What is the name of the DNA that traced the maternal (Mother) ancestry of all humans?
How many chromosomes are there in a human cell?
What is the biological name of all humans today?
Where do all humans originate from?

# Mathematics

*The Eye Udjat*

The eyes of the Ntrw were very important in KMT. They were all seeing eyes. They could see more than normal human eyes see. They could see the connection to the source of life. The eyes were two symbols of light, the Sun and the Moon. The right eye was called the eye of Heru - the son of Asar and Aset, the hawk headed Ntr - and symbolized the Sun. The left eye was linked to Djehuti - the Ibis headed Ntr – and symbolized the Moon.

The left eye of Djehuti was divided into parts. Each part was given a measurement in fractions. The symbols for the fractions were from ½ to 1/64 as you can see below. When these fractions were added together the total was 63/64. This amount is almost one. The missing part 1/64 is a mystery.

These fractions of the eye were called hekat. Hekat was a unit of volume used when measuring grain, like a bushel or basket for measuring wheat.

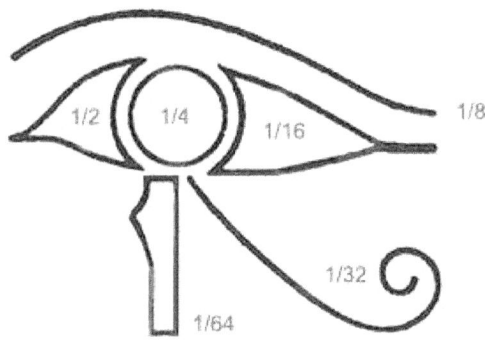

Please copy the eye, paint it and remember the measurements.

The eye was the symbol of the human ability to understand the source of life and know Truth.

The women and men of KMT used fractions. Fractions are a part of a whole. Like a sliced cake. Each slice is a fraction of the whole cake.

The top part of the fraction is called the numerator. The numerator shows how many parts we have.

The bottom part of the fraction is called the denominator and it shows how many equal parts the item is divided into.

## Adding Fractions

1/3 + 1/3 = 2/3 the denominator is in thirds so add the top numbers or numerators

1/5 + 2/5 = 3/5 the denominator is in fifths so add the top numbers or numerators

If the denominators are not the same, then they must be made the same in order to add the fractions successfully.

The denominators of 1/2 + 1/3 are not the same.

We must change them into the same fraction. What can the denominators of 1/2 and 1/3 divide into? They can both divide into 6ths.

Multiply the denominator of 1/2 by 3 to make six. Then multiply the numerator by the same number 1x3 to make 3. The new fraction is now 3/6.

To make the 1/3 into sixths, multiply the denominator 3x2 then multiply the numerator 1 by the same number 2. The fraction will now look like 2/6.

Now the fractions are both 6ths of a whole. They can now be added.

3/6 + 2/6 = 5/6

1/2 + 1/4 are not the same fractions, their denominators are not the same.

These fractions can both divide into 4ths.

Multiply the denominator of 1/2 by 2 and then multiply the numerator by the same number 2. The new fraction is now 2/4.

The other fraction 1/4 can remain the same. They are all 4ths or fourths or quarters. The fractions can now be added.

2/4 + 1/4 = 3/4

1/3 + 2/7 are not the same denominators. These denominators can both go into 21. The denominator of 1/3 can be multiplied by 7 to go into 21. Multiply the numerator by 7 too. 1/3 becomes 7/21. The denominator of 7 can be multiplied by 3 to go into 21. The numerator must be multiplied by 3 also. 2/7 now becomes 6/21.

7/21 + 6/21 = 13/21

Exercises[3]

1. 1/4 + 1/4 + 1/8 =
2. 1/4 + 1/8 + 1/16 =
3. 1/3 + 1/6 =
4. 1/3 + 1/6 + 1/12 =
5. 1/3 + 1/6 + 1/12 + 1/24 =
6. 1/4 + 1/16 + 1/32 =
7. 1/2 + 1/4 + 1/8 + 1/16 + 1/32 + 1/64 =
8. 1/5 + 1/10 + 1/20 =
9. 1/5 + 1/10 + 1/30 =

---

[3] Exercises from Robin Walker *African Mathematics* Reklaw Education Ltd: London UK 2014

10. 1/5 + 1/15 + 1/45 =
11. 1/5 + 1/10 + 1/20 + 1/40 + 1/80 =
12. 1/7 + 1/14 + 1/28 =
13. 1/3 + 1/4 + 1/6 + 1/8 + 1/24 =
14. 1/6 + 1/8 + 1/12 + 1/16 + 1/48 =

Answers for the Educators

1. 7/8
2. 7/16
3. 1/2
4. 7/12
5. 5/8
6. 11/32
7. 63/64
8. 7/20
9. 1/3
10. 13/45
11. 31/80
12. 1/4
13. 11/12
14. 11/24

**Converting Fractions to Decimals**

Change fractions into decimals by dividing the top number – the numerator by the bottom number – the denominator.

Here are some examples:

1/2 is 1 2 = 0.5          1/3 is 1 ÷ 3 = 0.33 infinity
1/4 is 1 4 = 0.25         3/4 is 3 ÷ 4 = 0.75
1/10 is 1 10 = 0.1        2/10 is 2 ÷ 10 = 0.2

Change the answers of the above fractions from exercises 1 - 14 into decimals.

Below are the answers for the Educators

1. 0.875
2. 0.4375

3. 0.5
4. 0.58333
5. 0.625
6. 0.34375
7. 0.984375
8. 0.35
9. 0.333
10. 0.2888
11. 0.3875
12. 0.25
13. 0.91666
14. 0.458333

Tiffany adding and subtracting fractions and mixed numbers
https://www.youtube.com/watch?v=tfZKwMdTt2w

## The Arts

Artist Omar Ba from Senegal

Renowned artist Omar Ba's work is of Africa. He says "I am an African artist but I create contemporary art". He did not want to lose his African roots. Africa is the heart of his work. He sees Africa in his mind. He is now living in Europe. His work inspires African people in Europe as well as European people who love Art.

He trained in Senegal and later in Switzerland. His paintings are exhibited in places like Dakar, Senegal; London, UK; Paris, France; and Biel, Switzerland.

Omar Ba begins his paintings with the background completely Black. He works with recyclable things. Often his work is on cardboard. He uses simple recycled containers to hold his paints. His painting is intense; he often mixes the violence with the peace. His paintings are based on his knowledge, memories, and his everyday experiences.

The work of Omar Ba has been chosen as an example of work that uses recyclable and simple things in its creation. His art reflects the culture, spirituality, history and present of Africa in symbolic ways.

The symbol is very much an African way of art. Remember the paintings of the people of KMT and the symbols that they used to show how life is very complex and spiritual as well as physical.

There is always so much in Omar Ba's paintings.

What is this painting showing? What can you see?

262  THE AFROCENTRIC SCHOOL

See the feathers and designs in the background, the seeds that make the hawk, the fallen warriors, and weapons on the red earth.
What is this painting showing? What can you see?
https://theartmomentum.com/traversing-boundaries-omar-ba/

This painting is called Les Autres
The women may be Mother and daughter. They sit on a comfortable high couch, looking down on a carpet that is like the world, in a white sea of important government type buildings and people.

What can you see?
Think of what you will do. You can copy one of Omar Ba's paintings. It will not be the same and you will do it in your own way. You can look at Omar Ba's other art online.

Find some old corrugated cardboard (like Omar Ba) that is recyclable. Find bits of things that are not needed, perhaps plastics, newspapers, magazines and scraps of cloth. Put these things in small boxes that you can keep tidy and put away when you are finished.

Make sure that you are wearing your old clothes or put on a cloth to cover your clothing. Play your music quietly in the background.

Work with as many colors as you can get. If you do not have many colors then glue on bits of material and magazines for colors to add. You can cut them or tear them. Begin your art with a painted Black background like Omar Ba. Be patient; painting takes time. Exhibit your Art at the next Afrocentric school conference.

# LESSON PLANS
# FOR AGES 12-13 YEARS

At this age, the scholars are maturing into young teenagers and preparing for adulthood. This age group is vulnerable to the negative aspects of maturing in western and Arab oriented societies that have less respect for African and Diasporic girls and boys. Culturally, the leaders in these societies know that the young person has to become very aware of her/his place in society. Here the manipulation of cultural identity is paramount. To control the mind is to control the individual and therefore the society.

In a culturally Traditional African oriented society, the young person will be expected to show or demonstrate her/his mental, physical, and memory skills, along with support or allegiance to family and society.

In societies where western Christian and Arab Muslim political values predominate, and huge social inequalities exist, girls and boys of this age may be called upon to look after their families. Under grievous conditions, they may also be called upon to fight wars, or encouraged to make money at any cost, which could include becoming prey to sexual predators or doing whatever is required of them for survival.

Cultural identity is essential to the scholars at this age which can be a vulnerable time. The young people are learning who they are, as well as who they are becoming. Developing cultural identity is ongoing in the Afrocentric School. Explaining why to the scholars is important. Claiming an identity outside the imposed 'racial' identity of people of African descent is imperative. Recognizing their own greatness and humanity and honoring self, community and their ancestors is a form of fortification for the child.

The significance of the baby, and the scholar's responsibility of protecting and teaching the child are paramount. Learning about the child is learning about the vulnerability of oneself. Traditional African children will remain involved in caring for younger siblings as well as learning their life skills as part of personal development. Whatever the home life situation of the Afrocentric school student, the importance of teaching, guiding, and setting an example for the younger children in their home, school, or community, should be expressed.

## Language Arts and Sociocultural Studies

### The Myth of Race

Across the world, the idea of race is used as an identity to recognize ourselves. It was invented in Europe in the 1700s about 400 years ago.

Race is a biological term, often used to show differences in domesticated animals and plants. As you learned, when it is used to show differences in humans, then it is a lie. It is a culturally constructed lie developed by pseudoscientists to assign human hierarchy. It is a lie because as we know today, scientifically, humans are only one race. This idea affects the mind and what people think of themselves and of others.

All humans that exist today are Homo sapiens sapiens. Archaeological and anthropological studies have shown that Homo sapiens sapiens is African. Humans are around 250-300,000 years old. Many humans stayed in Africa and millions migrated around the world between 80,000 to 50,000 years ago, forming the global populations that we see today.

Our differences in looks and color are linked to where people migrated from, and to, on Earth. Humans in Africa have many different phenotypes (characteristics relating to genes and the environment). People in different parts of Africa have different levels of melanin, different types of hair, different facial features etc., because the continent has different climates and environments. Those who stayed in Africa remained highly melanated in order to survive living in large amounts of sunlight. Those who went to the colder places became lighter over thousands of years because they did not need the high levels of melanin in such limited amounts of sunlight.

Another way that people's skin got lighter was that thousands of years later, people with less melanin and people with much melanin, met up again in their travels across the world.

The false idea of race has been used to separate humans. It has been used to say that the whiter that a person is, then the more intelligent, more beautiful, more mentally and physically superior that person is. This belief is built on a lie. The whiter a person is, the less melanin they have in their skin. The lighter a person's eye or hair color, the less melanin they have in their irises or hair follicles. The color of a person's skin, hair, eyes is decided by the amount of the pigment melanin they produce in those areas; it does not identify different race categories or separate human origins. It is important to understand this Truth so that people can be mentally freed from a destructive lie that has been used to oppress and divide humans globally.

The colonizers and enslavers imposed (forced) a false cultural identity on African people, based on 'race'.

The main lie is that:

- White women and men are the best
- White men are better than white women
- Yellow women and men are less than white
- Yellow men are better than yellow women
- Red women and men are less than yellow and white
- Red men are better than red women
- Brown women and men are less than red, yellow and white
- Brown men are better than brown women
- Black women and men are less than brown, red, yellow and white
- Black men are better than Black women

The older idea of White superiority and Black inferiority can be traced to the Christian and Muslim beliefs over 2,000 years ago.

Most people in the world have been made to believe this lie, including many African people both on the continent and throughout the Diaspora.

*Cultural Identity*

Culture is important for all people. It helps them to know who they are and what they must do to have a better life. Women and men want their children to live well and have good lives. Culture influences the mind and the mind influences the culture. Ideas come from the mind. The mind is very important.

A child will believe what it is taught by its parents as well as the wider society. If the parents and society believe that some people are better than others because of skin color and gender (girl or boy) then the child will believe this. If the parents believe that they and their children are superior or inferior to others then the children will believe this; especially when it is reinforced by the society in which they live.

It is important to know that all over Africa, Arab people were conquering Africa and taking the rich lands. After the Arabs became Muslim, they wanted to force the whole of Africa to become Muslim.

Enslavement and colonization of lands and people changed the power that people had to develop their own lands and lives.

People in Africa became Muslim to live. To stop the raiding, killing and fighting, it became a politically wise decision for African leaders to become Muslim. However, Africans who were converted to Islam, still believed in ancient African spiritual traditions that had existed thousands of years before the Muslim beliefs.

After Arabs took North Africa and enslaved African women and men, African people were no longer in political control there.

When Europeans colonized the Americas and First Nations women and men, then captured and brought enslaved African women and men to the Americas:

- First Nations people had no political power to decide what happens to their lands and people.
- African people had no power in their conditions in a foreign land.

The cultures of Arabian and European people were cruelly forced onto African and First Nations people.

Arabian and European people believed the source of life was masculine. They believed that African people should be enslaved. They believed that First Nations people and African people were inferior.

African people were taught by those responsible for their oppression that it was good for them to be colonized and enslaved. The culture of the enslavers and colonizers still teach this belief in their social institutions, which are:

Family – producing and caring for children
Spiritual system – guiding the spirit
Education system – teaching necessary skills
Political system – decisions of development
Legal system – creating, developing and using laws
Economic system – methods of production and exchange

Lies were taught by leaders so that their people as well as African people would come to believe these ideas.

The most detrimental lies were and are, that African women and men and children:

- Have no important history
- Have no important knowledge
- Gave no contribution to the world
- Are less important than others

Through these cultures, the world has been told that Africa is a frightening, uncivilized place, with a lack of rich history. After hundreds of years of Arab and European beliefs, there are millions of people of African descent all over the world who believe these ideas.

Thus, many people of African descent are scared of Africa. They are ashamed of their skin color.

In the places where Arabs and Europeans had political control over African people, there were still some Arabized and Europeanized African women and men who became some of the greatest parents, educators, farmers, conservationists, scientists, artists, musicians, mathematicians, soldiers, doctors, builders, lawyers, politicians, writers, film-makers, playwrights, psychiatrists, sociologists, nurses, travelers, explorers, archaeologists, researchers, biologists, surgeons, historians, athletes, dancers, sailors, pilots, astrologists, astronauts, sages, engineers, healers, manufacturers, and many more.

These great skills were and still are used to improve the societies that they lived in.

Some of these African women and men improved the lives of African people. Because of the Euro/Arab-centric cultural stigmas imposed on Africa and Blackness, some were never proud to be African. Some were never proud to be Black. Despite these constructed stigmas, some were.

Information about the True Africa and African people has been hidden for centuries.

*Some African women and men have never believed the lies. They have taught their children the Truth that they know. Some African women and men still remembered their Ancestors and their spiritual beliefs. Some African women and men studied the lies and found the hidden information written in the language of the enslavers and colonizers. Some studied history, science, anthropology, archaeology, and discovered Truth that had been withheld from people of African descent and much of the world in order to perpetuate the lies.*

Today we know that cultural identity is very important. A culture gives its people an identity. Identity is recognizing and knowing self – who you are.

Because this is not true, it is important to have a cultural identity based on Truth.

A cultural identity based on Truth helps people to know who they really are. It helps them to know where they come from and the importance of living life with purpose and leading righteous and good lives.

A cultural identity should be based on love as well as Truth. People need to love their humanity to know who they are.

The Truth is that Traditional African women and men:

- Respected women and men equally
- Built great societies
- Developed writing, architecture, spiritual values, sciences, medicine, mathematics, geometry, astronomy, history, literature, engineering, musical instruments etc.

- Tried to be Just and True
- Believed in democratic ideals
- Respected those who lived in countryside and the cities
- Welcomed people into their societies
- Were great warriors and protectors

These great accomplishments are hidden so that people will believe in the race construct. The cultural construct of race justifies the enslavement and colonization of people. It makes it easier to elude true history and keep it hidden.

To know the Truth of the history of humanity, is to also understand that 'racial' identity is a lie that impedes us from knowing who we are.

Cultural identity needs:

The history – what people have done
The language – the way people communicate
The psychology – how people think
The spirituality – the life force of people

They are important to culture and will influence the way that humans think and build their institutions that keep their societies going.

What is cultural identity?
What is race identity?
What cultures use race identity?
Why do people need to know their cultural identity?
Why is it important to have a True cultural identity?
What does a false cultural identity do to a person or a people?
What does a false identity do to white or light skinned people?
What does a false identity do to Black or dark-skinned people?
Name some ways/methods that societies use to make other societies believe in the race identity?

Discuss these ideas in the Education room, take notes, research, then present a talk and write a paper. This paper will be important for the Afrocentric schools conference at the end of the year.

## *Spirituality and Culture*

### The sacredness of children

Asar and Aset are considered a sacred couple. Asar is the god of nature, abundance and life. Aset is a Mother goddess and protector of life.

Below (as seen in the earlier lesson plan) Aset is breastfeeding her child Heru

*Asar and Aset (Heritage Museum Russia)*

Breastfeeding the baby is seen as a sacred work of Mothers, providing the baby with the food of life.

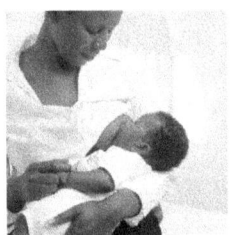

Even before the baby is born, s/he is aware of life outside the womb. Cultural identity is forming even before birth; the baby is learning about life. Inside the womb, the baby can hear sound, see light, and suck her/his thumb. Based on her parents' knowledge, s/he will grow to understand the world that s/he has entered. The closeness of her/his family before birth is important. S/he will be happy if s/he knows that she is wanted.

# Lesson Plans for Ages 12–13 Years

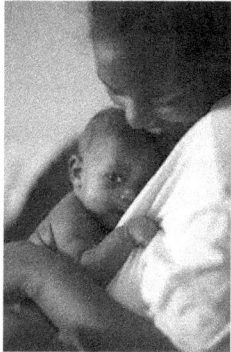

In the Traditional African societies, the child is welcomed. There is a celebration. A libation is poured. The Ancestors are thanked for the baby's safe arrival. The name of the child is chosen carefully. The name has a meaning. The parents and grandparents might use a name that is to do with:

- What the child might become
- How the child looks
- what was happening when the child was conceived or born
- If the child shares attributes of an Ancestor

**Adaoha** is a girl's name from Western Africa and it means **daughter of the people**. **Diop** is a boy's name from the Central Region of Africa and it means, **ruler, scholar**. **Chioneso** is a girl's name from Southern Africa and means **she is a guiding light**. **Oding** is a boy's name from Eastern Africa and it means **an artist**. **Yacoub** is a boy's name from Northern Africa which means **he is blessed**.

The African Pharaoh **Tutankhamun**[1] was a young man who ruled KMT in 1333 BCE.

His name means **in the living image of the Divine**.

---

[1] *Independent newspaper* (UK) 23 January 2016

The sound and the meaning of these names influence the life of the child.

The baby needs protection, care and love to grow well. In an ideal situation, the mother, father, family and community help to care for and love the baby. A Nation State government should also make sure that the baby and mother are cared for. Even today, African descended people believe that children should be loved and respected because they are the future.

If a Nation State believes that some people are of less value than others, then it will be more difficult for some families to live well.

The mother is the first carer of the baby. She has been carrying the baby until birth. The baby knows who the mother is and recognizes the people around the mother.

In Traditional African societies, the children also help to care for the babies. Even in non-Traditional societies, children of African descent often look after the younger ones. This is a remembered cultural tradition. Looking after babies and children, helps the older children to become responsible, strong, caring and loving adults.

Deciding to have children is a great responsibility. We look at our lives and we understand this. From the ages of 12-16 years, young people are becoming adults and imagining and preparing for their future lives.

Young people are learning who they are. African cultural identity helps the children to know who they truly are. They can have choices in what they might become. European and Arab cultural identity do not respect the African person. The choices of young people are often limited in these cultures.

*Discussion*

Look at where you live and discuss what choices there are for young people when they leave school?

- What types of work are available for young people?
- What work would you like to do?
- What type of life would you like to have?
- How would <u>you</u> change the world?
- What would you like the world to be like?

Talk about the community, state and world issues with your Educator. Take notes from the classroom discussion. Present your ideas based on ideas that you have heard and new ideas that you have (research ideas if you need more information). Write a paper after you have heard all the presentations. This discussion will be held in every Afrocentric school. At the annual conference these ideas will be presented.

## Logic and History

Logic is the ability to think clearly and to make sense of what is going on. In order to use logic, one must know or learn Truth. Logic cannot work without Truth. When people lie, they cannot use logic because they cannot understand what the effects of that lie will be. They will continue to lie in order to cover the Truth so that the lie is not exposed. These lies are devoid of logic and so rely on further lies and fabrication in order to seem like they are true. That is why it is important for people to learn Truth so that logic can be used to understand what things have happened, why things are happening now and what things can be done to improve the future.

Knowing the real history of Africa is important for developing cultural identity and logic – the ability to think clearly.

### *Archaeological Science*

We begin a history of Africa from where there is evidence to show where the people lived and worked. The evidence is the things that the people left behind.

Archaeological science includes the digging and finding of things, artifacts, objects, parts of animal and human bones, parts of buildings and rivers and tools and metals and so on. These things go through scientific tests to date how old they are. We can sometimes know what people did and thought thousands of years ago.

There are caves and mountains with beautiful African paintings that people left behind 12,000 – 40,000 years ago. The paintings in Chad and South Africa show what the people were doing then. The paintings cannot tell us everything but they can give us important information about the time.

There are also ancient bones like the 35,000 years old Lebombo bone found in South Africa that is a lunar calendar like the San people use today. There is the Ishango bone found in the Congo that is 25,000 years old. It was used as a calculator and lunar calendar. Bone tools 90,000 years old were found in the Congo near where the Ishango bone was found.

Bone was used for many things as there was no plastic then and bone lasted almost forever. Stones (including crystals) were also used. They last forever. The wooden artifacts that were carved did not survive as long. It is amazing that the paints of these ancient artists lasted thousands of years. Some of these paints were made from the powder of stones, crystals, and plants.

*Ta-Seti*

Ta-Seti is the oldest monarchy that is known. A monarchy is an area of land and people who are ruled by a Queen or King or both. It is a form of government. Royalty were expected to be the role models and wise leaders that the people looked up to.

It cannot be said that all African royalty was wise and good. What is important is that all over Africa there were standards for how to be wise and good. The standards were based on Maat.

Ta-Seti was built in Nubia, the Nile valley.

The Nile valley is where the Nile River runs down from Uganda and ends its journey to the Mediterranean Sea. The Nile River is about 6,853 kilometers long.

Ta-Seti was located in Northern Sudan and Southern Egypt. This land has been called Nubia, Ethiopia, and Kush. Tombs and artefacts like pottery, carvings and jewelry were found. There is not a lot known about Ta-Seti but its name means "land of the bow". This suggests that the people there were well trained and excellent with the bow.

Ta-Seti was ruled by African Pharaohs (who could have been called Kushite, Nubian or Ethiopian). It is believed that those who developed and built Kemet were Kushite and that the first people in that area were Kushite. The knowledge from Ta-Seti would have inspired the development of KMT. KMT also had Pharaoh rulers.

The map[2] below shows the Nile River running down from Uganda, Congo (which was called Zaire from 1965-1996 when this map was

---

[2] Map of the Nile River running down to the Mediterranean from Anthony Browder, Nile Valley Contribution to Civilization (1992).

made) to the Mediterranean from the South. Ta-Seti is located above Upper Egypt (KMT) in Sudan.

*Ta-Seti*

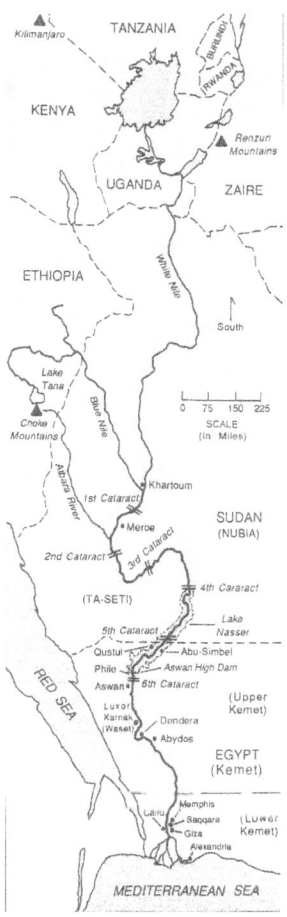

## KMT

The next major monarchy was KMT where there is so much evidence of what the people believed in and how they lived their lives. They left their pottery, tombs, buildings, writings, art work, jewelry, sculptures, technology, columns, stone carvings, ship building, astronomy, astrology and much more. Artifacts from KMT are in museums and private homes all over the world. That is why we know so much about them, although there is more to learn.

*The Mortuary Temple of Queen Hatshepsut is nearly 3,500 years old. Notice the work of the builders and engineers.*

Those who conquered KMT were:

- Hyksos (Semites)
- Assyrians (Syrians)
- Persians (Iranians)
- Greeks (Europeans)
- Romans (Europeans)
- Arabians (Muslims)

These people took control of KMT. They learned from the culture and beliefs of African women and men who were the first Queens and Kings or Pharaohs. KMT existed for possibly 10,000 years before it was conquered by the Muslim Arabs in 651 CE. The whole of North Africa was converted to Islam.

*Axum*

Another African monarchy was built in what is today's Ethiopia. It was called Axum and it began around 499 BCE. One of the major cities of Axum was Adulis, although it was not the oldest. The people of Axum were familiar with KMT.

Adulis was known as a beautiful city that many foreigners visited. It had palaces, and housing developments for the people. They traded with KMT, China, Sri Lanka, Arabia and India. The Axumites wrote down things that they thought and did. They could write and speak in many languages because they were traders. They also left their stone monuments, pottery and jewelry etc. Archaeologists and historians are still finding out about Axum. Axum was destroyed in 350 CE.

This is a monument[3] from Axum, Ethiopia.

There is a smaller Tekhen (Greeks called Obelisk) from KMT next to it. It is made to look like a building with windows and a door.

[3]Illustration from *When We Ruled* (2006) Robin Walker, Every Generation Media: London, UK

## Ancient Ghana

Ancient Ghana was ruled by the Soninke people of West Africa. It was located in southeast Mauritania, southwest Mali, and parts of Senegal and Guinea.

The name Ghana was said to be the title of the Kings. Among the Akan nation of today's Ghana, the name Nana is used as the title of a monarch to show her or his status.

Stories date the beginning of Ghana to the 25th Dynasty of KMT (circa 700 BCE). The 25th Dynasty of KMT was a Kushite Dynasty. This Dynasty kept its African values. Like KMT, ancient Ghana promoted education, literacy, and higher learning, as well as stone architecture, including temples and centralized water systems.

The people of ancient Ghana mined iron and made iron tools. They also mined gold and traded in gold. Many skilled workers were employed. The people of ancient Ghana were inventive farmers. The farmers produced enough food for thousands of people.

Ghana was ruled peacefully and democratically. It lasted over 1,500 years. People of many different cultures and countries came to settle there and share in the good life.

*Map of ancient Ghana*[4]

[4]Map from *Roots of Black History* (1999) Robin Walker, Bogle-L'Ouverture Publications Ltd: London, UK

Lesson Plans for Ages 12–13 Years 281

In ancient Ghana, King Tenkamenin 1060 CE, had an army of 200,000 soldiers; 100,000 of them were horse riders and were trained with the bow. They worked at their jobs and were on call when they were needed.

There were many cities in Ghana but the capital was Kumbi-Kumbi. Kumbi-Kumbi is often called Kumbi-Saleh, the Arabic name. In Kumbi-Kumbi, Mosques and Temples lived peacefully side by side. Gold was the center of the Ghanaian economy.

Archaeologists have recently found houses several stories high with underground rooms, stairs and hallways. One part of the city housed over 30,000 people.

In 1203 CE, the African Sosso Nation who had become Muslim, conquered Ghana. The Muslims who lived there helped in the conquest. Ghana's wealth in knowledge and gold was taken and its writing translated into Arabic.

We know that Ghana existed because of the:

- Arabic writings of travelers and educators
- Stories told by the Ancestors and remembered
- Archaeologists, who are still uncovering evidence

*Mali and Songhay*

The two next important monarchies were ancient Mali and ancient Songhay. They were built where ancient Ghana was located. Mali came first and then Songhay.

*A map of Mali and Songhay*[5]

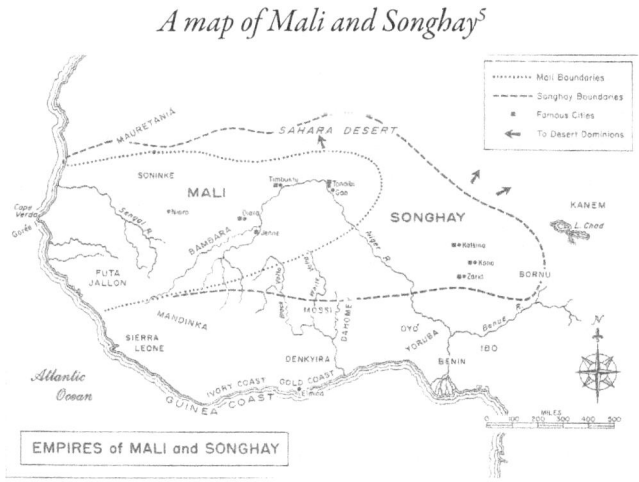

---

[5]Map from *The Destruction of Black Civilization*, Chancellor (1987) Williams, Third World Press: Chicago.

The Muslims learned from the knowledge of Ghana and its political organization.
Mali grew larger than Ghana and Songhay grew even larger. Their Kings were African Muslims.

### *Mali*

One of the greatest African Muslim Kings was the Malian Sundiata Keita who ruled from 1240 CE.

Sundiata Keita was a wise and powerful King. He was a military leader who defeated the enemies of Mali. He made peace with people from the nations around Mali and Mali was able to grow.

The Kingdom of Mali was larger than Europe. Sundiata was respected by the people. He developed good generals to take responsibility for different lands in Mali. The leader and his generals were able to protect and look after the Malian people. When he died in 1255 CE, Mali was the wealthiest and largest nation in Africa. Even today, Mali has one of the largest gold mines in the world.

### *Songhay*

Sunni Ali Ber wanted to unite the people of his kingdom Gao, who were Traditional believers and Muslim believers. He took a Muslim name and remained a Traditional believer. He came to power in 1464 CE.

He took control of Timbuktu, a city of 115,000 people. 25,000 people were at university and 20,000 were at school. When Ali Ber took Djenne it was after 7 years, 7 months and 7 days with no bloodshed. Gao, Timbuktu and Djenne were incredible cities. They became the foundation of the Songhay Empire. An Empire is larger than a Kingdom. Sometimes Empires are called Kingdoms, and Kingdoms Empires. There was a university in Timbuktu and one in Djenne. Djenne had a medical school attached to the university. Sunni Ali Ber kept peace. Sunni Ali Ber was a great African leader who never forgot his African traditions. People came from all over Africa and Europe to be educated. He died in 1492 CE.

Askia Mohammed was an African who was a devout (deeply religious) Muslim. He came to power in 1493 CE. He made Songhay even larger.

He conquered the Hausa states of Northern Nigeria and controlled over half of West Africa. Askia Mohammed ruled a state larger than the whole of Europe. He encouraged building, teaching, and learning and his government invested in writers, judges, doctors, and books. Askia Mohammed died in 1538 CE, and was remembered as Askia the Great.

*A picture of Timbuktu[6]
seen by Dr Henry Bath in 1851*

The Arts and scientific knowledge of KMT influenced the whole world.

### Review and Discussion

The Greeks and Romans learned from Africa before the Muslims. Like the Arabs; the Greeks and Romans do not say that African people gave them the knowledge that they still use today.

As the Arab Muslims conquered Africa, many of the Traditional African writers, thinkers, builders, intellectuals, scientists, doctors and agriculturalists etc., became Muslims. It was a matter of life, death and/ or enslavement.

---

[6]Timbuktu from *Roots of Black History* (1999) Robin Walker, Bogle-L'Ouverture Publications Ltd: London, UK

African knowledge was translated into Arabic. This knowledge was taught all over Africa. Arab Muslims made it seem as if they had created these ideas.

Why is it important to have a cultural identity?
What do you need to know to develop a cultural identity?
Why is it difficult to create a cultural identity if you are of African descent?
What was the name of the first known monarchy?
What does monarchy mean?
What were the names of 3 of the great Kingdoms in West Africa?
What did the Kushites of KMT's 25th Dynasty do?
Name an African King who had a Muslim name but remained an African Traditional believer?
How do we know that these places existed?
What is the name of the science that can date findings?

## Mathematics

### *Kemetic Multiplication*[7]

When multiplying two numbers together, the ancient Africans from KMT would make 2 columns. The first column would be the Multiplier and the second column would be the Multiplicand:

| Multiplier | Multiplicand |
| --- | --- |

If they wanted to multiply five by seventeen then five would be the multiplier and seventeen would be the multiplicand. Always beginning with one, they would keep doubling the number until the number five was reached. They would also double the multiplicand beginning with the number seventeen. Here is the example below.

| Multiplier | Multiplicand |
| --- | --- |
| 1 | 17 |
| 2 | 34 |
| 4 | 68 |

---

[7] African Mathematics from *African Mathematics History, Textbook and Classroom Lessons* (2014) Robin Walker, Recklaw Education: London, UK.

Since they were multiplying by five, the Kemites would use the information linked to the multiplier of 1 (and the corresponding 17) and the multiplier of 4 (and the corresponding 68). They chose these figures because 1+4=5. The calculation is 17+68=85. They did not need the 2 or the corresponding 34.

It would then be:

| Multiplier | Multiplicand |
|---|---|
| 1 Use this | 17 Use |
| 2 Reject this | 34 Reject |
| 4 Use this | 68 Use |
| 1+4=5 | 17+68=85 |

If they wanted to multiply six by seventeen, six would be the multiplier and seventeen would be the multiplicand. Always beginning from number one they would double the number until six was reached. They would double the multiplicand starting with the number seventeen. Here is the example below:

| Multiplier | Multiplicand |
|---|---|
| 1 | 17 |
| 2 | 34 |
| 4 | 68 |

As the Kemites multiplied by six, they would use the information relating to the multiplier of 2 (and the corresponding 34) and the multiplier of 4 (and the corresponding 68). They chose these figures because 2+4=6. The calculation would be 34+68=102. They would not use 1 or the corresponding 17.

| Multiplier | Multiplicand |
|---|---|
| 1 Reject | 17 Reject |
| 2 Use | 34 Use |
| 4 Use | 68 Use |
| 2+4=6 | 34+68=102 |

If they wanted to multiply fifteen by nine, then fifteen would be the multiplier and nine would be the multiplicand. Always beginning with number one, they would keep doubling the number until the number fifteen was reached. They would also double the multiplicand beginning with the number nine. Here is the example:

| Multiplier | Multiplicand |
|---|---|
| 1 | 9 |
| 2 | 18 |
| 4 | 36 |
| 8 | 72 |

Because they are multiplying by fifteen, they should use the information of the multiplier of 1 (and the corresponding 9), the corresponding 2 (and the corresponding 18), the multiplier of 4 (and the corresponding 36), and the multiplier of 8 (and the corresponding 72). They would choose these figures because 1+2+4+8=15. The calculation would be 9+18+36+72=135.

| Multiplier | Multiplicand |
|---|---|
| 1 Use | 9 Use |
| 2 Use | 18 Use |
| 4 Use | 36 Use |
| 8 Use | 72 Use |
| 1+2+4+8=15 | 9+18+36+72=135 |

If the African mathematicians chose 9 to be the multiplier and 15 to be the multiplicand the result would be the same but the method would look like this:

| Multiplier | Multiplicand |
|---|---|
| 1 Use | 15 Use |
| 2 Reject | 30 Reject |
| 4 Reject | 60 Reject |
| 8 Use | 120 Use |
| 1+8=9 | 15+120=135 |

Since they were multiplying by 9 the Kemites would use the information concerning the multiplier of 1 (and the corresponding 15), and the multiplier of 8 (and the corresponding 120) They chose these figures because the 1+8=9. Therefore, the calculation would be 15+120=135. They would disregard the 2 (and the corresponding 30) and the 4 (and the corresponding 60).

Using this method, multiply the following numbers together. Make the first number the multiplier. Make the second number the multiplicand.

1. 3x4
2. 4x6
3. 9x13
4. 13x16
5. 17x31
6. 19x36
7. 23x68
8. 47x149
9. 49x158.2
10. 51.25x2002

**Review and Discussion**

1. (a) Did you know the 13 times table before attempting these questions?
   (b) Did you know the 17 times table before attempting these questions?
   (c) Did you know the 19 times table before attempting these questions?
2. Could you do question 10?
3. Explain the advantages and disadvantages of using the Kemetic method.

Answers:

1. 12
2. 24
3. 117
4. 208
5. 527
6. 684
7. 1564
8. 7003
9. 7751.8
10. Cannot be done

The following questions are the same as the above. The numbers have been reversed and should come to the same answers. Make the first number the multiplier and the second the multiplicand

1. 4x3
2. 6x4
3. 13x9
4. 16x13
5. 31x17
6. 36x19
7. 68x23
8. 149x47
9. 158.2x49
10. 2002x51.25

Discussion questions:

1. Could you do question 9?
2. What difficulty did you have doing question 10?
3. Explain other advantages and disadvantages of using the Kemetic method.

Answers:

1. 12
2. 24
3. 117
4. 208
5. 527
6. 684
7. 564
8. 7003
9. Cannot be done
10. 102602.5

How did the Kemites Divide?

The method for doing division used the opposite process. If the Kemites wanted to divide 425 by 18 they would arrange the number in the two columns as they did for multiplication. The results might look like this:

| | |
|---|---|
| 1 | 18 |
| 2 | 36 |
| 4 | 72 |
| 8 | 144 |
| 16 | 288 |
| 32 | 576 |

Because 576 is larger than 425 the Kemites would use the number 16 (and the corresponding 288). Now from the 425 subtract the "partial products" starting from the number 288. It would look like this:

| | |
|---|---|
| 425 | |
| -288 | (16x18) |
| 137 | |
| -72 | (4x18) |
| 65 | |
| -36 | (2x18) |
| 29 | |
| -18 | (1x18) |
| 11 | remainder |

The answer is 16+4+2+1 -23. The remainder is 11.

Using this method, divide the first number by the second number. Make the second number where you begin doubling in the right-hand column. Make the number 1 the beginning for the doubling in the left-hand column.

1. 6÷2
2. 12÷3
3. 36÷4
4. 63÷7
5. 96÷12
6. 143÷14
7. 287÷15
8. 374÷17
9. 390÷18
10. 426÷19

Answers:

1. 3
2. 4
3. 9
4. 9
5. 8
6. 10 remainder 3
7. 19 remainder 2
8. 22
9. 21 remainder 12
10. 22 remainder 7

## The Arts

*Preparing a theatre presentation*

This year the scholars will write a play. The scholars will decide on a topic or story in a classroom discussion that interests them. The play should be around half an hour long. A lot of time will go into producing a play for that length of time. Music and dance will be incorporated into the play. It can be modern or ancient and should have a moral to the story.

One idea is the Haitian Revolution 1791-1804[8]

[8]*Image Ownership: Public domain*

The major scene could be the coming together of enslaved African women and men to discuss plans to take over and liberate the island. Imagine how this could be done if you were the revolutionaries. Below is the history of the Haitian Revolution to base your ideas on.

The Haitian Revolution is the only successful rebellion of enslaved people in world history, in which the enslaved population overthrew the government and liberated the country. Haiti was the name given to the island of Hispaniola after the revolution. Hispaniola was owned by the French on one side and the Spanish on the other. The French part was called Saint Domingue and the Spanish part Santo Domingo. Enslaved African women and men initiated the rebellion in 1791, and by 1803 they had succeeded in ending not just their enslavement but French control over the colony.

The Haitian Revolution was complex, consisting of several revolutions going on at the same time. These revolutions were influenced by the French Revolution of 1789. The French Revolution was the rise of the European poor against the European wealthy royals. The royals were killed and a change of regime took place. The revolution came to represent a new European idea of human rights, universal citizenship, and involvement in government.

In the 18th century, Saint Domingue, the French side of Hispaniola, became France's wealthiest overseas colony. It produced sugar, coffee, indigo, and cotton using an enslaved labor force. When the French Revolution broke out in 1789 there were five sets of interest groups in the colony. There were:

- White planters—who owned the plantations and enslaved African women, men and children
- *Petit blancs (small whites)*, who were artisans, shopkeepers and teachers. Some of them also owned African people

Together they numbered 40,000 of the colony's residents. Many of the whites on Saint Domingue began to support an independence movement. They wanted to become independent from France. This movement began when France imposed expensive taxes on items imported into the colony. The planters were extremely dissatisfied with France because they were forbidden to trade with any other nation. The white population of Saint Domingue did not have any political representation in France. The planters and *petit blancs* were devoted to the institution of enslavement because that is why they were so wealthy. The three remaining groups were of African descent:

- Those who were free
- Those who were enslaved
- Those who had run away

There were about 30,000 free African people in 1789. Half of them were mulatto, mixed African (mothers) and European (fathers). Some of them were wealthier than the *petit blancs*. The enslaved population was close to 500,000. The runaway enslaved African people were called maroons; they vanished deep into the mountains of Saint Domingue and lived off subsistence farming. Saint Domingue had a history of African rebellions; the enslaved African people were never willing to be enslaved and with their strength in numbers (10 to 1) colonial officials and planters did all that they could to control them. No matter how cruelly African women, men and children were treated, there were uprisings, even before 1791. One plot involved the poisoning of masters and probably mistresses.

At the time of the French Revolution, a number of Haitian revolutionary movements were also happening. African people were inspired by the French Revolution's "Declaration of the Rights of Man." The French government gave the island rulers the power to be French citizens. In Saint Domingue only the planter class had power in government but not the *petit blancs*. This legislation of citizenship allowed free citizens of color with substantial property to also have a say in government. This legislation created a three-sided civil war among the planters, free Black people and the *petit blancs*. All three groups were challenged by the enslaved African majority.

Led by formerly enslaved Toussaint L'Ouverture, African people rose up against the planters on August 21, 1791. By 1792 they controlled a third of the island. In spite of military support from France, the area of the colony held by the rebels grew. Before the fighting ended, 100,000 of the 500,000 Africans and 24,000 of the 40,000 whites were killed. The former enslaved Africans managed to fight off the French forces and the British forces that arrived in 1793 to conquer the colony. The French and British forces withdrew in 1798 after a series of defeats by L'Ouverture's forces. By 1801 Toussaint L'Ouverture took the revolution beyond Saint Domingue. He and his army conquered the Spanish colony of Santo Domingo (present-day Dominican Republic). He abolished slavery in the Spanish-speaking colony and declared himself Governor-General for life over the entire island of Hispaniola.

Napoleon Bonaparte, now the ruler of France, sent Général Charles Leclerc, his brother-in-law, and 43,000 French troops to capture L'Ouverture and restore French rule and enslavement. L'Ouverture was taken and sent to France where he died in prison in 1803. Jean-Jacques Dessalines, one of Toussaint L'Ouverture's generals who had also been enslaved, led the revolutionaries at the Battle of Vertieres on November 18, 1803. There the French forces were defeated. On January 1, 1804, Dessalines declared the nation independent and renamed it Haiti. The First Nations people had called the island Ayiti before conquest. France became the first nation to recognize its independence. Haiti became the first Black republic in the world (Ott, 1973).

# LESSON PLANS
# FOR AGES 13-14 YEARS

At this age, the scholars should be familiar with the significance of cultural identity as a way of understanding self. As previously highlighted, true historical knowledge, language, psychology and spirituality are the key to knowing self. In the special case of people of African descent, the knowledge of history, language, psychology and spirituality has been falsified, radicalized, demonized, debased and corrupted. The history of humanity that is generally being taught, is therefore a fabrication. It is the overall intention to enable scholars to be aware that their potential is being purposefully undermined through lack of knowledge.

The reality is that young people are resorting to ways of life that have been planned for them in the global economy. Working or not working, young people of African descent are making money for the system that ultimately undermines the humanity of people of African descent. Evidence shows that the young people are:

- Underemployed.
- Expected to receive less pay for the same work.
- At the bottom of any work that they can get.
- Criminalized by the authorities based on appearance.
- Encouraged to become involved in criminalized activity.
- Overrepresented in prisons.

- Underrepresented in universities.
- Becoming parents in destabilized families (as a result of the above-mentioned inequalities).

It is important that the young people understand that their choices in what to do in life are predominantly being directed by those in control of their society. It is vital that the young people learn to navigate this so that they can have greater control over finding their purpose, creating their future and in effect, positively impacting the world.

So far, the scholars have focused on enslavement as a heinous crime against African people specifically, and colonization as a crime against First Nations and African people.

This year the focus will be on colonization, and political movements in Africa to try to become independent from their colonial oppressors. The false history of African people and the role of finding cultural identity, underplay the continuous struggle for emancipation from cruelty, terror, debasement and the attack on the African persona and culture.

## History and Rhetoric

### Cultural Identity

To know yourself; a person must have a cultural identity. To have a cultural identity a person needs:

History
Spiritual belief
Psychology
Language

Based on Truth

To know yourself; is written by Kemites on the ancient Temples in Egypt. This vital philosophical knowledge is reiterated here to remind us;

Know Thyself

S/he who knows not and knows not that s/he knows not, is a fool – shun him/her;

S/he who knows not and knows that s/he knows not, is simple – teach him/her;

S/he who knows and knows not that s/he knows, is asleep – wake him/her;

S/he who knows and knows that s/he knows, is wise – follow him/her;

All of these reside in you so to thine own self, be true.
To be an African and to not believe in the African source of life, the energy that is both female and male, is to be confused.

*Colonization*

What is involved in colonization is cruelly forced on the colonized. Colonization was not just about using people's skills and personal power (energies) to work for the colonizer; it was about taking the lands, resources, minerals, water, and knowledge. When Europeans and Arabs divided Africa, it made it possible for them to colonize and control smaller areas of land. Inside these colonial boundaries, countries were created. African people from different Nations, who had for years had their own governments, laws and remarkable societies, were forced to be divided and speak different languages. Colonization was a war against African people and the gun was instrumental in winning. Those who chose not to participate went into the hinterland (The remote areas of a country away from the coast or the banks of major rivers) like the maroons. They stayed away from the colonizers and lived in fear of losing their lives and lands. The San people of South Africa left their lands after almost being wiped out by the Europeans and went to live in the Kalahari Desert. They sacrificed their lands for life. Great depression and sadness took the hearts of the people across Africa. People lived in fear.

Colonization could be called the great depression, terror and destruction of Africa. This depression was built upon the enslavement of countless millions of African women, men and children. When Africa lost millions of people; mothers and fathers, farmers, scientists, doctors, lawyers, priestesses and priests, wise people, builders, political leaders, boat builders, cooks, child carers, astronomers and so on, it was difficult to carry on.

The true figures of how many lives were lost in Africa enslaving people; how many lives were lost on the boats taking people to other parts of the world; how many lives were lost when African people reached places that would become their homes for generations; are still not known. Europeans and Arabs downplay these heinous crimes.

Arabs called black African people Zanj. They enslaved the Zanj for centuries. They created a false history of African people. The Zanj fought a war with the Arabs from 869–883. They fought in today's Iraq, at Basra. Between 500,000 and 2,000,000 people lost their lives. This stand against Arab supremacy was equal to the Haitian revolution. Although the Zanj were eventually defeated, African people's fight for liberty has inspired and continues to inspire the world towards the understanding and recognition of human rights.

European Christians ruled most of Africa from the 1884-5 Berlin conference. Europe forced and taught their culture including their god, to those who they had colonized, conquered, enslaved. The colonizers imposed their religion onto people whilst committing heinous crimes against humanity. It is taught globally, that the European governments are the best types of governments in the world (by Eurocentric teaching). These governments did not and cannot help the majority of African people. They still exist to help Europe at the detriment of all others. This is a huge problem for Africa and the Americas. The African leaders within these systems struggled to make sense of their history.

In every new colonial country, African people were forced to speak the language of the colonizers. Those in the hinterland kept their culture, values and beliefs as well as languages. Many of the farmers, living in villages and working on their lands to grow crops for Europe, kept their culture and languages too. The people in the hinterland made do with their meagre resources to live as best that they could. They sacrificed their wealth to be free. They were free mentally and physically but not free to develop their societies in the ways that they would if there was a choice.

As people grew to speak and understand the new languages, European and Arab schools along with Christian churches and Arab mosques multiplied. They trained people to not only speak the languages but also to believe in the source of life (God) as male with no mercy or respect for the African man and woman. Their gods could only respect them; the colonizers.

The belief in Ancestors was banned and demonized (to teach that something is evil). Inside these colonial cultures, African culture was considered backward and a false history of Africa was developed. It is a history still taught all over the world.

Even within these colonial systems, Africans rose to be great leaders. African people still rose to be great leaders 2,000 years ago when Muslims controlled large parts of Africa. Arabs continue to control the North of Africa and in some countries like Sudan and Mauritania, there are African people who are still enslaved. The film *I am Slave* (2011) starring Wunmi Mosaku focuses on this.

The Struggle for Independence

The fight for independence from colonial rule was full of contradictions for African women, men and children. The Arabs (Muslim) and Europeans (Christian) colonizers fought wars over African resources between. African people were the main soldiers either fighting for the colonials or the new African leaders.

African leaders rose up to demand freedom from Europe. In reality, the results of this achieved Neo-colonial (meaning new colonial) rule, that is, they took over their colonial countries but carried on running them like the Europeans and Arabs that had colonized them. This is because most of the leaders were educated at colonial school systems, teaching disciplines grounded in Eurocentrism. Some of the leaders tried to understand who African people were before colonization.

African currently comprises 54 sovereign countries. The countries listed in the below table are arranged by the earliest date of independence (from Wikipedia).

| Country[33] | Colonial name | Colonial power[34] | Independence date[35] | First head of government | Independence won through |
|---|---|---|---|---|---|
| Liberia | Commonwealth of Liberia | American Colonization Society | 26 July 1847 | Joseph Jenkins Roberts | Liberian independence referendum, 1846 |
| Union of South Africa | Cape Colony Colony of Natal Orange River Colony Transvaal Colony | United Kingdom | 31 May 1910[36] | Louis Botha | South Africa Act 1909 |
| Kingdom of Egypt[37] | Sultanate of Egypt | British Military Administration | 28 February 1922[39] | Fuad I | Egyptian Revolution of 1919 |
| Emirate of Cyrenaica | British Military Administration | United Kingdom | 1 March 1949 | | |
| United Kingdom of Libya | British Military Administration Territory of Fezzan-Ghadames Emirate of Cyrenaica | United Kingdom French Fourth Republic Emirate of Cyrenaica | 24 December 1951 | Idris I | Western Desert Campaign |

*Lesson Plans for Ages 13–14 Years* 301

| | | | | | |
|---|---|---|---|---|---|
| Republic of Sudan | Anglo-Egyptian Sudan | United Kingdom[41] Republic of Egypt | 1 January 1956 | Ismail al-Azhari | Egyptian Revolution of 1952 |
| Kingdom of Tunisia | French Protectorate of Tunisia | French Fourth Republic | 20 March 1956 | Muhammad VIII al-Amin Habib Bourguiba | _[42] |
| Morocco | French Protectorate in Morocco Tangier International Zone Spanish Protectorate in Morocco Spanish West Africa Ifni | French Fourth Republic Francoist Spain | 2 March 1956[43] 7 April 1956 10 April 1958 4 January 1969 | Mohammed V | Ifni War |
| Ghana | Gold Coast | United Kingdom[44] | 6 March 1957 | Kwame Nkrumah | - |
| Guinea | French West Africa | French Fourth Republic | 2 October 1958 | Sékou Touré | Guinean constitutional referendum, 1958 |

| | | | | | |
|---|---|---|---|---|---|
| Cameroon | French Cameroons / British Cameroons | France / United Kingdom | 1 January 1960[45] / 1 June 1961 / 1 October 1961 | Ahmadou Ahidjo | [46] |
| Togo | French Togoland | | 27 April 1960 | Sylvanus Olympio | - |
| Mali | French West Africa | France | 20 June 1960[47] | Modibo Keita | - |
| Senegal | | | | Léopold Senghor | - |
| Malagasy Republic | French Madagascar | | 26 June 1960 | Philibert Tsiranana | |
| Republic of the Congo | Belgian Congo | Belgium | 30 June 1960 | Patrice Lumumba | Belgo-Congolese Round Table Conference |
| Somali Republic | British Somaliland / Trust Territory of Somaliland | United Kingdom / Italy | 26 June 1960 / 1 July 1960[48] | Aden Abdullah Osman Daar | - |

## Lesson Plans for Ages 13–14 Years

| Country | Former status | | Date of independence | Head of state | |
|---|---|---|---|---|---|
| Republic of Dahomey | | | 1 August 1960 | Hubert Maga | - |
| Niger | French West Africa | | 3 August 1960 | Hamani Diori | - |
| Upper Volta | | | 5 August 1960 | Maurice Yaméogo | - |
| Ivory Coast | | France | 7 August 1960 | Félix Houphouët-Boigny | - |
| Chad | | | 11 August 1960 | François Tombalbaye | - |
| Central African Republic | French Equatorial Africa | | 13 August 1960 | David Dacko | - |
| Republic of the Congo | | | 15 August 1960 | Fulbert Youlou | - |
| Gabon | | | 17 August 1960 | Léon M'ba | - |
| Nigeria | Colony and Protectorate of Nigeria / British Cameroons | United Kingdom | 1 October 1960<br>1 June 1961<br>1 October 1961[49] | Nnamdi Azikiwe | - |
| Mauritania | French Equatorial Africa | France | 28 November 1960 | Moktar Ould Daddah | - |

| | | | | |
|---|---|---|---|---|
| Sierra Leone | 🏴 Colony and Protectorate of Sierra Leone 🇬🇧 United Kingdom | 27 April 1961 | Milton Margai | - |
| Tanganyika[50] | 🏴 Tanganyika Territory 🇬🇧 United Kingdom | 9 December 1961 | Julius Nyerere | - |
| Kingdom of Burundi | 🏴 Ruanda-Urundi 🇧🇪 Belgium | 1 July 1962 | Mwambutsa IV of Burundi | - |
| Republic of Rwanda | 🏴 Ruanda-Urundi 🇧🇪 Belgium | 1 July 1962 | Grégoire Kayibanda | Rwandan Revolution |
| Algeria | 🏴 French Algeria 🇫🇷 France | 3 July 1962 | Ahmed Ben Bella | Algerian War |

## Lesson Plans for Ages 13–14 Years

| | | | | | |
|---|---|---|---|---|---|
| Uganda | 🇺🇬 Protectorate of Uganda | 🇬🇧 United Kingdom | 9 October 1962 | Milton Obote | - |
| Kenya | Colony and Protectorate of Kenya | | 12 December 1963 | Jomo Kenyatta | Mau Kay-adanda Uprising |
| Sultanate of Zanzibar[50] | Sultanate of Zanzibar | | 10 December 1963 | Jamshid bin Abdullah | _[51] |
| Malawi | Nyasaland | | 6 July 1964 | Hastings Kamuzu Banda | - |
| Zambia | Northern Rhodesia | | 24 October 1964 | Kenneth Kaunda | - |
| The Gambia | Gambia Colony and Protectorate | | 18 February 1965 | Dawda Kairaba Jawara | - |
| *Rhodesia* Zimbabwe | Southern Rhodesia | | *11 November 1965* 17 April 1980[52] | *Ian Smith* Robert Mugabe | *Rhodesia's Unilateral Declaration of Independence* Lancaster House Agreement |
| Botswana | Bechuanaland Protectorate | | 30 September 1966 | Seretse Khama | - |
| Kingdom of Lesotho | Territory of Basutoland | | 4 October 1966 | Leabua Jonathan | - |
| Mauritius | Mauritius | | 12 March 1968 | Veerasamy Ringadoo | - |
| Swaziland | Swaziland | | 6 September 1968 | Sobhuza II | - |

| | | | | | |
|---|---|---|---|---|---|
| Republic of Equatorial Guinea | Spanish Territories of the Gulf of Guinea | Francoist Spain | 12 October 1968 | Francisco Macías Nguema | - |
| Guinea-Bissau | Overseas Province of Guinea | | 24 September 1973 | Luís Cabral | Guinea-Bissau War of Independence |
| People's Republic of Mozambique | State of Mozambique | Portugal | 25 June 1975 | Samora Machel | Mozambican War of Independence |
| Republic of Cape Verde | Overseas Province of Cape Verde | | 5 July 1975 | Aristides Pereira | Guinea-Bissau War of Independence[53] |
| Union of the Comoros | French Comoros | France | 6 July 1975 | Ahmed Abdallah | Comorian independence referendum, 1974 |
| São Tomé and Príncipe | Overseas Province of São Tomé and Príncipe | Portugal | 12 July 1975 | Manuel Pinto da Costa | - |
| People's Republic of Angola | State of Angola | | 11 November 1975 | Agostinho Neto | Angolan War of Independence |
| Republic of Seychelles | Seychelles | United Kingdom | 29 June 1976 | James Richard Marie Mancham | - |

## Lesson Plans for Ages 13–14 Years

| Republic of Djibouti | French Territory of the Afars and the Issas | French Fifth Republic | 27 June 1977 | Hassan Gouled Aptidon | Afars and Issas independence referendum, 1977 |
|---|---|---|---|---|---|
| Sahrawi Arab Democratic Republic[55] | Spanish Sahara *Southern Provinces* | Francoist Spain *Morocco* | 27 February 1976 *independence not yet effectuated* | El-Ouali Mustapha Sayed *Mohamed Abdelaziz* | Western Sahara War *Western Sahara conflict* |

## African Freedom Fighters

African leaders were aware of the effects of the colonial control of the African mind and tried to decolonize their own minds. In order to decolonize their minds, they had to learn how their minds had been colonized. They wanted African people to be free from European control. Some of these leaders come from areas where great African civilizations existed before, like Ghana, Mali, Songhay, and ancient Zimbabwe. As a result of their European education, they did not know the ancient history of Africa. It was difficult to learn African history because colonization was predicated on the false history of the colonizer. However, many refused to believe the lies and searched for Truth despite this. They fought for the freedom of African people and risked their lives. African freedom fighters often worked with each other. They had the same intention to remove colonial terrorism out of Africa.

Some African freedom fighters who led the struggle against colonial rule are mentioned below.

### Ghana: Kwame Nkrumah

*I am not African because I was born in Africa but because Africa was born in me.*

Born in 1909, Kwame Nkrumah was the first leader of independent Ghana, which the Europeans had called the Gold Coast. The Gold Coast was colonized and ruled by the British. Ghana's major gold mine is in the Asante area. It is one of the largest in the world. Kwame Nkrumah became Prime minister from 1957-66. He was an important pan-African leader who influenced other independence movements. He was the son of a goldsmith and was educated in Catholic schools. He became a teacher at a catholic school after gaining his qualifications and then progressed to become a headmaster. Following on from teaching, he studied economics, sociology, and theology at Lincoln University (a historically Black university or HBCU) in the U.S. He took degrees in education and philosophy, before eventually teaching political science at Lincoln. Nkrumah also studied law at the London

School of Economics and the University of London. He was active in the West African Students Union and there he met George Padmore, a fellow pan-Africanist. Together they co-chaired the Fifth Pan-African Conference with W.E.B. Dubois from the U.S. Kwame Nkrumah returned to Ghana and became Head of the United Gold Coast Convention (UGCC). He formed a youth organization called the Convention People's Party (CPP), which is still a political party in Ghana today. He was imprisoned for three years for political demonstrations led by the CPP. During this time his party won elections and after his release he was made prime minister of Ghana. After a series of African led uprisings, Nkrumah called for independence which they achieved against the will of the British. It was the first African country to achieve independence from the colonizers. In 1956 Kwame Nkrumah renamed the gold coast, Ghana, after ancient Ghana. He called for a United States of Africa. Nkrumah died in 1972 at the age of 62, and in 2019 his birthday, 21st September, which is an official holiday in Ghana, was named Kwame Nkrumah Memorial Day.

SENEGAL: LÉOPOLD SENGHOR

*My inner life was split early between the call of the Ancestors and the call of Europe, between the exigencies of black-African culture and those of modern life.*

Léopold Senghor was born in 1906. He was the first African President of Senegal after French colonization. Unlike the majority of Senegalese who are Muslim, Léopold Senghor was a Catholic. He went to Paris to study and entered the Sorbonne. He was the first Black African person to gain an 'aggregation' degree in Europe, which is a degree of a number of subjects. He was one of the first African intellectuals to challenge French cultural assimilation. Cultural assimilation is the process of making a culture like that of another group. It was about forcing European ideas on African people. French cultural assimilation created a false cultural identity for African people. After fighting for the French against Germany in the European World War 2, he became a politician. He was a great poet. He and Alioune Diop founded *Présence Africaine* in 1947. *Présence Africaine* was a pan-African quarterly cultural, political, and literary magazine which was based on the philosophy of Negritude. Negritude was the idea that the African was equal to the European. It was an attempt in the 1930s and 40s by African people, to decolonize their minds and create a cultural identity. Because they did not know the true history of Africa, the cultural identity was based on the opposition of the injustice and cruelty of Europeans. This cultural identity challenged the European lie because the contributors knew that injustice was based on skin color and greed. Some of the greatest thinkers of the time, like Cheikh Anta Diop and Franz Fanon wrote in the magazine. Léopold Senghor believed that the French colonies should join together to have more strength. Like Kwame Nkrumah, Léopold Senghor was unable to achieve African cultural unity while he was president but is remembered for his efforts towards it.

CONGO: PATRICE LUMUMBA

*The colonialists care nothing for Africa for her own sake. They are attracted by African riches and their actions are guided by the desire to preserve their interests in Africa against the wishes of the African people.*

Patrice Lumumba was born in 1925; he became a nationalist leader in the Belgian Congo. He knew the history of the treatment of people by the Belgian king Leopold II, when 8 million Congolese had been murdered during his reign from 1885 to 1908. Patrice Lumumba was the first prime minister of the independent Congo in 1960. He was born in the Kasai province and educated at Catholic and Protestant schools. He became a civil servant and then assistant post master. He did a number of jobs and joined in a petition asking for independence. He was a good orator and writer of pamphlets. Pamphlets are small booklets or leaflets with information or arguments about a subject. As political movements developed, asking for independence, Patrice

Lumumba led mass demonstrations. He helped to form and make the *Mouvement National Congolais (MNC)* a national party. He spoke at a national independence conference in Belgium. His support was massive. In 1958, Lumumba was invited to Ghana by President Kwame Nkrumah, who organized the All Africa People's Conference. In order to keep peace back home, Patrice Lumumba was asked to form a government as prime minister. The Congo gained its independence in 1960. Moise Tshombe, an African military leader supported by the Belgians, created chaos. Tshombe took the Katanga province, which was rich with cobalt, copper, tin, radium, uranium, and diamonds. Patrice Lumumba would have used Africa's wealth for the Africans. He tried to get the UN to help remove the Belgians from Katanga. They did nothing. Joseph Mobutu led the army against Lumumba. Patrice Lumumba was eventually captured by the Congolese army and assassinated in Katanga in 1961.

### Mozambique: Samora Machel

*The liberation of women is a fundamental necessity for the revolution, a guarantee of its continuity and a precondition for its victory.*

Samora Machel was born in 1933 in Mozambique, a country colonized and ruled by the Portuguese. He was born in Gaza Province and became a nurse in Maputo, which was then called Lourenzo Marques. He loathed the treatment and inequalities of African people by the Portuguese. He went to Tanzania to join the freedom fighters called *Frelimo*. He trained in guerrilla warfare in Algeria and returned to Tanzania to train his people. In 1964 Frelimo fought against the Portuguese in northern Mozambique. He became Frelimo's secretary of defense and eventually commander in chief. In 1969 he became the President of Frelimo. Frelimo took over large parts of Mozambique and politicized the people and created socialist farms like Tanzania. While the Portuguese fought in Mozambique, Portugal had a revolution and the new government granted independence to its African colonies. It was very difficult to change an economy run for Portuguese needs to an economy to serve the needs of African people. He shut off the links to Rhodesia which later became Zimbabwe. Samora Machel supported their African freedom movement. The South African government supported an anti-Machel movement. After signing an agreement with South Africa for peace, he was murdered by the South African government in 1986.

### Zimbabwe: Robert Mugabe

*I am termed dictator because I have rejected this supremacist view and frustrated the neo-colonialists.*

Robert Mugabe, born in 1924, is the President of Zimbabwe. He was born in what was called Southern Rhodesia. He was educated in Catholic schools including a Jesuit school in Matabeleland. He graduated from college in South Africa and taught in Southern Rhodesia, Northern Rhodesia (Zambia), and Ghana. Heavily influenced, he joined the National Democratic Party. The party was banned and he became deputy in Joshua Nkomo's, Zimbabwe Africa People's Union (ZAPU). He escaped capture and went to Tanzania and helped the Zimbabwe African National Union (ZANU), where he became secretary general. When he returned home, he was captured and spent the next ten years under arrest. He read and earned college degrees during the time he was imprisoned. On his release he went to Mozambique in 1974 and became political leader of ZANU's liberation army. Joshua Nkomo and Robert Mugabe continued to war against the white Rhodesians. Mugabe's support by the people, led to an election that gave Africans the vote. He shared the victory with Joshua Nkomo and together they became a coalition government. However, this did not work, as Joshua Nkomo was against a one-party state. He governed the new Zambia and Robert Mugabe the new Zimbabwe. During his lifetime, Robert Mugabe as leader, has developed the concept of *indigenization*.

This is the attempt to respect ancient African ideas by taking back the European owned African lands and growing food for the people and encouraging the practice of Traditional African medical care.

### Guinea Bissau and Cape Verde: Amilcar Cabral

*The colonists usually say that it was they who brought us into history: today we show that this is not so. They made us leave history, our history, to follow them, right at the back, to follow the progress of their history.*

Amilcar Cabral was born in the Cape Verde islands off the coast of West Africa in 1924. It was known as part of Portuguese Guinea. He attended school and went to Portugal to study at the University of Lisbon. There he trained as an agronomist (the scientific study of soil management and crop production, including irrigation and the use of herbicides). He also trained as a hydraulics engineer (concerned with the flow and carrying of water and sewage as well as systems that use gravity to cause the movement of the fluids – like the screw pump of ancient Africa). When Amilcar Cabral returned to Cape Verde in 1952, he was one of the few "university educated" African people. He took work as an agricultural engineer. He spent two years going through the country, mostly on foot, showing his anger with the Portuguese colonialists. The government was disturbed by his attitude and he returned to Lisbon. He later went to Angola, another Portuguese colony, where he joined the freedom movement. In 1956 Amilcar Cabral returned home and created a freedom party. He named the party PAIGC the Partido Africano da Independência da Guiné e Cabo Verde which means African Party for the Independence of Guinea and Cape Verde. The party was intending to work peacefully in its demands. The murder of 50 dock strikers gave the PAIGC its revolutionary goal; to free Africans from Portuguese colonialization. Sekou Toure, the first president of the Republic of Guinea, a French colony, allowed the training of the PAIGC freedom fighters in the capital Conakry. Cabral believed in the people. He tried to educate through programs. He knew the need to involve women. He was assassinated in 1973 by a Portuguese agent in his own organization. He was one of the most respected leaders of the anti-colonial wars.

*Review and Discussion*

The independence of Africa from European control did not mean that Africa was now free. It meant that the European governments were run by African people. These governments were never meant to help Africa or her people. They were meant to help Europeans.

Look at the map of Africa and locate where each one of these freedom fighters is from.

Look at the map of Africa and discuss these important leaders and what they did to get independence.

Why was it so important to get independence?

Remember that they studied and show how that helped them?

These leaders knew that they had to decolonize their minds, why?

Why is it important to have a cultural identity based on Truth?

Choose a leader of African descent and research, give a talk and write about that leader.

Listen to all the presentations and learn from other scholar's ideas and how they speak.

How important is it to speak well about your subject?

One of the fundamental purposes of this type of school is to educate the children to be able to gain clarity and use logic, allowing them to speak clearly and with confidence so that they may teach others.

Why is it important to teach others?

Why is it important to teach others something that is good?

Why are the leaders all men?

## Mathematics

How to find the volume of a cylinder

Finding out the volume of a cylinder is really finding out the area of 2 circles (one on top and one at the base) and the height or length of the cylinder.

The volume of a cylinder is how much space is inside. It is a 3-dimensional object. So, its measurement is cubed, that is by 3 ($^3$)
The radius is 2 and the height is 10
The calculation for finding the volume of a cylinder is written as
V =r²h (Pi which is 3.14 x R² x height)
Find the area of the circle which is r².
The radius is 2m so 2m² is 2x2=4
Multiply x 4
This is 3.14 x 4 = 12.56m²
Multiply 12.56m² by the height or length which is 10m
This is 12.56m² x 10 = 125.6m³
Remember that the radius is half of the diameter.
If a cylinder has a diameter of 5mm and is 6mm high then the formula will be 5mm ÷ 2 = 2.5mm radius.
Using the formula r² x height
The 2.5mm radius² = 2.5mm x 2.5mm = 6.25mm
6.25 x 6 = 37.5
37.5 x 3.14 = 117.809mm³
V= 117.81mm³
Try these examples below; use a calculator and make sure that the answers are in mm³, cm³ or m³

1. Cylinder with a radius of 9mm and a height of 10mm
2. Cylinder with a radius of 63cm and a height of 20cm
3. Cylinder with a radius of 13.5m and a height of 5m
4. Cylinder with a diameter of 45mm and a height of 40mm
5. Cylinder with a radius of 40.5m and a height of 80m
6. Cylinder with a diameter of 108cm and a height of 200cm
7. Cylinder with a radius 49.5m and a height of 180m
8. Cylinder with a diameter of 36mm and a height of 50mm

9. Cylinder with a radius of 36m and a height of 90m
10. Cylinder with a diameter of 54cm and a height of 60cm

The answers are:

1. $2560mm^3$
2. $62720cm^3$
3. $2880m^3$
4. $64000mm^3$
5. $414720m^3$
6. $1843200cm^3$
7. $1393920m^3$
8. $51200mm^3$
9. $368640m^3$
10. $138240cm^3$

*Medicine*

The practice of medicine is as old as human beings. It was always important to find ways to heal. As we know plants are very important to medicine and healing. Being healthy meant having a healthy mind, body and spirit.

The ancient medical doctors were priestesses and priests. In Africa today among the Traditional people, children still train as priests and priestesses to learn how to heal.

Some of these medical traditions still exist in places where African people live. There are priests and priestesses who heal in North America, South America and the Caribbean.

Through enslavement, colonization and decolonization, Traditional medicine was sometimes the only way that people survived. European medicine was not available to the majority of people.

The Priestesses and Priests were responsible for the mental, physical and spiritual health of the people. In KMT the mother Divinity Het-Heru, was a protector of the Pharaoh or King. She was also a healer. Het-Heru was known as the Lady of the Sycamore tree. The Sycamore tree had medical properties. Many doctors of the time used it. Its fruits, bark and leaves were used.

The Greeks came to learn from KMT. In order to learn, they trained to become Priestesses and Priests equivalent to Professors. Roman and Arab invasions banned the priests and priestesses and closed down the Temples.

The Romans were Christians and the Arabs were Muslim. They wanted African people to become Christians and Muslims. It was difficult then, to be healed.

Reminder: We know that the ancient African Kemites practiced medicine because it is written in the books below

1. Kahun Papyri
2. Ramesseum Papyri
3. Edwin Smith Papyrus
4. Ebers Papyrus
5. Hearst Papyrus
6. London Papyrus
7. Berlin Papyrus
8. Carlsberg Papyri
9. Chester Beatty Papyri
10. Brooklyn Papyrus

The Europeans and Arabs appropriated this medical knowledge. They learned from the books they had taken, but they did not use the spiritual connection, energies or the Ancestors in their healing and they did not acknowledge where they learned the information from.

Dr Charles S. Finch writes that the information found in the Edwin

Smith Papyrus, is as ancient as the time of the Old Kingdoms. This would make that papyrus at least 5,000 to possibly 10,000 years old.

Although it was written, the medical information was also passed on orally for thousands of years. People had great medicinal knowledge all over Africa. Today, people still carry much of this knowledge. The Zulu nation of South Africa knows of the medicinal uses of 700 plants.

Some enslaved African people took plants to where they were taken. Spiritual systems were set up wherever they went. Some of the plants in South America were like the plants in Africa. They continued to heal.

In Carolina in the U.S., there are 14 healing plants that are the same as in countries in West Africa. First Nations people used similar plants and healing methods. They believe in the Ancestors too. Some plants and foods are healthy and some plants and foods are not. There are strict rules for what to eat or not to eat for your health.

It has become more important for these African medical traditions to be saved and not lost.

*Become a Researcher*

We are trying to find out if the ancient ways of healing are still used today.

Find out if there are any medical plants in your area.

If there are none in your area, find out from your family or the community what they use to get better.

Ask what plants or herbs they use to heal.

Write down the names of plants, herbs, or fruits/vegetables that you find have healing properties.

Find out what they are good for.

Find out how and where they grow.

Read some of the books on medical herbs like the work of:

Stephanie Y. Mitchem, *African American folk healing* (2007). She writes about the African Traditions of plant healthcare that have been handed down in her family for generations.

Perhaps your family has important knowledge about healing too. Perhaps you know a family member or friend who is a healer.

This research and discussion are very important. If there are no longer healers where you live, that is important to know too.

## Music

Africa has a history of sending messages through music. These messages have helped people to survive. Musicians have been like the Professors of sound, playing instruments, singing and dancing the important messages. They have been the historians telling stories of the past so that people can remember who they are and who their Ancestors were. To be a historian musician, one needed an excellent mind and memory. The details of past lives were vitally important in war or peace. The historian musicians were called different names across Africa but they all were important messengers. They were orators. They used their instruments and movements to send the messages. As well as being historians they were storytellers and poets.

*Women musicians in KMT*

*Dogon Mali historians*

These women and men musicians had a high status in society. They were important to the people. They helped the people to remember who they were. They used sounds to heal. Sometimes their messages were a matter of life and death. They could travel with messages from place to place. This is how they knew what was happening and could spread the news. They were the ancient sacred newscasters.

What are the messages that we are receiving from our musicians today?

The messages are sometimes profound (insightful) and sometimes profane (disrespectful). Those with profound messages often do not get enough play. Those who have nothing important to say; that speak of women or men as sexual objects; that speak of themselves as all knowing; that promote guns and drugs; are promoted.

They are commonly the artists who are most wanted by the record labels and mainstream media. They can become very wealthy and make countless millions for their record companies. These are the young artists who have learned a corrupted cultural identity.

It is not their fault. They do not know and often do not care who they are. The schooling that is usually in place is not there to educate them about self, purpose and true history. That is the plan of the culture in which they live.

These young people believe in individualism. This is important in European culture. Individualism is when the individual makes her/himself more important than anyone. Getting wealth by any means necessary is an individualistic trait and a core feature of capitalism.

In Traditional African culture, the individual is nothing without the community. It is said in Africa *I am because we are*. This signifies that the collective is as important as self; we need one another to live and we exist because others existed before us.

In European culture, the individual is more important than the collective. The French philosopher Rene Descartes coined the phrase *I think, therefore I am*. This famed philosophical sentiment signifies that the individual simply exists because one knows that they exist. It is about the self and reliant on the self.

For this study of music and its effect on society, please find/choose one popular female music artist and one popular male music artist. Listen to their music. What are their messages? Find the words of their songs online. Look at the words and analyze what they are saying.

Can you tell if the artists each have an African cultural identity?

If the artists do not have African cultural identities, then choose a male and female artist who you think have African cultural identities.

Explain in the Education room why you think that these persons have African cultural identities.

Take notes from the other students.

Write your thoughts in an essay about the female and male artists who you think have African cultural identities, and why their message is different from those who have European cultural race identities.

# LESSON PLAN
# FOR AGES 14-15 YEARS

At this age, the scholars will be looking toward studying in areas of academic and scientific skills. Potential career options should be provided with examples of how the students can contribute to the development of themselves and African descended people. Their skills in the seven disciplines will be evident to the Educator. For the first six months the students will become apprentices of skilled professionals. Examples of some professions are:

Professors, psychologists, sociologists, writers, artists, dancers, poets, farmers, scientists, archaeologists, engineers, astronomers, sculptors, film makers, illustrators, book publishers, doctors, historians, language experts, biologists, microbiologists, singers, musicians, recording engineers, computer programmers, pilots, pottery makers, social workers, veterinary surgeons, researchers and so on.

Efforts will be made to find these contacts to make them available to the students who will learn with them and gain experience in the chosen field.

The students and Educators will go through a process of finding out what the scholars are suited to; helped by the professionals in their assessment of the students in relation to what they would like to do. The next 6 months will focus on entry to University.

## Language Arts and Sociocultural Studies

*The Mdw Ntr*

This year, the focus will be on learning and translating the Mdw Ntr. The importance of this subject is for the students to join the upcoming new translators of this most ancient writing. The history of the Mdw Ntr will be the context in which students will study and learn. The African cultural background is the key to understanding the meaning of the letters and words. There are Egyptologists who have translated the words of important documents like the Mathematical and Medical books.

In France, there is a group of African translators of the Mdw Ntr who would possibly allow access to their growing knowledge. A lesson plan for learning the Mdw Ntr can be developed through the work of Educators who have been teaching how to translate it for years.

As the students learn the meaning of the writing, their translation into different languages will provide knowledge for future Afrocentric school students.

*Basic Needs*

The focus will be on inventions that relate to the basic needs of African communities. Choose the location that the school is in and research the needs of the area. Regard the school as a community-based education center.

Basic needs of the community are:

- Clean Water
- Uncontaminated Food
- Safe Shelter
- Good Healthcare
- Sanitation
- Relevant Education
- Electricity
- Roads
- Transportation

**Review and discussion**

What does your community need?
How could the needs of the community be accomplished?
These questions will be asked and worked out jointly by discussions with the other Afrocentric schools and professionals associated with the schools. This year the Afrocentric school will hold its Science conference where inventive ideas can be developed and exhibited from all the age groups. Your six months of professional training will have helped to give you ideas about what you as a class or group can invent that can be useful. Keep the community needs in mind.

Research the countless inventions, designs and creations by people of African descent that have helped to change the world including many of the tools and scientific instruments that we use today. Present your research findings at the conference.

*Logic and Philosophy*

What the childhood of a generation is will be what that generation becomes in its adulthood. A ruined childhood is a ruined society.[1]

The sacred speech will relate to *Selections from the Husia* collected and translated by Professor Maulana Karenga to show the sacred wisdom of Africa written by the women and men of Kemet. This important book will be used as a learning tool. A study group or groups will be formed to study and explain the meanings of some of the educational and philosophical instructions.

*The Egyptian Philosophers: Ancient African Voices from Imhotep to Akhenaten* (Asante, 2000) is a useful book for understanding the background to the thinking and philosophy of great African leaders.

Anthony Browder's book *Exploding the Myth vol. 1. Nile Valley Contributions to Civilization* (1992) will be an excellent resource for Afrocentric school Educators teaching information concerning KMT.

---

[1] Kindezi: The Kongo Art of Babysitting (1988), Fu-Kiau & Lukondo-Wamba, Black Classic Press: Baltimore, U.S.

## The Book of Ptah Hotep

(I) The wise instruction below is the first of XXI. It is based on the teaching of Maat.

Be not arrogant because of your knowledge. Take council with the ignorant as well as with the wise. For, the limits of knowledge in any fields have never been set and no one has ever reached them. Wisdom is rarer than emeralds, and yet it may be found among the women who gather at the grindstones.

Think carefully, go through thoroughly, line after line and analyze, discuss and explain this wise instruction. What is Ptah Hotep teaching? Ptah Hotep[2] lived during the reign of Menkauhor 2396 – 2388 BCE during the Old Kingdom. He was the mayor of the city and wrote this work at the age of 110 years old.

### The 42 Maatic Declarations of Innocence

The teaching of Logic is grounded in Truth. *The 42 Maatic Declarations of Innocence* (formal sayings) will be studied in order to understand their importance to life and death. These 42 Declarations are made before the person's heart is measured against Maat's feather of Truth. They are based on the moral standards that a person is expected to live by.

The 42 Declarations of Innocence were written 1,500 years before the 10 commandments of the Hebrew religion known as the <u>Decalogue</u> (meaning the 10 sayings). The commandments are a set of biblical laws relating to morals, beliefs in the idea of right and wrong. The 10 commandments are important to Judaism, Christianity, and Islam. Ten were chosen from the ancient African 42 Declarations of Innocence.

1. I have not done iniquity (crime, wickedness, evil)
2. I have not robbed with violence
3. I have not stolen
4. I have done no murder; I have done no harm
5. I have not defrauded offerings (offered less than I could)

---

[2] *The Teachings of Ptahhotep The Oldest Book in the World* (1987) Asa G Hilliard III, Larry Williams and Nia Damali

6. I have not diminished obligations
7. I have not plundered the Ntr
8. I have not spoken lies
9. I have not snatched away food
10. I have not caused pain
11. I have not committed fornication
12. I have not caused shedding of tear
13. I have not dealt deceitfully
14. I have not transgressed
15. I have not acted guilefully (craftily, treacherously)
16. I have not laid waste the ploughed land
17. I have not been an eavesdropper
18. I have not set my lips in motion (against any man or woman)
19. I have not been angry and wrathful except for a just cause
20. I have not defiled the wife or husband of any person
21. I have not defiled the wife or husband of any person (twice)
22. I have not polluted myself
23. I have not caused terror
24. I have not transgressed (repeated twice)
25. I have not burned with rage
26. I have not stopped my ears against words of Right and Truth
27. I have not worked grief
28. I have not acted with insolences
29. I have not stirred up strife
30. I have not judged hastily
31. I have not been an eavesdropper (repeated twice)
32. I have not multiplied words exceedingly
33. I have done neither harm nor ill
34. I have never cursed the King
35. I have never fouled the water
36. I have not spoken scornfully
37. I have never cursed the Ntrw
38. I have not stolen
39. I have not defrauded the offerings of the Ntrw
40. I have not plundered the offerings to the blessed dead
41. I have not filched the food of the infant, neither have I sinned against the Ntr of my native town
42. I have not slaughtered with evil intent the cattle of the Ntr

*Review and Discussion*

What does having a moral order or set of standards to guide us mean?

Look at the history of the African experience and list how many of these moral laws were broken during enslavement and colonization.

Do politicians practice these laws? If they do, name the politicians.

Do religious leaders practice these laws? If they do, name the leaders.

What does number 19 mean? Can it be used to understand the wars against enslavement, colonization and injustices?

Write an essay on the meaning of 19. Pick an African or African Diaspora movement, uprising, or war against injustice and racism. In the essay name the morals that have been broken to create these dehumanizing racist injustices. Show how 19 can be applied.

## Mathematics

By now, the scholars should be able to measure the areas of circles, triangles, squares and other shapes, and the volumes of 3D shapes.

Use *African Mathematics: History, Textbook and Classroom Lessons* (Walker, 2014) to build upon and enhance mathematical knowledge and understanding.

## Music

Write a musical play that is current with the times. Write a true or imaginative story based on reality. Write a story of a person becoming conscious of her/his cultural identity. Point out the triggers or ways in which the person grows to learn. It can be a spiritual intervention; or meeting an elder or young person or a person who had a brutal life who is the messenger. Use the African wisdom of the sacred knowledge or the fables of Aesop the enslaved African storyteller or someone who you know that tells the stories as a way to guide you. Watch the movie of *Sugar Cane Alley* to help inspire your ideas before you begin writing the musical play. Be inspired by today's music and write your own poetry to music that fits into the story. Choreograph the dance that will run through your play and add meaning to the story. It is a story of realization. Not only does the person become conscious but the music and dance can also change in the same way.

# CONCLUSION

*The Afrocentric school: A Blueprint*, is based on ancient indigenous African cultural beliefs that live within our memory. Afrocentric theory is applied throughout the Blueprint to study the his- and herstorical movement of humanity from Africa. It is incumbent on us as educators and students to understand the true meaning of education, which is to develop ourselves to ultimately have inner vision and become enlightened in order to improve the world. Our Ancestors left us a legacy that we must continue to uncover. We pour libation to those African women, men, girls and boys across the world, known and unknown, who have throughout the ages, continuously laid out a path for us in spite of conquest, domination, imperialism, colonization, deculturalization, enslavement and untold cruelty; for our survival and for the future. We have to go backwards and reclaim our past, to go forwards. Ultimately, this Blueprint is to cultivate within the child a cultural identity which is the basis for cultural unity. May the Afrocentric school Blueprint, humbly help in this endeavor.

Here are some answers to important questions.

Q  If humanity came out of Africa, what happened to the African white skinned people that led their elite/privileged to betray their own Ancestral connection to the motherland?

A  They lost touch with their Ancestors and their culture.

Q   Why did they construct a falsehood about the Blackness of humanity, centered in their cultural configuration, to debase and demonize their own origins?
A   They lost their spiritual balance and focused on individualism, materiality (greed), aggression and domination.

Q   Why did they fabricate the idea of "race"?
A   The root of this fabrication lay in the disrespect for women, the opposite of female-male reciprocity. The men languished in the power and privilege afforded by patriarchal domination. The men and women collaborated so that they would both prosper. They applied their desire and greed for power and domination, to dominating others. Through aggression, they could access the wealth of nations. The cultural construction of race justified the conquest and control of the world, in particular Africa and Black people.

Q   What made them later deny the source of their spiritual knowledge and create religions that demonized the authorship of their Black African mentors and educators?
A   They were jealous of and greedy for, their teachers' beauty, wealth of knowledge and abundance.

Q   How have they successfully claimed to be superior to their own educators?
A   After plagiarizing the knowledge and stealing the wealth, they hid the truth, distorted history and herstory, took control over African episteme by creating a belief in race, thereby cunningly placing their teachers at the base of the hierarchy of humanity through enslavement.

Q   Why can they not live the lives that they religiously espouse should be lived?
A   Patriarchal cultures are antithetical to those beliefs.

Q    Why do they withhold knowledge from those whom they call their own people?

A    To maintain a system within which the most debased will view themselves as superior to the supposed 'races' and align themselves with their oppressors. In this way, the elite maintain a race-caste, gender and class control over the minds of the oppressed women, men and children.

From the teachings of Ptahhotep written around 4,500 years ago:

If you want to have perfect conduct, to be free from every evil, then above all guard against the vice of greed. Greed is a grievous sickness that has no cure. There is no treatment for it. It embroils fathers, mothers and the brothers of the mother. It parts the wife from her husband. Greed is a compound of all evils. It is a bundle of hateful things. That person endures whose rule is rightness, who walks in a straight line, for the person will leave a legacy by such behavior. On the other hand, the greedy has no tomb. (Hilliard, 1987, p.25).

In the words of **Molefi Kete Asante,**

> *Afrocentric education centers the child in history, herstory and culture, rather than outside it.*

May the *Afrocentric school: A Blueprint,* humbly contribute to this endeavor.

# BIBLIOGRAPHY

Ainsworth, M. D. "Infant Development and Mother-Infant Interaction among the Ganda and American Families" In *Culture and Infancy: Variations in the Human Experience*. Edited by Leiderman, H. P. Tulkin, R. S. Rosenfeld, A. 119-149. New York, San Francisco, London: Academic Press, Inc.

Asante, M. K. (2000). *The Egyptian Philosophers: Ancient African Voices from Imhotep to Akhenaten*. Chicago: African American Images.

Asante, M. K. (2007). *An Afrocentric Manifesto: Towards an African Renaissance*. Malden MA: Polity Press.

Asante, M. K. (2017). *Revolutionary Pedagogy: Primer for Teachers of Black Children*. New York: Universal Write Publications LLC.

Ben-Levi, A. J. (1986). "The First and Second Intermediate Periods in Kemetic History." In *Kemetic and the African Worldview: Research, Rescue and Restoration,* edited by M. Karenga and J. Carruthers, 55-69. Los Angeles: University of Sankore Press.

Browder, A. (1996). *Nile Valley Contributions to Civilization*. Washington: The Institute of Karmic Guidance.

Chandler, W. B. (1988). "The Jewel in the Lotus: The Ethiopian Presence in the Indus Valley Civilization." In *African Presence in Early Asia,* edited by R. Rashidi and I. Van Sertima, 80-105. New Jersey: Transaction Books.

Chandler, W. B. (1999). *Ancient Future*. Baltimore: Black Classic Press.

Chivaura, V. (2015). "Dance in African Societies, Role of." In *Encyclopedia of*

*African Heritage in North America.* Edited by Shujaa, M. Shujaa, K. 349-353. Thousand Oaks, California: Sage Publications, Inc.

Clarke, J. H. (1991). *Notes For An African World Revolution: African at the Crossroads.* Trenton, NJ: Africa World Press.

Diop, C. A. (1991). *Civilization or Barbarism: An Authentic Anthropology.* New York, NY: Lawrence Hill.

Diop, C. A. (1989). *The Cultural Unity of Black Africa: The Domains of Matriarchy and of Patriarchy in Classical Antiquity.* London: Karnak House.

Dove, N. (1998). *Afrikan Mothers: Bearers of Culture, Makers of Social Change.* Albany, NY: SUNY Press.

Fairservice, Jnr, W. A. (1988). "The Script of the Indus Valley Civilization." In *African Presence in Early Asia,* edited by R, Rashidi and I. Van Sertima, pp. 64-79. New Jersey: Transaction Books.

Finch, C. S. (1990). *The African Background to Medical Science.* London: Karnak House

Harrison, V. (2018). *Little Leaders: Bold Women in Black History.* London: Puffin Books.

Hilliard III, A. (1984). *Kemetic Concepts of Education: The African Perspective of Education.* Presentation, Nile Valley Conference, Morehouse College, Atlanta, Georgia. London: Hackney Black Peoples Association.

Hilliard III, A. Williams, L. Damali, N. (1987). *The Teachings of Ptahhotep: The Oldest Book in the World.* Grand Forks: Blackwood Press & Co.

Hilliard III, A. (1995). *The Maroon Within Us.* Baltimore: Black Classic Press.

James, G. M. (1989). *Stolen Legacy.* (Republished) Virginia: United Brothers Communications Systems.

Jok, M. J. (2001). *War and Slavery in Sudan.* Philadelphia: University of Pennsylvania Press.

Kia, K., Bunseki Fu-Kiau, A., & Lukondo-Wamba, M. (1988). *The Kongo Art of Babysitting.* Baltimore: Black Classic Press.

Ott, O. (1973). *The Haitian Revolution 1789-1804.* Knoxville, Tennessee: University of Tennessee.

Rajshekar, V. T. (1987). *Dalit, the Black Untouchables of India.* Atlanta:Clarity Press.

Rashidi, R. and Van Sertima, I. (1988). *African Presence in Early Asia.* New Jersey: Transaction.

Twumasi, R. A. (1975). *Medical Systems in Ghana: A Study in Medical Sociology.* Accra, Ghana: Ghana Publishing Corporation.

Walker, R. (2006). *When We Ruled.* London: Every Generation Media.

Walker, R., and Matthews, J. (2014). *African Mathematics: History, Textbook and Classroom Lessons*. London: Reklaw Education Ltd.

Walker, R. (2016). *Blacks and Science Volume One: Ancient Egyptian Contributions to Science and Technology*. London: Reklaw Education Ltd.

Woodson, C. G. (1933). *The Mis-Education of the Negro*. Washington, DC: Associated Publishers.

www.ingramcontent.com/pod-product-compliance
Lightning Source LLC
LaVergne TN
LVHW011927070526
838202LV00054B/4524